SEA RUN

March 24, 1993

For Howard,

SEA RUN

Surviving

My Mother's Madness

At last!

❊

MARY LOU SHIELDS

❊

As the summer of their spawns nears its close, old females go out to sea in great numbers to die. Inexplicably, lesser numbers of these ocean-journeying crabs may return the next year to eke out a purpose-less existence for yet a few more summer days. Those that return can be easily recognized. Barnacles stud their shells and sea moss dulls their once bright colors. They are known as "sea runs."
　　　—WILLIAM W. WARNER,
　　　Beautiful Swimmers:
　　　Watermen, Crabs and the Chesapeake Bay

Thanks

Sea Run Enterprises
16 Mead Street
Cambridge, MA 02140

Mary Lou Shields

Title-page quote from *Beautiful Swimmers: Watermen, Crabs and the Chesapeake Bay* by William W. Warner, illustrated by Consuelo Hanks. Copyright © 1976 by William W. Warner. By permission of Little, Brown & Company in association with the Atlantic Monthly Press.

Hardcover edition was published by Seaview Books, New York 1981.

Manufactured in the United States of America.

FIRST EDITION

Library of Congress Cataloging in Publication Data

Shields, Mary Lou.
    Sea run.

        1. Psychotherapy patients—United States—Biography. 2. Shields, Mary Lou. I. Title.
RC464.S54A37   616.89′009′24 [B]   80-52406
ISBN 0-87223-665-X

Designed by Tere LoPrete

For Frank, Christopher, and Elizabeth—
my growing pains cost them the most

The extreme kindness and forbearance of family and friends have freed me to write, so as I bring *Sea Run* to a close, I have many people to thank.

Paul Lorris, whose love, support, and counsel were my "anchor to windward."

John Fallon, Patrick Ames, Florence Murphy, Alice Nauen, and John Hurley, each of whom helped to make possible my initial departure from Cambridge to Long Island.

Harriet and David Christman, Paula A. Lieberman, Edward J. O'Shea, and the staff of the Emma Clark Library made my stay in Setauket, New York, a productive period.

Tim Crews, James Fallon, Jack Neuwirth, Ulrich Figge, and Jack Walsh made it possible for me to come home to Cambridge and continue to write.

The special kindness of Rowena and H. Bernard Fisher, Ellen Burofsky, Gladys Madeiros, Elizabeth Badger, Irene Koronas, Donna Wooldridge, Virginia Greenblatt, and Trudy Goodman got me *and* my family over separate rough times.

I thank Rhea and Vincent Shields, Doris and James Charles, Juanita and Sumner Barton, Olga Chavis, and Barbara Hoffman whose trust in my work has sustained me.

I thank Janet Stone, Marge Piercy, and the anonymous contributors to the "survival fund" without whom life would have been far more difficult.

For sharing home, hearth, and support, I am deeply grateful to Phyllis Chesler, Donis Dondis, Rebecca and Cyrus Harvey, and Esther Begell.

Florynce Kennedy, Thomas Teal, Cynthia Rich, Stuart Diamond, Susan Bolotin, Christine Steinmetz, Raphael Sagalyn, Adrienne

Rich, and Hal Davis encouraged me from the start, sharing freely of their own knowledge and skills.

Marge Piercy, friend and teacher, provided the environment and the guidelines . . . my first pages were written in her Wellfleet home.

Ellen Frankfort, friend and teacher, too, persisted with love and loyalty as she taught me how to write, edit, and revise. Together she and I moved beyond a metaphorical "sisterhood."

Carol E. Frame, Wanda Lee Woodford, and Roseanne McCusker met a manuscript deadline with typing precision. I am indebted to them for their kindness and generosity.

The unflagging dedication of Elaine Markson and Sherry Huber transformed the manuscript into a finished book.

Finally, I must acknowledge my good fortune to have chanced upon Dr. Egbert Mueller, whose sensitive interpretation of the art of psychoanalysis was then—and still is—rare throughout the profession.

MARY LOU SHIELDS
Cambridge, Mass.
September 24, 1980

Part One

And I saw the figure and visage of madness looking for a home.

—THOMAS HARDY

Chapter One

Once again I'm on my way to McLean, a familiar trip—the Waverly bus from Harvard Square to the end of the line, then a brisk walk to the rear gate of the hospital grounds. I follow the paved road a half mile through the trees up the hill to the clearing. The stone chapel and well-kept mansions are just as I'd remembered them. McLean always did seem to me to resemble a university campus more than a mental hospital.

Eight years ago, for a brief time, I'd been an attendant here. I was just out of college and uncertain about whether or not I should go on to graduate school in psychology or social work. The job gave me my first insider's view of a private mental hospital. At the time, though, what I found myself thinking was how would it have been for my mother if she'd been sent here instead of to the state mental hospital?

This return to McLean's stately grounds evokes even earlier memories. Trips to the state mental hospital to visit my mother were a regular part of my adolescence. A particular day comes to mind.

"You go now. See mother." My grandmother stood in the kitchen doorway as I climbed the back stairs home from school. "Bring Mary these things," she said in her broken English.

"But I don't know the way."

"You go now. You find way. Bring these to Mary." She
handed me a brown paper bag and my carfare.

Rebuttoning the coat I'd begun to remove, I turned and headed
for the trolley stop just around the corner from where I lived
with my aunt and my grandmother. I'd rather try to get to the
hospital than fight with Nana. Besides, I wanted to see Mummy
anyway. It was Wednesday, one of two weekly visiting days.
Usually I went on Sundays with Aunt Tilly in her car.

Snowflakes swirled around me as I boarded the trolley. I was
ashamed to ask for directions to the state hospital, so I asked the
driver the way to nearby Mattapan.

"Stay on this to the Arborway. Then catch the bus that will
take you out Hyde Park Avenue."

My vague sense of direction told me I could walk from there
to the hospital grounds.

I looked for landmarks; each stop moved away from those
that I recognized. The snow thickened, the day darkened. I came
forward to stand behind the conductor in the near-empty bus.
"How close do you come to Morton Street?" I asked.

"Not very."

"You better let me off as close as you do come."

At the next set of lights, the driver turned and gave me the
once-over from my wool cap and braids to my knee socks and
oxfords. "Don't you know there's a blizzard coming up? Where
are you going anyway?"

"The hospital."

"What hospital?"

"Boston State." I admitted it.

He shook his head no, then looked puzzled. "Boston State?"
I nodded and felt my face flush.

"I don't go by *there*, kid."

I flushed again.

"Look at this weather. It's too nasty to walk in. Stay on with
me to the end of the line. When we get back to the Arborway,
I'll show you the right way. There's a trolley that goes real close
to the hospital. You'll have a short walk from there."

But too long a ride, I thought. Thank God he's not judging me.
He's just trying to help. A glance at his watch showed the time to

be after three. Visiting hours ended at four. I'd barely make it. "Thanks," I said, "but I'm late. Better let me off as close as you do come."

"This is it." He pulled the bus to a stop. "But I hate to think of the walk."

We both peered through his snow-blanketed windshield. I could barely see to the other side of the street.

"Morton Street's way over there. Beyond the cemetery." He beckoned me to go in front of his bus. He didn't start up until I was safely across.

I waved good-bye, then put my head down. The fierce wind mixed new snow with old and made drifts. Thick snow kept falling.

I walked a long time and passed no one. How could I have stumbled upon a wilderness in the city of Boston? It felt like a blizzard. Where had it come from so fast? Both hands in my pockets, I tucked the bag into my armpit, keeping my head down.

I'd made a mistake. I should have listened to the driver and stayed on the bus. Even if I made it all the way to the hospital, visiting hours would be over by the time that I got there.

I moved out into the street, where an occasional car had left furrows. It was easier to walk in them than in the deepening drifts. It was taking lots of energy just to keep moving my legs. My knees were all chafed from rubbing each other. The wind blew right through me.

I felt lost but I wasn't. I could always turn back. I wasn't lost. I just didn't know where I was going.

I will make it. I must, I said to myself. I pushed on to the cemetery.

If I'd asked the first driver straight out for directions to Boston State Hospital, I'd have been there by now. Why didn't I ask? Did I think he'd think someone in my family was crazy? Was I afraid he'd think it was me who was the crazy one? Yes, I was.

No cars anymore. There was no one in sight. Into my head came a poem I'd learned that year in seventh-grade English. Francis Thompson's "Hound of Heaven." I began saying out loud:

"Down nights and down days
Down arches and years
I fled him down labyrinthine ways
Of my own mind

. . . and in the midst of tears, I fled from Him
All things betrayest thee who betrayest me."

My lungs felt close to bursting. Crying didn't help. I was talking to God. Could her daughter's love set my mother free?

I made one last push and collapsed.

"Oh, Mummy, I'm tired. I'm cold. I don't know the way. It's late and it's dark and I'm scared." I slumped against the gate of the cemetery. "Please forgive me."

The paper bag that Nana had given me to take to my mother had dissolved. Waxed paper and postage stamps, lettuce and bread were all stuck together. Seeing the waste made me cry all the harder. Mummy loved her mother's sandwiches; Nana made her triple-deckers.

I pushed myself away from the gate. My legs felt stiff and were numbing up. I knew I had to go back, but it was so far to walk. Could I still make it? Then a new scary thought: were the buses still running?

I set out again. At my back, the wind carried me. Here and there, snow had failed to bury my footsteps, so I made a game of looking for them. When I looked up and saw the shimmering lights of the avenue off in the distance, I knew the worst part was over.

I propped myself against a pole. The lights in the shops comforted me. Up ahead, I saw coming toward me, moving slowly— the bus! Almost over. But wait. It wasn't stopping.

"Hey," I shouted, "hey!" My legs moved woodenly.

The bus lurched to a stop. The back door opened, and I pulled myself on.

"Where'd you come from?" asked the driver when I came forward to pay my fare. "I didn't see you."

"Over there," I croaked. "At the stop."

"Umph. Well, I must not have seen you with all that snow on

you." It was melting already. I stood in a puddle. "What are you doing out anyway? Don't you know it's a blizzard? You must be crazy."

It was an offhand remark, but the driver confirmed one of my deepest fears—I carry marks on me and strangers can decipher my secrets.

Nana greeted me once more at the door. I pulled the soggy cigarettes from my pocket. She hit me.

"No-good liar, you never go to the hospital," she said, "you eat sandwich yourself." She hit me again.

I was too numb from the cold and I was too weak to protest.

"I never see daughter like that," she muttered. Then she left me alone in the kitchen.

I thought of my mother. I beamed my thoughts to her. I told her I loved her and I begged her forgiveness. I knew she believed in me.

Back at a mental hospital, I think as I walk the last lap of the hill to McLean, but this time it's not for a job *or* to visit my mother.

"Which way to Dr. Mueller's office?" I ask the receptionist. "I have an appointment. My name is Shields."

"Take a seat around the corner. I'll tell him you're here."

A glance at the clock shows me to be early. Being on time is always an effort. A troubled sleeper by night, I'm a slow starter in the morning. It's a very old pattern. Knowing how awkward and significant it would be to be late for my very first appointment with my prospective psychoanalyst, I'd taken all kinds of care, set two alarm clocks. Now I had time to organize my thoughts for our meeting.

Ahead of me, the long carpeted hallway is lined on both sides with great heavy doors. What goes on behind them? I'd never stopped to wonder before.

Men in dark suits pass by. They must be psychiatrists. The young men and the young women in long hair and army clothes must be the patients. At thirty-two, I seem too old for this crowd. I wear a plaid skirt and black sweater. My hair's in a bun. I feel out of place.

Who might Dr. Mueller be? From our one telephone conversation, I picked up a slight Teutonic accent, so I suspect that he's German. I scan the passing doctors. Some seem too young, others too old, most too American-looking. I spot only two likely candidates: one a balding man in a brown suit; the other dark-haired, early forties, and close to six feet.

Now that I'm here, what if he won't accept me as a patient? What if I'm not ready? Which door is his?

Despite this relatively posh waiting room, I feel more and more anxious. This administration building triggers memories of one from bygone days.

"At least she's not on the East Side," said my mother's sister as she brought her gray Plymouth to a stop in the parking lot of Boston State Hospital's West Side administration building.

"What's so good about that?" I asked Aunt Tilly.

"The East Side's where they put the ones who never go home."

"You don't really mean never?"

"Never," she said.

What crime would someone have to commit to go to the East Side? I followed my aunt into the administration building carrying the bag Nana had packed for my mother.

"Mary Frazier," my aunt announced crisply.

"Relationship?" asked the nurse at the desk.

"Sister and"—Tilly pointed to me—"daughter."

"How old?"

"Thirteen," Tilly lied.

I was eleven but tall. Children under twelve weren't allowed in the acute wards.

"Take a seat." The nurse gave my aunt a pass and wrote something in a ledger.

It was a Sunday in 1947. It was summer. I looked around at the waiting room of anxious relatives. My aunt appeared to be the best-dressed; and, heaven knows, she'd worked very hard at it. That morning she'd taken great pains with her hair, doing it and redoing it until it was right. The front was rolled in an upsweep, the back was wrapped in a snood. She'd powdered and rouged her pale skin and used mascara and pencil on her dark brows and eyelashes. With a dab of red gloss on her finger, she'd widened her lips by spreading the color beyond her mouth's natural edges. "You're beautiful," I'd said in admiration.

In this crowd, she was surely the most fashionably attired. She wore a brown cotton dress with a matching bolero. Chalk-white jewelry and white gloves topped off her ensemble. She carried a purse of shiny patent leather. Tilly was armed: *she* would never disappear into the hospital's quicksand—but what of the rest of us?

"Are they inmates?" I asked my aunt.

"No, they're visitors," she said of the drab couple across from us.

How could she tell?

Would those in charge know that I didn't belong here? Know that I was a child? Too young to be crazy? What if they mistake me for a grown-up? Everyone says I'm so tall. I huddled closer to Tilly. I bit my nails. She chain-smoked Old Golds.

"Frazier's in L," called out the nurse at the desk.

Except for the grates on the window, L looked like a regular hospital building.

"She's better since hydrotherapy," said a nurse at the door as she took Aunt Tilly's pass.

"What's hydrotherapy?" I whispered.

"They wrap her in sheets and put her in a big tub of water."

"Why?"

"It calms her down."

The nurse reappeared. A woman was with her. I almost didn't recognize my own mother.

Our eyes met. Then the flicker. I knew the look. I froze in her gaze.

By the time my mother and I took the remaining steps to reach each other, the glow of recognition was gone. She was no longer "there."

We took a bench near the wall. "Well, Mary," Aunt Tilly said, "you're really lucky to be here."

My mother gave her sister a dirty look but said nothing.

I gave her the bag. She reached for the cigarettes she knew would be there. Tilly lighted one for my mother and one for herself. I watched as my mother dragged deeply and sucked on the cigarette.

I couldn't take my eyes from my mother's face. She seemed unaware of my presence.

"You can't get out of here until you behave," Tilly said. "If you're good, you'll get to go before staff. They'll decide when you can come home for a visit."

My mother's lips curled into a sneer. She scowled at Tilly, then tensed as if she were going to hit her. But she didn't. She slumped down and looked away from both of us off toward the wall.

I ached to reach out to my mother.

Tilly got up and walked toward the nurse. As she moved, my mother swirled toward me and grabbed my arm. "For God's sake, Mary Louise, tell Nana to get me out of here," she pleaded desperately.

The nurse took my mother's arm. They went out of the room. The visit was over.

Following my aunt back to the car, I tried not to cry. It made Tilly furious when I cried for my mother.

After all, Tilly and Nana were making a home for my brother and me. I didn't want to be ungrateful, but why was my mother in this horrible place?

"What's wrong with her?" I asked Tilly when I could keep my voice steady. "What's wrong with my mother?"

"She's got to learn her lesson. Once and for all, she's got to learn," Tilly declared.

In McLean's administration building, from where I am sitting I can see a door open just down the hall, and out steps the dark-haired man I'd seen in the corridor earlier. He appears not to notice me. Does he know I'm here?

"Mrs. Shields?"

I nod and look up at him. He's slim, clean-shaven, has dark brows and dark eyes. Rather attractive.

I get to my feet. We shake hands. I follow him back to the open door.

His office is uncluttered and bright, not the dark book-lined sanctuary I had anticipated. Morning light shines in through a large window. The beige walls and high ceiling seem to bounce back the light. A few cushioned chairs, a few end tables, a desk, and a brown tweedy couch make up the furnishings. On one wall is a painting of a lone sailboat heading toward the horizon.

Dr. Mueller closes first the outer door, then the inner one, his manner one of European formality. He gestures me to a chair, not the couch. I am relieved. His presence, the double doors, and the high ceiling create a comfortable atmosphere. I feel drawn in.

He settles into the chair opposite mine. He is attentive, calm, and relaxed.

I sit on the edge and smile nervously.

Here we are, face-to-face.

"Well, what brings you to psychoanalysis?"

I'd rehearsed dozens of answers, but now I don't know what to say. I feel my face flush. "When you called from the Institute and said you could take on a new analysand, I made the decision to drop out of graduate school on the spot." I smooth my skirt. "It was the mid-winter break, so all my course work was finished. They're holding my fellowship, so I can go back anytime." My heart is pounding. "Something about graduate school upset me. I'd been out of college for several years. The program was new. My hopes were too high."

The graduate program was designed to train people to become teachers in Boston's poorest neighborhood schools. The curriculum focused on ways to categorize poor kids more than it did on developing new ways to teach them. "Culturally deprived" the kids were called. They were viewed by the program as having the same social limitations as the families they were born into. Thus, the curriculum presented a rigged game as fair.

But I'd grown up poor. Aunt Tilly and Nana collected welfare for me and my brother. Yet in the Boston school system, I'd had a few teachers who'd seen me as a child with potential. Thanks to their high expectations, I held on to my dream of becoming a writer. I finished high school and was admitted to Radcliffe and awarded a scholarship.

"I find it a struggle to believe in myself," I tell Dr. Mueller. "I never quite do. I care so much about what people think of me, I always feel vulnerable."

"You have a high need for approval?"

"I do."

He draws the connection. "You expect psychoanalysis to help?"

I nod. "And there's something else."

"What is that?" He enunciates every word in the manner of one for whom English is not the first language.

"I'm afraid I'll go crazy." I speak quickly to get the words out.

"Do you know why?" he asks after a while.

"My mother. I never understood what made her schizophrenic. I've gone to college, I've read psychology. I've been in mental hospitals as a visitor, a volunteer, an employee. I've even been here." I point over to Belknap, where I'd worked as an attendant. "But I always feel it's only a matter of time before I end up somewhere as a patient." I take a deep swallow. My throat has gone dry. "This place is better than most. Too bad I won't be able to afford it."

He doesn't laugh.

Drained of composure, I slump back in my chair. "I wish I knew what else to tell you." I flutter my hands to indicate I can no longer speak.

He shifts in his chair and recrosses his legs. "Can you give me a specific example of something that bothers you?"

"Crossing streets. I walk blocks out of my way to avoid crowded intersections."

"Does this happen often?"

"Only when I'm afraid I might walk into a car"—I shrug my shoulders—"but mostly I just bump myself a lot." I expose a bruised elbow. "A few weeks ago I tripped on a toy while cleaning my son's room. I banged my arm and sprained my ankle. It was Sunday, so my husband was home. He put me to bed, took care of the kids, cleaned up the house. I couldn't walk for a day."

"What meaning do you see in these events?"

"Anxiety, I guess."

"You guess?" He peers at me over his glasses.

"When I get very depressed, I drink too much." I look away from his face and down to his shoes. "And that scares me too. My father is an alcoholic and my aunt was one too. Alcohol ruined their lives. I saw the destruction, but I have to admit alcohol sure kills the pain." I can feel my mind wandering. "I'm sorry." I reach toward him. "Now that I'm here, I don't remember."

"What don't you remember?" he asks sympathetically.

"The reasons I want psychoanalysis. Is anything I've said reason enough?"

"There are many reasons to want psychoanalysis," he says in a tone that manages to avoid sounding patronizing. "The things you've told me are some of them, but you do know it takes time."

Ah, that's what I was afraid of. He thinks my problem is too acute. He can't help me. "My declines come and go in relation to pressure." I speak urgently now, my adrenaline pumping. I know the analytic process is slow and exacting, isn't good in a crisis. "Graduate school was an experiment to see if I could handle a career and my family. I can't. Now that I've dropped out, the pressure is off. I'll have time to devote to analysis. I want to use it to help me figure things out."

He still hasn't said yes or no, so I speak even faster.

"Ever since college, I've wanted to be in analysis. I wasn't ready for it then, but I'm sure I am now. At my job, my hours are flexible. I can adapt to your schedule." I suddenly stop.

"What is it you're feeling now?" he asks, leaning forward closer to me.

I'm fighting back tears, but I don't say that to him. "I feel tired . . . run-down. I believe that if I'm ever to get over the fear I'll go crazy, it's going to have to be in analysis." I look him in the eye. "I'm not really sure I can do it, but I am sure I do want to try."

"And you feel you can do this work with me?"

An image of him in the hall before I knew who he was flashes to mind, but I'm too embarrassed to speak of it. "Yes," I answer.

"Yes?" He seems to know I am holding something back.

"In the hall, before I knew who you were, you were one of the ones whose faces I liked."

He seems neither flattered nor critical.

What's left to explain? Have I left something out?

"Very well." From his breast pocket he removes a small date-book. He flips through its pages, then looks up at me. "Let's set up a schedule then, shall we?"

After nearly a year on the Institute's waiting list, I feel suddenly rushed. In a daze, I say, "Fine."

"Can you come mornings?"

"How early?" My heart skips a beat.

"Wednesdays at eight. The four other mornings, nine."

"I have a problem being . . . no, never mind . . . mornings are fine. I can see you and still get to work fairly early. The store doesn't open till ten."

"Have you thought about what you can afford to pay? The Institute's sliding scale will apply."

"Without it I couldn't afford to be here."

He nods.

"My husband . . . his name is Mike . . . he and I have discussed it. We can afford fifteen dollars a week. Perhaps I can afford to pay more in the fall, but for now that's the most . . ."

"That will be fine."

What a relief.

"That's three dollars a session. On the first of each month, I'll hand you a bill. You can make the check payable to me, not the Institute."

"I wondered about that."

"So," he says, pen poised over his datebook, "shall we make our next appointment for Wednesday at eight?"

"Yes."

He makes some notations and we both rise. So accustomed am I to endless preliminaries, it's hard to believe that arrangements for this next big step in my life have been made so quickly—almost easily. I have an urge to embrace him.

"Thank you, Dr. Mueller," I say, extending my hand. His

touch reassures me. "I want you to know that I'll try very hard."
"I'm sure that you will." He bows by way of farewell. "Until next Wednesday at eight then?"

It is over and I'm back out in the cold March air. The sky is cloudless, and off in the distance I can see the tall buildings of Boston. I pass through the gate lost in reverie.

Chapter Two

My very first psychoanalytic session prompts me, on my own time, to try to revive my earliest memory.

Atwood Square. A short unpaved alley of run-down tenement houses in the Jamaica Plain section of Boston. My mother, father, and I had moved there to be close to Aunt Tilly and Nana, my mother's sister and mother, who lived only two blocks away. For some unexplained reason, the first sight of the kitchen linoleum in that top-floor apartment of the wooden three-decker cheered me enormously. It was a black-and-white-checkerboard floor. I was four, and it was the winter of 1939.

I remember being home from kindergarten. I was sick and the weather was bad.

"Please, can we go through your trunk, Mummy, please?" I asked.

"But, Mary Louise, you've been through that trunk so many times."

"I never get tired of looking. Can we get out your reporter drawings?"

"How many times do I have to tell you that I was a newspaper illustrator, not a reporter? There's a big difference." Her voice was impatient, and she rubbed her temples as if she had a headache.

I waited to see whether she would stay in touch or withdraw. She absentmindedly inhaled on a Pall Mall. Her expression grew more relaxed. "All right." She beckoned me to her side. "All right." She broke into a rare smile.

I scrambled out of bed, and together we sat on the cold floor under the window next to the wooden chest stapled over with bright yellow chintz.

When she was young, my mother had worked for a daily newspaper called the *Boston Post*. One by one, she took her illustrations out of the trunk. Many pages were filled, top to bottom, with her drawings, lots of them in bright-colored ink.

I looked at my mother. Her auburn hair was cut in a short, girlish bob. Her face was heart-shaped. I loved her nose. She called it "pug" and hated it, but I thought that my mother was even lovelier than the women she drew. The flapper, the aviatrix, and the ladies in ball gowns—there they were, just as I'd remembered them.

Out from the trunk came some cutout dolls my mother had drawn for the *Post*'s Sunday comics. There was my favorite—Marie Antoinette—with a wardrobe of ball gowns complete with changes of wig. Then came one of the cover pages the *Boston Post* paid my mother to do for the Sunday pictorial section. So many details and bright colors—fountains, flowers, and women in elegant ball gowns.

"Could you teach me to draw the way you do?"

"You should go to business school. Learn bookkeeping, not art. I became an artist, and what did it get me? Stay away from deep water, Mary Louise. Learn practical things, not foolishness." Gingerly, she set her illustrations aside.

On top of the pile was a gray cardboard folder I'd never noticed before. Inside was a studio portrait of a baby girl clutching a Mickey Mouse doll.

"Put that away," said my mother.

"Why, Mummy?"

"That's baby Jean Andrea," she said in a faraway voice, gently touching the photograph. "A man came to the house, said 'I have a special.' I took from the rent money. He took Sissa's picture. I gave her the toy to keep her hands still. . . ."

My mother got to her feet lovingly holding the photograph. I held my breath.

"I don't remember her," I said softly.

"That's because you were only two and a half at the time. A few weeks after the man took this picture, Sissa came down with the croup. Daddy went out to get medicine. Aunt Tilly came by with fresh oranges. 'That child has to go to the hospital,' Tilly said, 'she's turning blue.' I left you with a neighbor. You had the croup too, but you were stronger than Sissa. Tilly drove us to the hospital. It was strep. There were no sulfa drugs then. They put that dear baby into an oxygen tent, but by the time Daddy showed up, she was gone." My mother moved farther away from me, into a chair. "She was the quiet one. A perfect baby, everyone said. Not even a year and a half," my mother muttered. "Not even a year and a half."

Please stay with me, Mummy, I silently prayed, please don't go off in your head. Don't leave me alone.

"I feel unprepared," I tell Dr. Mueller, "but I think I know why."

Dr. Mueller says nothing. The warm glow from the lamp standing next to his chair lends his office some coziness on this dark, drizzly morning.

"Take Radcliffe, for instance. 'You'll never get in,' said my guidance counselor, 'so apply to State Teachers—that way you'll be sure.' But I'd already decided on Radcliffe. My seventh-grade history teacher, a very important person for me, had gone there. I looked up to her. That's how I decided. In spring of senior year, before I knew whether or not I'd been accepted, I couldn't bear to hear one word from anyone about how hard it would be if I got in. On the day the fat envelope arrived with the good news, I cried for three hours. I was over my head and I knew it. I was poorly prepared." I search his face for a reaction.

"What brings this to mind now?"

"Psychoanalysis. I've done it again. I'm not really prepared."

"How so?"

"When I made up my mind in college that one day I would

have psychoanalysis, I knew about as much about it as I knew about Radcliffe when I made up my mind to go *there*. I just decided it was something I wanted to do."

"You had no reason?"

"My mother."

"Radcliffe or analysis?"

"Which one did you mean?"

"Why change your answer? Which one did *you* mean?"

I am intrigued by how readily "mother" slipped out. Which one *did* I mean?

"I don't understand why my mother went crazy."

"But how does psychoanalysis fit in?" he asks.

"Because if she went crazy, it means I could too."

"Yes?" He finally interrupts my long silence.

"I'm not sure I can do it."

He doesn't offer me the encouragement that I wish he would.

"Since I last saw you, I've resisted the urge to run to the library and read every book written about psychoanalysis. That's not the way—is it?"

He shakes his head no.

"I know how regular therapy works, but I don't know how it's different from what we do here in analysis."

Dr. Mueller sits motionless.

"Just tell me what you want"—I make an attempt at a joke—"ask me some questions—the ones you want answered."

He doesn't smile.

"There must be more to it than what you've already told me," I hastily add.

"Speak freely and honestly. Say what comes into your mind with as little censoring as possible."

"But you must have some expectations?"

"It is your analysis. It must be the way you want it to be."

"I've been meaning to ask you when I go over there." I nod toward the wall . . . where the couch is.

"Whenever you're ready. Now if you like." He pauses. Using the same courtly gesture with which he'd ushered me into his office, he nods toward the couch.

What to do? My boots are still wet from the rain. Should I

take them off? Feels too intimate in front of a stranger. But boots on a couch? The mattress cover has a piece of plastic sewn on at the foot. Must be for shoes and boots. I go to the couch and lie down. I set my feet on the Naugahyde strip, my head on the wedge-shaped bolster. Dr. Mueller changes chairs. He's now behind me, out of my line of vision.

I'm physically comfortable but psychologically embarrassed. All I can think of are *New Yorker* cartoons, line-drawn psychoanalysts with little books perched on their knees, their strange-looking patients stretched out before them.

"I feel silly, Dr. Mueller."

"Uhmm?"

"You can see me. I can't see you."

"Does that bother you?"

"Yes."

"Why?"

"I can't see your face. I can't even guess what you're thinking."

"Lying down on the couch helps you focus on your thinking—on your own thoughts, not mine."

"What about dreams? Do you want me to tell you?"

"When you have them. Remember that some thoughts you have will seem irrelevant, but you should say them anyway. And try to be truthful even if it's embarrassing."

"Won't that take trust?"

Silence.

"I'm not sure I'm ready to trust you. Right off the bat, I mean." It's unnerving. A man I don't know and can't see is sitting behind me. Watching and waiting. This whole arrangement feels scary. But I can't tell him that. I signed up on my own . . . knew what I was in for. "I trust your thinking, but I don't know how you feel."

I am aware of sounds from the radiators. Old pipes make a clatter in the basement below. I look up to the ceiling, down to my feet, over toward the door. By turning my head slightly, I can see the sailboat on the opposite wall.

The analyst's lack of verbal response is a device I know all about from my reading. It's supposed to offer a mirror for the analysand's own reflections. I know all about that. So why do I feel as if I'm about to throw up?

Before my son, Christopher, was born, I read lots of books about childbirth . . . talked to my friends who had already had babies. Yet when Christopher was actually born, it wasn't like what I'd expected. It hurt. He came quickly. Nothing softened that shock. I felt very alone. Very frightened.

"Yes?" Dr. Mueller says, as though he detects my wandering thoughts.

Be honest. Speak my mind. That shouldn't be hard. I'm outspoken anyway.

"Yes?" he repeats.

"This is not how I expected to feel."

※

Chapter Three

※

"How did it go?" DeeDee clatters into my kitchen, one arm in, one arm out of her camel's-hair coat. She untangles herself, then gives me a hug. "I'm dying to hear," she says breathlessly.

DeeDee Dante, my friend of ten years, is ten years older than I. More than anyone else, she's reinforced my strong interest in psychoanalysis. She was the first person I knew who'd actually done it. Her analysis unearthed an inner core that longed for self-discipline. A free-lance designer and photographer, she's now a professor. She is no more talented than she was before her analysis—but she *is* more organized, more in control, less frightened of life.

I don't know what to say to her.

"You're not disappointed?"

"I just wish I had more to go on than this dreadful feeling something is wrong with me."

"But, Lou, that feeling is your way of telling yourself you're unhappy."

"If I did lots of things, the way you do, I could use the analysis to learn to do them all better."

"That's the way I did it, but you're different from me. You've got to do your analysis your way."

"That's the second time I've heard that today, and believe me, it's no consolation."

"Look," she says, putting her arm on my shoulder, "I was a

dilettante before my analysis and I still am. Too bad this isn't Florence in the Renaissance instead of Cambridge in the Sixties, but I bet the food didn't taste any better." She leaves my side to bend over the stove. "What's this sauce in the pot?" She makes a breeze with her hand to draw the smell toward her.

"Chicken Marengo."

"I'm glad I was invited to dinner. I see Suzy Homemaker is at it again."

"Suzy Homemaker?" asks Dr. Mueller during our next session.

"It's only a joke."

"I don't get it."

"My friends call me that. Sometimes I refer to myself that way, too."

"Under what circumstances?"

I wish I could see his face. Does he think I'm crazy?

"It's harmless, really," I add, a little defensively. "If I've been doing a lot of cooking or canning or sewing, I say, 'Suzy Homemaker's at it again.' I started doing it a few years back. I don't remember when exactly. Suzy Homemaker was the brand name of toy mops, tiny brooms, little stoves. The tools of the trade, I used to call them. Make sure little girls get the message."

"What toys did you play with?"

"That's not the point."

"Then I'm afraid I don't see what the point is."

"Calling myself Suzy Homemaker is a way to show I don't take housewifely things seriously."

I wait for his comment, but all I can hear is his breathing.

For several sessions, I digress to tell Dr. Mueller all about my best friend through childhood, Nanette O'Dwyer. Nan and I dreamed of growing up to be writers.

All through high school, we excelled: honor roll, dean's list, National Honor Society; yearbook, school magazine, officers of our class.

Our teachers thought we should both go on to college, but

Nan's family made her switch to secretarial in her senior year. I promised my aunt that I would, but I didn't, so I made it to Radcliffe.

"What for?" Tilly said. "Waste of time if you ask me. You'll only end up getting married."

She was right, of course. Both Nan and I did.

But I never gave up on my dream of becoming a writer. It's part of why I hold on to my past, part of my motivation to do psychoanalysis; I don't know what to hold on to, what to let go of.

Suzy lends me a double identity, like a character in a story I wrote when I was nine. She had an identical twin.

A double identity fills many needs, and it's all part of the muddle I bring to Dr. Mueller.

"The real point is I never held high expectations for marriage."

"Uhmm?"

"I got married in black."

"Black?" Now his voice registers the surprise I'd anticipated.

"I worked the night shift here at McLean. A friend picked me up at eleven. Back home, I changed from my white uniform into my favorite dress—full skirt, wide collar. It just happened to be black. At the time, I thought nothing of it. Mike and I were married by a justice of the peace right about midnight. Now I see that what I did was odd, but maybe I should tell you . . . I was three months pregnant with Christopher."

"What about the pregnancy?"

"It was 1959. Not only abortion was illegal in Massachusetts, so was contraception. I'd been using a diaphragm. I'm not sure I was properly fitted."

I interpret his silence as criticism. "Dr. Mueller," I ask with some indignation, "are you aware of how hard a woman has to work *not* to get pregnant?"

"Don't forget, I'm a medical doctor."

"That's too easy an answer. When I was pregnant with Chris, the friend I'd last known to have an abortion was picked up on a corner, blindfolded, and taken to someone's kitchen table. I could never have done that. Besides, Mike wanted to marry me, even before."

How to describe the reasons I married Mike? How can I say them and not sound like a dope?

Mike was twenty-two, two years younger than I, and less than a year out of Harvard. It never occurred to him to set up our household without including my sixteen-year-old brother, Frank, and my eighty-two-year-old grandmother, Nana. That's the way they did things back in Ohio. Nothing odd about that.

Mike wanted to teach, but decided to postpone graduate school until after the baby, so he stayed on at Good Design, the furniture store in Harvard Square where he'd worked part-time his last year at Harvard. When I got pregnant, I left my job at McLean to go work there too. Mike did the woodworking and I sold the furniture.

As a new wife, the first thing I learned to do was to cook. It came naturally. Having our friends over for dinner not only made our place homier, it gave them a home to go to as well. Our friends would chip in on the wine and the groceries. I did the cooking.

"We were so happy. . . ."

"Is something wrong, Mrs. Shields?"

"Not really. I'm just thinking back. Nana lived with us until she died of a stroke. She was eighty-six, and active right up to the end. Frank grew up and moved out, now has a place of his own and a good job in computers. Four years after Christopher was born came Elizabeth. They're both wonderful children, so loving and spirited. Now Mike and I own our house. We both work at the store. Everything has turned out better than I ever imagined it could. . . ." I feel myself overcome with an indescribable emotion.

"Mrs. Shields, what's the matter?"

"All that reading and schooling . . ."

"Could Suzy Homemaker," he asks softly, in a tentative voice, "be a way of letting yourself do all that's expected of you while you save a part of yourself for something more?"

"I never looked at it that way."

"That's what we're here for—to find new ways to look at things."

"My mother didn't cook much. She never liked housework.

Nana and Tilly always said she was no good as a housewife." My speech is faltering. "The police took my mother away . . . I was there."

"And you weren't going to let that happen to you."

"No." I gulp on my spit. "I cook. I sew. I'm a very good mother."

"Therefore you're not crazy." He carries my thoughts one step further.

"They'll *never* take me away." I cover my face with my hands so he can't see my embarrassment. "To think I began by telling you Suzy was a joke."

"It must be frightening to recall a time when you were unable to understand what was happening to your mother."

I nod.

"Dr. Mueller," I ask after a while, "who do you think I should be?"

"You must decide. No—let me put it another way—*only* you can decide. My sole expectation is that you use this analysis to decide for yourself who and what you want to be." Then he adds gently, "There is time."

❀

Chapter Four

❀

"I brought in a letter I'd like you to read," I start a new session. "There's no date on it and I've lost the envelope, but I'd guess that my mother sent it to me when I was about two. I must have been away with my aunt and my grandmother, but I don't recall . . ." I hand it up over my head to him.

"Why don't *you* read it?"

" 'Dear Mary Lou,' " I begin. Saying my own name out loud makes me aware that my mother chose to give me her name, Mary, and yet she is—and was—always careful to call me "Mary Lou" or "Mary Louise." Did she make that distinction deliberately?

I clear my throat and continue:

" 'I am so glad you are having such a good time. I hope you are being a very good girl and doing just what Nana and Aunty Tilloo say.

Baby Sissa says she would like to see the new baby cow and the horseys, but she seems satisfied enough with her new Popeye digging set.

Your dolly has a new suitcase for her dollclothes and a new doll broom which you will see when you come home.

I will probably have some more things here by the time you get back but those will be only for the good Mary Lou.' "

I move the letter toward him again. "See. She signs it with a big kiss. And look." I open the folded paper. "She wrote another letter inside to my aunt and my grandmother." I clear my throat again:

" 'Dear Tilly and Nanny:
     The weather has been wonderful here—a little cool maybe but comfortable, especially at night. Pretty soon I'll have to pin Sissa up in blankets as it's getting too cool for her without them.
     I've done the ironing around here and have started the curtains and as I can borrow a stretcher from upstairs, I hope to get them all done.
     As you know we have a new phone for Ralph's business, but so far I haven't seen any.
     I expect Ralph home early today (Sat.) and will try to send up a couple of bucks to Mary Lou before you start back for home. Sister is squally and pulling my dress here every minute since I've sat down to write so I must close now as she is making me nervous. Will write again. Love to all.

                                                    Mary.' "

     "You seem to see great significance in these letters. I'm not sure I know why." Dr. Mueller sounds perplexed.
     "When I became a mother myself, I thought I was embracing a role that my mother had always rejected. These letters prove otherwise."
     "It still isn't clear to me what you are driving at."
     "She *did* try to play Suzy Homemaker, but she apparently stopped as I grew older—which is why I don't remember."
     "And?"
     "In these letters, my mother sounds like she's trying. She reminds me of me—relieved when she has just one of two children to take care of—the way I feel when Mike takes off with Christopher. She's washing curtains, doing housework. She sounds normal—not crazy. When I was little, my mother taught Anna, the girl downstairs, how to draw. Instead of teaching me too, she

gave me dolls and brooms. I thought it meant she loved Anna better than me."

"I'm sorry. I still don't understand."

"I *did* get pregnant. I *did* have to get married. In her own way, my mother was trying to prepare me for what she thought I couldn't escape. She'd tried herself."

"Tried what?"

"Rising above being a woman."

"In what way?"

"Being an artist. She made lots of money free-lancing her art work. That was in the Twenties. She was young. She was beautiful. She didn't get married until she was thirty-two."

"Wait a minute." Dr. Mueller interrupts my flow of thought. "Are you trying to tell me that your mother *had* to get married?"

"You mean I didn't tell you?"

"I would have remembered."

"Oh. She was seven months pregnant with me."

At Waverly Square, a dime in the pay phone gets me Mike at the store. "I just can't come in."

"You do sound upset. That's okay. We can manage. Take the day off and don't worry."

Another dime reaches DeeDee. "Come right over," she tells me, "I'm home packing today. Take a taxi. I'll put up some coffee."

On the other side of her front door, I hear footsteps. I remove my dark glasses.

"Oh, Lou, you look awful." DeeDee stands in the doorway, still in her nightgown. "Are you all right?" I let her help me into the living room.

"I am now."

She settles me on the couch before going for coffee and cigarettes.

"What bothers me," I finally confide to her, "is that I don't think I'm doing it right."

"But why?"

"All I do is talk about my marriage and the kids. And my mother."

"What did you imagine you'd talk about?"

"My identity, I guess . . . some new direction for my life."

"Right now, your family *is* your identity. Being a wife and mother takes most of your energy. Even I can feel that. You used to have more time for me. Don't forget, I knew you before you were married. I felt the change after you gave birth to Christopher."

"What did you see?"

"You're driven to prove you're a good wife and mother."

"Is that so bad?"

"Of course not. It's just that . . ."

"Yes?"

". . . you're trying too hard."

"What's wrong with that?"

"Marriage seems to mean more to you than it does to the rest of us." She flutters her hands as if groping for words. "For you, it's more like a state of grace, and that's what I bet you're having such a hard time trying to explain to Dr. Mueller."

Her words hurt. They ring true.

I don't want to admit how important my marriage is. Having Mike makes me feel secure; as his wife, I know where I stand and what's expected of me—even though the work's hard. It takes time . . . drains my energy.

"Oh, Lou"—DeeDee's tone is gentle—"you still hear Nana criticizing you. God, what a hard woman!" DeeDee shudders.

"You knew her only in old age. She wasn't always so bad."

"If you want to forgive and forget, that's your business." DeeDee sounds impatient. "She wasn't *my* grandmother. I don't owe her—or her memory—anything. The awful thing is that even from the grave she still gets to you. She made you believe you were worthless. She used to tell me—your best friend—that you were no good, but the pity of it all is that *you* were the one who believed her. You know you did. Now you think that if you can surround yourself with people who love and respect you, your inner feelings will change." She shakes her head. "It doesn't work that way. The change must come from you."

"You've been in analysis for such a long time. How long do you think mine will take?"

"It all depends." She comes to sit next to me. "It's a very slow process. Like water dripping on stone. It takes a long time to make an impression."

"Oh, DeeDee, how I'm going to miss you."

The next day she'll be gone for the summer to her house on Martha's Vineyard. "Now remember," she says as we part, "you can come anytime."

"We'll see," I say, hugging her. "Thank you for everything."

I start missing DeeDee even before she leaves town. On the Vineyard, DeeDee won't have a telephone, so I won't even be able to call her. I'll miss her companionship, but I'll also miss our long talks. I'm dreading the loss of feedback I get from my dear friend.

My friend Abby, whom I met through our antiwar work, is, like me, in Cambridge all summer to see her analyst. She's single and younger than I am, but our common bonds make for a deepening friendship, and were anyone to eavesdrop on our long conversations, the gaps in our upbringings would not be readily apparent. It astonishes me that we have so much to share. Abby's last name is Rockefeller, and she is an heir to one of America's largest family fortunes.

In her family, as in mine, males were preferred, the extremes painfully obvious: Abby's father and uncles share in the Rockefeller Brothers Trust Fund left to them by John D.—the one female sibling was simply left out. Abby's own brothers are expected to marry and do something meaningful with their lives; Abby is expected only to make a good marriage.

"My independence they label rebelliousness," Abby tells me. "They want me to 'act like a young lady.' I'm twenty-seven years old and they keep telling me to stop acting like a tomboy."

"But I don't see why you care."

"Don't you think I want their approval the same way you wanted your grandmother's?"

"It doesn't seem quite the same." I shake my head.

"Well, it isn't. You *know* you can survive on your own. You've been tested. When I bring myself to be able to forget about my family, there's always someone around to remind me that whatever recognition I earn is because of—not in spite of— being a Rockefeller."

I look closely at Abby. Her naturally wavy long hair is loosely pulled back, leaving soft tendrils around her face. She never wears makeup, the way I do. Her face is intelligent; she is perceptive and witty. She could persuade me of anything. "But," I protest, "you're so strong."

" 'Willful,' they say in my family."

"Strength is strength."

"I don't have yours." She is serious.

"What *are* you talking about?"

"Lou, coming through all you have is quite an achievement. You should face it as such."

Isn't that odd?

We each seem to need psychoanalysis because we both lack self-confidence.

"You should plan a day when we can go to the beach without them," Abby says.

Abby drives and I don't, and she's been more than good-natured about taking my kids along with us. "But that doesn't seem fair," I say nervously.

"You sound as though you need to be in some sort of crisis to justify a day off from being a mother. Sometimes a day off is in order, Lou—whether you deserve it or not."

Why does a day off from the children feel like such a big deal? It probably goes back to my adolescence. My brother was nine years younger than I was, and when my friends and I went to the beach, we always took him. I didn't feel that I had to—I just didn't want him to miss a good time.

Then I remind myself: Christopher and Elizabeth have lots of good times. Besides, they have a father.

"Okay. You win." I give Abby's shoulder a mock punch. "I'm

sure Jeannie will sub for me at the store. She's done it before. If
we don't bring my kids, we can take your canoe to Plum Island."

After her own appointment, Abby arrives on the grounds of
McLean to pick me up in front of the administration building.
The green canvas canoe is strapped to the roof rack of her green
Volvo and overhangs front and back.

"The next time," she says as I get into the car, "we'll take the
kids to swim in the pond."

"Promise?"

"Promise. You choose the day and I'll pick you all up."

"Let's go then."

We arrive. "How do we get it *there?*" I ask Abby as I stare at
the long distance between Plum Island's parking lot and the
water.

Abby unties the rope on the rack and hoists part of the canoe's
weight to the top of her head.

"You're kidding!"

"My sister and I do it all the time."

"How long *is* it?"

"Seventeen feet."

"I don't know . . ."

"Need some help?" call two guys from a car near to us in the
parking lot.

"No," Abby shouts.

I was prepared to let them give us a hand.

"Here." Abby stands me next to the car and begins easing the
canoe over my head. "It's fun. You'll get used to it."

She takes the front, leads the way. I struggle to hold up my
end. I'm taller than Abby and would have guessed I was stronger
—but apparently not.

"How did we do it?" I puff with exhaustion when the canoe
finally slips into the water.

"Strength." She laughs. "Now get in. I'll push us out."

"How do you see analysis?" I ask Abby.

We're not far from shore. Our arms drag in the water as we
relax in the sun.

"Like hitting a tennis ball on a backboard. It always comes back just the way you hit it. How about you?"

"Like a mirror. I see myself as I am, and"—I sit up—"that's not always what I want to see."

"I know what you mean," Abby says as she picks up the paddle.

❁

Chapter Five

❁

Ever since I began seeing Dr. Mueller in March, I'd assumed he'd be gone during August, the month psychoanalysts traditionally take for vacation. When he tells me he'll be gone for just a week over Labor Day, the news does nothing to relieve my panic. I am baffled by the tension. I feel claustrophobic.

"What form does it take?" asks Dr. Mueller.

"Shortness of breath in elevators. I always feel a slight tinge of panic in them."

"Do you know why?"

"The locked doors. I get afraid they'll never open."

I hear Dr. Mueller sigh.

"It's not too hard to figure out, I suppose, what with my mother locked up and my father in and out of jail for nonsupport and petty larceny." I heave a deep sigh of my own. "It's not the most reassuring way to grow up."

"I should say not."

"It's left me with a tremendous need to establish my own set of institutions to relate to. It's a way to be recognized."

"Recognized? I don't know what you mean."

"I've always felt that somehow Radcliffe is my mother, and my marriage and this analysis I think of as home. If they try to take me away, I'll have people on my side who'll fight for my rights . . . won't let me be swallowed up the way my mother was. The record will show that I went to a good school, was a good wife, and was in analysis with a good—"

"Mrs. Shields?"

"Yes."

"You're twisting your finger."

"What's wrong with that?"

"Don't you notice anything?"

I hold up my hand. God, my fingernails are a disgrace. Bitten right down to the cuticles.

"Isn't the finger you were twisting your ring finger?"

"So what?"

"You don't wear a wedding band. Isn't that somewhat unusual?"

I turn around, check his finger. Just as I thought. A gold band on his finger.

"Well, you're German. Perhaps that's why it seems strange to you," I say, turning back to the couch. "I know you want to read something into it, but I just took it off because it was too tight."

I wait for a reproach, but it doesn't come. "I had a dream," I say, in an effort to start a new subject. This work on the couch is unsettling.

"Why don't you tell me about it."

"Nothing much to tell. No train—just the tracks."

"And?"

"That's it. It was sort of picture dream—not very much action."

"Does anything come to mind?"

"We have a routine. When you go away for your week of vacation, you'll break it."

"Yet every time I've asked you how you feel about the upcoming change, you tell me it doesn't matter to you."

"You certainly have the right to take a week off."

"Is that all there is to it? Let's look at your dream. Broken tracks, missing trains—what do these things suggest?"

"Danger," I whisper.

"Yes?"

"I don't feel safe. I can't explain why."

"We're here to analyze, not explain."

"Jesus, Dr. Mueller, don't you think it's a bit obvious? My father abandoned me and my mother. She got locked up. He did too. What more do you want?"

"What about the tracks?"

"They had a break."

"Precisely."

"There you go again. To you everything has a meaning."

"Do you think there's none?"

"A few days of vacation. It's hardly abandoning, would you say? You never miss an appointment. You're always on time. You deserve a break . . ."

A break. A break? Broken tracks. Missing trains.

"Okay, okay, you have a point. You're taking a break and I'm supposed to miss you, right?"

"Supposed to, Mrs. Shields?"

"Look at it this way, Dr. Mueller, we've got a whole month to work on it. That should be enough time."

August 4. Was it the fourth or the fifth? I cannot remember. The ferry steams toward Martha's Vineyard. I stand over the railing to let the salt air spray my face. We were married at midnight. Is that Vineyard Haven already? No. Too soon. Let's see, what did the justice of the peace decide? The fourth, that's what he wrote on the marriage license. We got there before midnight, but he didn't marry us until a few minutes after. Today is the fourth, so it doesn't matter. Either way, Mike and I will not be together for our anniversary.

Vineyard Haven! The ferry pulls in. I scan the faces. There it is. The gondolier's hat. Leave it to DeeDee to stand out in a crowd.

DeeDee whisks me off to my favorite beach. There is no one in the water, and the horizon is cloudless.

"Now, Lou," DeeDee cautions, "don't go out too far. Please be careful. I'll watch you from here."

"Remember, DeeDee, I'm a mother now. I don't set out for the horizon the way I used to."

The pull of the undertow surprises and frightens me. With fast strokes, I swim hard for the shore. Dripping wet, by DeeDee's side, I reach for a towel.

"I'm glad you saw me waving you in."

I hadn't, but I don't tell her that.

"That man down the beach says you shouldn't be swimming. The undertow is too strong," she tells me as she dries my back.

"It was fine. I just wanted a dip. I'm through for the day."

Later, I call Mike from a pay phone not far from DeeDee's.

It rings and rings. I think that it is strange that no one is home.

"Oh, hello, you *are* home. I was just going to hang up. How are the kids? . . . Good, they'll like that. By the way, Mike, did you remember today was our anniversary? . . . You remembered last week and then forgot again? You know what Dr. Mueller would say about *that*. Never mind, though, I forgot too."

"Martini?" I look up to see John Donlon's broad Irish grin. DeeDee has brought me along to his party as her houseguest. I accept the frosty glass that John offers.

"That's not gin you're drinking!" DeeDee looks askance at my glass.

"Try it."

"But, Lou,"—she pushes the glass away—"I thought you'd given up gin."

"I just wanted a change," I lie—because I continue to drink until I go numb.

Chapter Six

"I nearly called you last night." I start talking even before Dr. Mueller closes the inner door. "There was a drowning on Martha's Vineyard at the same beach I'd been swimming at. No one I knew, but it seems to have thrown me into a depression." I lie down on the couch, grateful it's there.

My words are faltering. The hangover. I cover my eyes with one hand. The visor effect hides my face from his view. I recall the sea spray, the fumes from the engine, the way I felt on the ferry, and I begin to feel queasy all over again.

I speak of the undertow.

"I was at a party with DeeDee when I heard the news. That's all people were talking about." I swallow hard to suppress the reflex to vomit. "I think I'm still sick from the gin."

"Let me get this straight," he interrupts me. "You felt the undertow, experienced fear in the water—and that was the day *before* the drowning?"

"Yes. I don't think my panic had anything to do with the water even though the danger was real. The feelings seemed to be coming from inside me. I felt as though I were drowning—but not in the water. Do you understand?"

"Not yet. Tell me more."

"I returned to Wood's Hole on the same ferry that carried the hearse." I take another deep breath.

Can this be hyperventilating? I never did that before.

The sound of a power mower shatters the morning tranquility. Dr. Mueller gets up to close the window.

Pull yourself together, Mary Lou, try to say something meaningful.

I hear Dr. Mueller come back to his chair. I know I should say something to him about Mike—not Mike as a father, not Mike as a husband, but Mike as a man . . . how I *feel* about him.

"You've noticed, haven't you, that I hardly ever speak about Mike to you?"

"You mean you censor yourself?" he asks.

"Not exactly. Let me try to explain."

How to describe Mike? My Rock of Gibraltar? I'm so high-strung, he's so steady. Left on his own, he'd see only close friends or family, go fishing or birdwatching, play poker or read. He's quiet by nature, loves family trips to the country. The less anyone knows about him, the safer he feels. His family loves him and he loves his family. They meet all his needs. It's the way he grew up. Maybe that's why he feels so self-sufficient.

I'm just the opposite, I tell everyone everything. That's my security. I need for the world to know that I'm here. If I hadn't had help outside my family, I'd be done for by now. Teachers, librarians, my friends, and especially Mike. Without him, I'd have never managed to take care of Nana and Frank. Mike was always so good to them, it seemed to come from his heart. And he looks out for me in ways I can't for myself.

I turn around on the couch.

"I can't talk to you about Mike unless I can see your face. Will this be all right?" My eyes meet his.

Dr. Mueller nods.

"I have always respected Mike's need to keep his private life private. Take DeeDee, for instance. She's my best friend. I don't keep secrets from her, but if they're Mike's, I do."

"Excuse me." Dr. Mueller shifts in his chair. "You mentioned the forgotten anniversary, and I'm losing track of how all this ties together."

"I have to talk to you about Mike, but I'm sick at the prospect."

"Can you tell me why?"

"He would never be in analysis. Confiding to strangers is his very worst nightmare. He doesn't know how I do it or why I would want to."

"Do *you* understand why?"

"Oh, yes." I nod my head up and down. "Like it or not, Dr. Mueller, I'm desperate. You're my last resort, and you know it." I swallow again. Maybe I won't be sick after all. "I have no other alternative. My fear of going crazy is one I've lived with for my lifetime. I've done all I can to dispel it—ridicule it, make light of it, even outrun it. Nothing works. The fear has a life of its own in my head. Doing analysis makes intellectual sense to me. Not that I don't have doubts of my own. I do. I'd be a liar if I told you I didn't."

"And Mike?"

"He's afraid of this process. It's too much like confession. He grew up a Catholic and now has nothing to do with the Church. When you called me from the Institute, Mike urged me to think it over very carefully. Not that he ever asked me not to do it. He respects my wishes. . . ."

My eyes brim with tears.

"To Mike—in some way I don't understand—my coming to you means his personal defeat. He's disappointed. He thought his love would meet all my needs, undo my past. Of course, that's too much to hope for, although . . ."

"Yes?"

"It did work for a while."

Dr. Mueller looks confused.

"I've told Mike I can't leave him out of my analysis. He's too important a part of my life. Mike and I are drifting apart, and I don't know why."

"I see."

"Before I forget, let me tell you a dream. I don't think it means much, but I did remember it."

I lie back down on the couch. I hear Dr. Mueller put a new piece of paper into his clipboard.

"I was at a party. I met a psychologist. He tells me there's a new therapeutic technique that takes only six months." I struggle to bring back the dream. "To tell you the truth, I was shocked. I asked the psychologist how anyone could possibly do anything in such a short time. This fast cure is best, he told me, shrugging his shoulders nonchalantly. It will make traditional psychoanalysis obsolete."

"That's it?"

"That's it."

"And what do you make of this dream?"

"We've been at it six months and we're just getting started, wouldn't you say?" Before he can answer, I make a connection. "Of course, you're going away . . ."

"For a one-week vacation."

"I know that."

"I think you're afraid that if I take some time off, I won't ever come back." Dr. Mueller's tone is unusually forceful.

"Ridiculous." I think back to the dream. "It's just that it's taken me six months to feel that the analysis is special. It's mine. I want it to last."

"It?"

"You."

"To last?"

"To come back." Maybe he's right. "When I was a child and things weren't going my way, I'd act as if I didn't care."

"So you denied needing a father."

"I suppose."

"Are you also aware that you rarely speak of *him* here?"

"Hard for me to talk about him, too. Like Mike. Different reasons. I don't mean Mike's like my father. Neither are you. You're both very different from him. Hard to believe my father is living in Boston. So close. I haven't seen him for eight or nine years. He called me when Chris was born. I haven't heard from him since. Not like you at all. I see you every day. I always feel close to you. Even when we're not together."

"Oh?"

"I write in a journal. It's a way to hold on."

"It's funny, Mike, I find it almost impossible to talk to Dr. Mueller about you."

Mike sits across from me in the living room. The children are asleep. The house and the neighborhood are unusually quiet. Still in his work clothes, Mike looks tired and worried.

"So what do you say?" He takes a sip of his coffee.

"That I can't talk about you, which is a way of saying nothing at all." The rumble of a train passing the back of the house momentarily disrupts the quiet. "It's been so long since we've had a serious talk," I say after the train passes, "are you up to one now?"

I look into his eyes. That sandy hair, those green eyes. Goddammit, I still find him so attractive. I steel myself to get through.

I'm going to try to speak of the forgotten anniversary, what may have been behind our both forgetting . . . but that's not what comes out.

"Do you remember when we first were married, I used to say that if you ever found someone else, not to tell me?"

He nods and looks down at his shoes. "Why bring it up now?"

"But I also told you that if I ever asked, you *had* to tell me the truth."

"Lou, you've been such a good wife and mother."

"Not now, Mike. I don't want to hear that now. The anniversary, Mike. It was our eighth. I have a question." I take a deep breath. I can feel my heart pounding. "Is there someone else?"

"It's not that simple, Lou."

"The question is simple. Have you been unfaithful?"

His eyes fill with tears. He sits motionless in his chair. Then his head begins moving. Up and down slowly.

I clutch at my sides. I feel as if I've been kicked in the stomach. "Oh, no. One woman or many?"

"Just one," he whispers.

"Isn't that odd?" I struggle to keep my composure.

"What?"

"I hoped there would be many." I reach for a cigarette. "Is it love?" I inhale. "Never mind. I don't want to hear it." I start pacing the floor. "Yes I do. Is it love or a fling?"

"It's no fling." He looks wounded.

"Then it's love," I say angrily. I head for the stairs.

"Where are you going?"

"Out for a walk . . . I'm all right. Stay here with the children."
Slamming the downstairs door behind me, I head for Harvard
Square. One thought gets through. I see Dr. Mueller tomorrow.

"I knew we had trouble. I knew bad times were coming. That's
why I was so desperate to get into analysis. I couldn't face it
alone. Remember when I told you I took off my wedding ring
without knowing why? In graduate school, I used to stay up
late studying. It was a legitimate way to avoid sex and intimacy.
Mike and I had always done things independently. I knew that
what was happening to us these days wasn't the same. I just didn't
know why."

"So what are you going to do?"

"I don't know—and I don't want to see Mike until I do. Oh,
Dr. Mueller, look what I've done! Brought this all to a head just
as you're leaving. What shall I do?"

"What do you want to do?"

"Run away."

"Where?"

"I'll go back to the Vineyard."

"Oh, Lou, what's the matter?" DeeDee looks worried.

"It's Mike. He has somebody else." I stare from her deck off
into the woods.

"That bastard . . ."

"I can't talk."

"Weeping is good, Lou. Don't try to apologize."

Chapter Seven

Who is she? The other woman, who can she be? One of my friends? Someone I trust?

Could it be Jeannie? No. Besides, we all work together at the store. How could they keep it a secret? It would make life too complicated.

Does sexual energy exist in pure form? I once read that it does. If I can transform mine into energy for the analysis, Mike and I can go on living together. That's it! I'll repress my sexual energy, that shouldn't be hard. Mike's the only man I want anyway. He can have his life. I will have mine. We can appear to the world as husband and wife. Yes, that's what we'll do.

Jeannie is pretty—and sexy. Everyone says so. No, she's out of the question. Let's see. Who else? I'd better stop before I have all my friends under suspicion.

"Here you are," says the waitress in the ice cream parlor where I sit mulling over my predicament.

"Thanks." I wait until the waitress turns her back before I smile. Thick fudge. Very hot. Cold vanilla ice cream. I smile because hot fudge sundaes always make me think of Mummy. I recall a childhood trip into Boston with her.

"Wait right here, dear." We were in Bailey's, and Mummy left me to go up to the fountain.

From where I sat in the wire soda chair, I could see the long counter of tray after tray of candies. A woman in a white cap and apron used delicate tongs to pick up, one by one, two of this, three of that, as she made up boxes of chocolates. How I wanted to go right up to the counter and jam one into my mouth. "Here you are, Mary Louise." My mother set down in front of me a circular tray. In the center was a stemmed dish of vanilla ice cream overflowing with fudge sauce, marshmallow, and nuts. Napkin on my lap, my chin up close to the marble tabletop, I spooned the ice cream. Across from me, sipping her strawberry soda, Mummy smiled.

Why don't they serve liquor here? A drink's what I need. Oh, what the hell. "Miss, can I have another fudge sundae?

The humiliation. That's the worst part. No doubt about that.

Anyway, Jeannie's not really close to me. We're co-workers more than best friends. All these years we've worked together at the store, we mostly see each other coming and going. We work different days, different hours. She *is* pretty, though, and I wish I had more of her confidence. I also have to admit she looks great in a mini-dress. She wears them with no trace of embarrassment. She blonds her dark hair, uses makeup just right. Compared to me, she looks like a coed, but she's nearly my age with two kids of her own. No, it couldn't be Jeannie.

"You think *she's* sexy?" I now recall Mike and the billboard episode, because it was rare for him to look at one with lust.

"She's sexy," he murmured as if in a trance.

That dumb movie billboard. What an awful scene we had over that. Up there was Carroll Baker. Pouty mouth. Shortie nightgown. Blond hair. She was curled up in a crib or something. How I hated her.

Mostly because she looked nothing like me.

I never did go to see *Baby Doll*. It was my way to protest.

Protest what?

I was eight, maybe nine the Christmas that my father gave Cousin Jane a dear baby doll. She had a sweet little face and was

dressed in a blue dress and bonnet. She had tiny lace gloves. Oh,
how I wanted her.

I always believed Mike loved me just the way I was. And still
am. Me—for myself. Now somewhere out there is a woman he
loves. She knows his body the way I do. Oh, my God—he knows
hers.

Baby Doll was a vamp, and who gives a damm about baby dolls
anymore?

How could he do it?

"Welcome to marriage, Lou," DeeDee had said only yesterday.
"It isn't perfect, but the difference between you and the rest of
us is that you thought it was."

Good old DeeDee. Always tries to talk sense to me. "You
better grow up," she said, "and just take it easy. Don't make any
decisions you won't be able to live with. You must think of the
kids, not just of your pride. I've seen marriages in far worse
trouble than yours."

Of course she makes sense. Why do I wish she'd shut up?

"You'll get over this, Lou," she says, "just give yourself time."

"I can't come home, Mike," I tell him on the phone, "I'm not
ready yet."

"Take your time," he says softly.

"I will," I snap back.

"You'll get over this, Lou. You're very sexually desirable, you
know."

If I am, then why don't you desire me? was the question I was
too proud to ask.

"The kids think you're on a vacation," he says.

"That's good. Tell them I'll be away a while longer."

"Do you know how long?"

"I really don't."

"We can manage. Don't worry."

I go to replace the receiver, then: "Oh, Mike . . ."

"Yes?"

"Who is she?"

"You're not serious? You don't want to know?"

"Yes, I do."

"Don't torture yourself, Lou."

"You haven't answered my question."

Silence.

"Her name, Mike, her name."

"All right." I hear him take a deep breath. "It's Jeannie."

Chapter Eight

I must stop acting on impulse. Learning to reflect on problems before taking action is the essence of psychoanalysis. What I get from Dr. Mueller in our sessions of talk is invisible, an unseen net should an acrobat fall.

At the top of the stairs, I glimpse the macramé tapestry I'd bought from a scrawny girl selling her wares in the Square. Blackie is asleep on the living-room couch. Usually she sleeps with the children. Do cats react to separation? I stroke her, then tiptoe into the children's rooms. The sight of each child curled up and asleep reassures me they're safe. Their sweet vulnerability touches a wellspring of sadness.

I make my way into the kitchen.

Mike is hunched over the sink. Hearing my step, he looks up.

"Want a cup?" He points to the pot on the stove. "It's fresh. I just made it," Mike says, drying his hands.

I go to the pantry for my favorite mug. I turn to give it to Mike, but he's right behind me, arm stretched out toward me.

"Lou," he says, reaching.

"Don't touch me, Mike Shields!"

The sound of his last name makes him seem a stranger.

Mike backs into the stove.

"I'm sorry. I didn't mean to scare you. I scared myself, too. It's just that I don't want you to touch me." I pour my own cup of coffee and sit down at the round oak table. "You did fix the upstairs room?"

"I did."

"Good."

Light from the wicker shade over the table glows in the oak's grain, mellowed yellow with oilings. Across from each other, we sit as so often we have.

"You probably want your sexual freedom."

"Mike, you've missed the whole point." I shake my head hopelessly.

"Are you saying you've never been tempted?"

"I've been tempted." I feel my mouth twitch. "Twice I was tempted, but I didn't give in. I made a conscious decision not to be ruled by my genitals."

Oh, how I wish I were back in the safety of DeeDee's.

"Can you honestly say you didn't sleep with another man because you loved me more, or"—he doesn't give me a chance to respond—"were you holding on to a good thing? Protecting your interests?"

"I was keeping our marriage intact. I knew that sleeping with somebody else would have jeopardized our marriage, just as you must have known sleeping with Jeannie would."

That shuts him up.

"I'm not saying I know why I've been faithful, but the fact is, I have been, and what's more"—my voice involuntarily drops to a whisper—"you're still my first choice."

"You mean as the father of Christopher and Elizabeth?"

"As my lover . . ." I nearly choke on the word. "I'm not a machine. I can't make myself stop loving you. And God knows I've tried these last few days."

I drag on a cigarette and let my eyes wander to the pegboard over the stove. Behind the hodgepodge of casseroles and frying pans is the bright orange paint; I was eight months pregnant with Lizzie when Mike and I painted it.

"It won't last," DeeDee had declined when I tried to persuade her to come to the enamelware closeout at Raymond's. But the red porcelain pot for fifty-nine cents is still up there, and it still looks nice on the pegboard.

I must try to tell Mike what I'm feeling.

"Because of the way I was treated in my childhood . . ." My voice breaks. "Rejection . . . my childhood . . ."

"I never meant to . . ."

"I know. . . ."

He takes a step toward me.

"Ssh." I extend my arm in a gesture that stops him. "Your option is on the whole me. Take it or leave it. We have some time." I tilt my head up to the ceiling. "Not everyone has a third floor. We're lucky. We have separate spaces." I head for our bedroom. He follows. "For God's sake, Mike, if it's Jeannie you want, let's find a way to make it work out for all of us. That's all I can say."

I close the bedroom door tightly behind me.

I hear her soft patter.

"Mummy!" Lizzie cries. She presses her warm little body to mine. "They got lost, Mummy and Daddy, but they found their way back. The mummy didn't find the wrong way, did she?"

Tousling her blond ringlets with kisses, I hold her close a long time before together we go to rouse Christopher.

"Oh, Mum," he says drowsily as I hold him in my arms, "I'm so glad you're home."

For the next week, Mike and I share a sense of strain and relief: the strain comes from having to pretend to our friends that nothing is wrong; the relief from having things out in the open between us.

Saturday, September 16, is unseasonably warm. A handful of family and friends gather in Harvard's Appleton Chapel. The university crest reads "Veritas," and under scrolled candelabra and filigree panels, Ramona appears. She and Ben did much of their courting over soufflés in my kitchen. Ben takes his place next to her between the banks of pews. He wears a dark suit and his full black mustache is neatly trimmed, yet he still looks as though he'd be more at home in the garb of a cossack.

Ramona, some years his junior, imparts the congregation's sole note of dissonance. Her dress, a simply styled dotted Swiss, sports a very brief hemline. Were it not for her aristocratic features and bearing, the whimsical incongruity of her costume would be sacrilegious.

The nondenominational ceremony fininshes quickly. Outside the chapel, we laughingly throw all our rice. At the other end of the yard, a lanky girl walks down the steps of Widener Library. A floppy Garbo hat covers her hair, and she has tied a turquoise balloon to the strap of her brown leather saddlebag purse. I watch as she unlocks her bike from the rack. As she rides, she tosses the balloon in the air toward us.

I remember myself at her age. Never could I have been so cavalier. Harvard and Radcliffe meant privilege right down to one's dress. Everything seems so changed.

We leave through the large iron gate that separates the Yard from the rest of the city. The prospect of the elegant reception awaiting us at the Grand Turk restaurant distracts me from my reveries.

A parrot in an ornate golden cage welcomes the wedding party. Seafaring charts, lithographs of Rangoon and Burma, and a glass-encased model of a ship—all the appropriate paraphernalia of the Grand Turk.

I slump into a cushiony black leather couch next to my brother.

"How did the wedding go?" Frank asks over the blare of the Rolling Stones' "Ruby Tuesday."

"It's too noisy to talk. I'll tell you later."

Two blacks in form-fitting silver get up to dance.

Matrons in long gowns chat with girls in scant minis. The men are dressed more uniformly. "The theater is real. My life is like theater." I recognize at the bar an actor I know. "Here she comes!" someone cries. I don't recognize that voice. "Look at her dress," cries out another.

I focus on Ramona's white top. It's cut like a fencing jacket. Wait. There's something red stitched over her breast.

"Touché," jokes a guest, gently tapping the red with a swizzle stick. The red seems to light up.

"Touché yourself." Ramona giggles. Ben takes her hand. The red lights up again.

"It's a heart, Frank. Look at that, it's a goddamn heart."

"Have you had too much to drink, Lou?" Frank asks, staring strangely at me.

"There it goes again. Oh, you missed it."

"I do it with batteries," I hear Ramona explain as she turns back her sleeve. Ben takes her hand. The heart lights up red. He lets go; it goes out.

After the reception, I join the small group going over to Dee-Dee's, but, once there, I head for her bedroom. "Too much going on," I mumble, "too much in my head."

"Well, now you can rest." DeeDee closes the door.

I keep seeing a heart lighting up red, going on, going off with the touch of Ben's hand.

"Wake up, Lou." I hear voices. Patrick and Jan, here from New York for the wedding. Ironic, I think through my stupor, they were witnesses for Mike and me at *our* wedding ceremony.

"Come on, Lou. Jan and I are driving you home. No one else here is sober."

"Don't want to go home. No more home to go home to."

"Oh, Patrick, maybe we should just leave her here."

"How can we go back to New York and not know Lou is okay?"

"I'm not okay," I shout over the strains of *My Fair Lady*, "but I want you to leave me alone."

"She's more than just drunk. Snap out of it, Lou."

"Mind your own business." I pull the covers over my head.

"We just want to help. Let us take you home."

"No home to go to. I want a drink."

"You've had enough."

"Not enough. I still feel."

"Oh, Patrick, I'm worried. This isn't like Lou at all."

"That's what I told you. She's more than just drunk." His voice is impatient.

"Lou." Patrick takes me by the shoulders. "Sit up."

"Don't touch me. Don't you dare touch me."

"Patrick, I'm scared. Let's get DeeDee. She'll know what to do."

"Lou," Patrick persists, "it's Saturday night, and Jan and I have to drive all the way back to New York. Please let us take you home now."

"Saturday's over. It's not Saturday night."

"Yes it is."

"Can't be."

"Well, it is."

"Jan, do you know where Mike is?"

"I think he's with the children."

"Dammit."

"Damn you! Why did you wake me up?"

"What's the matter with you, Lou?"

Oh, why don't I just tell them? No. I promised Mike I'd keep it a secret until we decide what we're going to do. I start to cry. "My heart. Mike won't make it beat." I pound my breast.

"Stop it, Lou," Patrick and Jan say in unison.

They both grab me.

I continue beating my breast.

"What's going on in here?" I hear DeeDee's voice.

"Thank God you're here. Stay with her, Jan. Something's the matter with Lou." Patrick and DeeDee go outside the door.

No more "Rain in Spain." The house is all quiet.

"Here, Lou." DeeDee comes in with the telephone. "It's Dr. Mueller. If you want to go to the hospital, we'll take you."

"The hospital? The hospital? Are you both crazy?"

"Take it, Lou." DeeDee puts the receiver in my hand.

"Mrs. Shields?"

From a light-year away, I hear Dr. Mueller's voice.

"Yes?"

"What's the matter?"

"I'm drunk. I don't know what day it is. I'm a mess. What should I do?"

"What do you want to do?"

"What did you say?"

"What do *you* want to do?" he repeats. He sounds closer now.

"I want to be home. No hospital."

"Do you want someone to be with you?"

"My brother. I want my brother." I put the phone on the bed. DeeDee picks it up and drags the long cord out of the room.

Mike turns on the light in our bedroom.

"Oh, no—not you."

"Frank came to get me. I was about to take the kids to the country."

"Get them out of here."

"They're not with me. They're at Frank's with Jan and Patrick."

"Thank God." I begin pounding my breast.

"Don't, Lou," pleads Mike. He and my brother force my arms to my sides.

Writhing free of their grip, I start beating my breast again. "You did this, you son of a bitch. Now get out of this house and leave me alone."

DeeDee appears in the doorway. "We're in for it now."

"Go fuck yourself, DeeDee."

"Librium." She waves a bottle of pills at Mike. "I found them in my medicine chest. Now, if we can just get them into her."

"*Leave me alone. All of you!*"

"We can't," says my brother, "and you know that."

"I hate all of you, and"—I glare at Mike—"you most of all."

DeeDee approaches me with the pills. Frank and Mike grab at my arms. I struggle free and bang my head deliberately into the wall.

"Hold her still. Quick," DeeDee shouts. She shoves pills down my throat.

"Hit me," I hear Mike sobbing, "for God's sake, Lou, hit me. Don't hurt yourself!"

As the water runs into my ears, down my neck, down my throat, I gag on the pills, but they go down.

I feel sweat on my body. My head aches inside and out.

I'm in my own bed. It's dawn or it's dusk of what day I don't know. I squint, and DeeDee comes into focus.

"What can I get you?" she asks quietly.

"Water. And a cigarette."

She returns carrying both.

"How do you feel?" she asks.

"Like shit."

"I'm not surprised, that was quite a performance you gave."

"Call it that if you want to."

I drag on the cigarette.

"What day is it?"

"Sunday."

"Saturday's over at last."

"I'll do whatever you want," says Mike, coming into the room. "I'll stop seeing Jeannie. DeeDee and I have been up the whole night."

"Doing what?"

"Talking. About you, about me, the marriage, the kids."

"You know how I feel about marriage," DeeDee butts in.

"Are either of you interested in how I feel?"

"How *do* you feel, Lou?" DeeDee asks.

"I don't want to go on living with him." I point my finger at Mike. "I want you out."

"Where would I go?" Mike reacts with a start.

"That's your problem."

"She won't feel that way later," DeeDee reassures Mike.

"Yes I will," I say through clenched teeth, "oh, yes I will. I'm going to get up now and take a hot shower. I'll talk to you both in the kitchen."

They leave me alone.

My God, did I do that with my head? I place my hand over the missing piece of plaster. The size of a baseball. I must have wanted to hurt myself. I sit down and rub the bruise on my scalp.

Under the shower's spray, my senses revive. I stand under it until the hot water runs out. I feel ready to face them.

"While you were sleeping, Mike and I worked everything out," DeeDee says. "You know I have no illusions about marriage, but if two people *are* married—and they have children— they should stay married. Grow up, Lou. Infidelity exists in the best of marriages."

"Not in mine."

DeeDee ignores my response and turns to face Mike. "As for you, let me warn you that finding your manhood through women will doom you to replace one with another. You must come to grips with yourself."

"I've loved you the best that I could." Mike turns to me.

"I know that. . . ."

"And I was wrong. . . ."

"No, you weren't. Let's face it. You now feel about Jeannie the way you once felt about me."

His eyes meet mine in panic. DeeDee stares at the both of us, falls back in her chair.

"If I can say it, you should be able to." I choose my next words carefully. "Whatever your feelings were toward me when we married, that's not what they are now. You were the virgin, Mike. I was the one with a past. You asked me if I was faithful because I loved you or needed you. The truth is I can't sort out the one from the other."

Mike pours me coffee.

"Stop." I push his hand away. The gesture reminds me of his tenderness, and I do not want to be reminded. "What you've done to our marriage is poison. If I hadn't let out my feelings last night, I'd have gone crazy. Surely you know that?"

He nods.

"See this." He pushes a news magazine toward me. On the cover, a wounded soldier, his face contorted with pain, is holding his guts. "That's how I feel when you hurt yourself. If you can't go on living, then neither can I." He breaks into sobs and puts his head down on the table.

"Mike, don't cry," DeeDee says, "Lou will take you back."

"This time you're wrong, DeeDee."

"Are you telling me that this whole night has been wasted?"

"I can't"—I take my friend's hand—"as you say, take him back. I can't and I won't."

Chapter Nine

"It sounds like you're contemplating a divorce," says Dr. Mueller.

"Not contemplating. I think I'll just do it and contemplate later."

"And are you aware"—I hear him tap on his pipe—"that in one breath you say you're afraid you can't manage without him and in the next breath you tell me you're the one who's pushed him out?"

"I am," I answer quietly.

"You know, Mrs. Shields, you do speak of stress. You tell me you're concerned for the children. You talk of fatigue. But I've noticed that you never mention any stress you might be under from the work we do here in analysis."

"You don't think I want to stop?"

"I don't know *what* you think. Psychoanalysts," he adds, "can't read minds."

"Of course, there's pressure here too, but, of all the things that I do—or have ever done—analysis feels like the only thing that's completely for me."

"Do you doubt it?"

"Never—but sometimes I forget."

That can't be what's on his mind, can it? That I *should* stop?

"What's on your mind?" he asks gently.

"Disapproval. I'm afraid you think my approach is un-orthodox."

"To your life or to analysis?"

"I'm not sure." I think of all the times I've turned around on the couch. I'm not sure that's "correct." I give in to my impulses. "Not the analysis, I don't think it's that. It's Mike. I think you disapprove of my asking him to leave."

"You never brought it up here. You confronted me with a fait accompli. You know that, don't you?"

I nod. "Was that wrong?"

"We lost it as work here. You didn't analyze . . ."

"I wanted him to stay . . . perhaps even more than I wanted him to go. I was afraid to talk about it. I just had to do it . . . while I had the strength."

"What's on your mind now?"

"It would be wrong to use the children against him." That thought just flashes to mind.

"You think you could?"

"I know I could."

"How?"

"Mike believes in the family. He gave so much of his energy to Nana and Frank. He did it spontaneously . . . out of his love for me and his sense of family loyalty. He knows what a hard childhood I had. For the sake of his own children, I think he'd do anything."

"And?"

"It would be cruel of me to let him—or get him to—give Jeannie up because of the children."

"I don't understand . . ."

"When he loved me, Mike loved me completely. I know that. I was his first love—and nothing can change that. It should make me strong. I should be able to let go. Not force him to stay past the time when he gives his love freely. I know what it's like to be a charity case. I never want that again. I have too much pride. I think I'm the one who has to move on. See myself whole. See my own life worth the living—whether Mike wants me or not."

"Is that what you believe?"

"It's what I want to believe."

* * *

"Oh, Frank. The Sunday papers. Just what I wanted!"

The bell rings again and Abby comes up the stairs carrying oranges, her juicer, corn muffins, and a jar of marmalade.

Sunday brunch. What a nice way to spend the day while the children are at Mike's.

When the doorbell rings in the evening, I'm refreshed and relaxed. All the same, it makes me feel uneasy to greet Mike downstairs at the door. We did decide, though, that it makes the point to the kids: there's no chance he's staying.

Lizzie stops on the threshold. Doesn't budge.

"Tell Daddy goodnight."

Nobody moves. A family tableau in the hallway. Seven-year-old Christopher stands next to his father. Two-and-a-half-year-old Lizzie is plunked down between them and me. Mike is, seemingly, paralyzed. I, alone, stand on the other side of the threshold.

I yank Lizzie across, and as I do, Christopher gives us both a shove, pushes past me, and runs up the stairs.

"Don't you ever have trouble leaving someone you like?" Christopher shouts on the stairs. "Like Mummy." He turns back at Mike.

Mike and I stand helplessly.

"I have problems you don't understand," Christopher says, leaning over the banister, his blond bangs falling forward. "I want to live with my mother *and* father."

Upstairs, his door slams.

"We'll have to talk." I clutch Lizzie's head to my belly. "Tomorrow. Not now."

Without a word, Mike closes the outside door behind him.

I watch as he goes down the stairs.

Call him back now. *Do it!* Before he gets to the car.

I take Lizzie's hand, and we walk up the stairs.

"The kids can live with whatever you can," DeeDee tells me over the telephone after the children are asleep. "You're the one who has to make up your mind. The decision's not theirs, and, I may add, it would be rotten of you to let them think that it is."

"Taking Mike back wouldn't solve anything."

"Then that's what you have to learn to live with."

"Thanks, DeeDee. You've helped a lot. I'll work something out."

I replace the receiver.

How easy it would be to pick up the phone and beg Mike to come home.

The effort it takes not to do it nearly kills me.

Chapter Ten

"But I thought it was settled."

"Well, it's not, Lou, so you better get yourself a good lawyer."

"A lawyer?"

"I'm going to sue you for custody."

"You can't be serious." I collapse on the nearest thing—a mailbox. "But we agreed not to have lawyers."

"I'm getting my own, so you better get yours."

"What about trust?" I try to be reasonable. "Don't you trust us to decide what's best for our children?"

"Jake says I can sue."

"On what grounds—and for what—did Jake"—I spit out our friend's name—"say you can sue?"

"If a judge knew the number of years you've been in therapy . . ."

"What does that have to do with anything?"

"Jake said mental health."

"Mental health?" The truth quickly dawns. Insanity. That's what he's talking about. Proving I'm crazy. I back away from the mailbox in horror. I no longer care that we're making a scene on the street. "Oh, Mike, how could you even consider such a terrible thing? You. Of all people."

"I don't mean to hurt you, Lou. I just want my kids. I'll do whatever I have to."

"I can't talk to you anymore." I back away, leave him on the corner. I walk and then run down Boylston Street into the Square.

Between the Harvard Coop and the Yard is the kiosk, and all around it are pay telephone booths. I call my ally.

"Oh, DeeDee, I'm so glad you're home," I groan, and describe the scene almost verbatim.

"Mike adores those kids, Lou," she says mournfully. "I was afraid of something like this."

"What shall I do?"

"Stay where you are. Give me the number. I'll call Donald. He'll find you a lawyer. I'll call you back as soon as I can."

I wish I hadn't seen Dr. Mueller already this morning. Well, I'll see him tomorrow.

The ring of the phone startles me.

"Joseph Napoli," DeeDee says, "he's a good divorce lawyer, a classmate of Donald's. He'll see you today. I said I'd call him right back. He's in Boston. How soon can you be there?"

MTA RAPID TRANSIT 8 MINUTES TO PARK STREET, says the sign over my head.

"To be in psychoanalysis is no proof of anything," Mr. Napoli tells me. "Mike hasn't a case."

"Mike says he'll reconcile for the sake of the kids. I'm the one who wants the divorce."

"If you want a divorce," Mr. Napoli says calmly, "you have a right to one. You don't need Mike's consent."

"You're punishing me, Lou. I gave you all the cards when I didn't have to." (That sounds more like Jake than like Mike.) "I could have lied about Jeannie."

"Are you asking me to be grateful that you told me the truth? That you told me you were having an affair?"

Mike's not like my father. That's why I married him. Mike loves his children. It's ironic that his being such a good father should hurt me so deeply.

My father never saw my brother and me as his to take care of. Because of my father, I had to deal with parole officers, social workers, and judges. Meddlers. I hated them all. I won't let that happen to my children.

I try a new tactic. "Mike, if you contest this divorce you'll be risking our personal freedom by entangling us with the law. Don't you see the irony? You, a child of the middle class, voluntarily getting us caught in that mire? If we want to be free to decide our own future, we can't fight with each other. Think of the children."

I press him with my sense of urgency.

I can see I'm wearing him down.

"I'll sign the agreement," he says wearily, "if that's what you want."

"That's what I want." I sigh with relief.

Later, in bed—exhausted—I try to figure out Mike's reasoning.

His father is a judge, so Mike tends to see judges as kindly and wise. That's not been my experience. Mike overlooks the power of the law to meddle and botch.

It must be Mike's Catholic upbringing: the prospect of divorce is getting him down. I bet he's ashamed to tell his parents what's going on.

Yes, that must be what's driving him. Desperation. He probably thinks that if a judge orders him to give up his own children, then he can face his parents. I'm sure that's what it is.

He's scared.

So am I.

I need him. I need his cooperation. I can't raise these two children alone. My mother tried that—and look what happened to her.

Divorce should be a way to give us a new start in life. A chance—not a failure. It's a challenge, that's all.

I must make myself remember everything.

When Mike and I first met, I was the one with experience, the one who'd had a few lovers. Our circumstances were the reverse of the norm.

And his affair with Jeannie. Nobody knew. I appreciate that. Even there, Mike was trying to protect me. Jeannie didn't even tell her very best friend.

He was faithful to me for almost ten years—if you count from before we were married. That's a long time for any man to be faithful, let alone to his first love. Perhaps it wasn't a desire to teach poor city children that propelled me to graduate school but a sense that my life was in a state of change, whether I was ready or not. I know Mike tried not to feel "that way" about Jeannie. Yes, that's what he told me: "I fought it," he said.

Now it's clear that he loves her.

Mike wanted to marry me right from the first. When I got pregnant, he wasn't alarmed. Seemed to take it for granted we'd get married.

Even if abortion had been legal, he wanted that baby. He met the prospect with joy.

I made him swear at the time that if I had that baby, he'd never abandon it.

Too bad he's going to such an extreme to make good on his promise.

What I grasp theoretically is one thing; what I feel is another.

I want Mike to have his chance with Jeannie, but another part of me hates him for putting me in this position.

I wish things were the same as they used to be.

I miss him.

So do the children.

The house isn't the same.

If I don't figure out something soon, we won't make it through.

I stop fighting sleep.

Chapter Eleven

Pizza. I could swear that I smelled pizza, but the only noticeable scent in my bedroom is the perfume that I'd put on in the morning.

That dream was so vivid!

"Daddy," I cried. I jumped out of bed. I ran into the kitchen. In my dream, there he was—big as life. When I hugged him, I smelled fuel oil and kerosene, tobacco and whiskey—the smells of work and my father. He must have been out cleaning oil burners.

In the bathroom of Atwood Square, where my dream took place, I watched as he scrubbed his palms with the pink gravelly paste. "There," he said, holding up his clean hands. He toweled dry, leaned down, and said, "Go ahead."

And I kissed his bald spot.

"Your kisses will make the hair grow back."

Out in the kitchen, Mummy was awake too. It must have been almost dawn. One reason the dream seems so vivid is that Daddy, in real life, arrived unexpectedly more often than not.

"Can I untie it?" I asked, pointing to the waiting pizza box.

Mummy pulled strands of Bugler tobacco out of her pouch and scattered them over thin paper. She put the whole thing in the roller and—presto!—a cigarette.

"Isn't she beautiful?" Daddy asked while I untied the box.

"Oh, yes."

Mummy appeared not to hear.

"I'm the luckiest man in the world. A beautiful wife and a smart little girl. Who could ask for more?"

Mummy dragged on the cigarette.

"Oh, Daddy, I love you."

He pulled me onto his lap as we prepared to dig into the pizza.

"My little girl," Daddy said, "Daddy's little girl."

In real life and time-present, on Mead Street, the doorbell rings.

"Open the door. Daddy's here!" Christopher shouts.

"Daddy! Daddy!" Lizzie shrieks gleefully.

The doorbell *is* ringing. I get out of bed and put on my robe and hurry downstairs in a slight state of confusion.

It's Saturday evening, of course, and that's Mike at the door. He's come for the children. I had intended to nap, never thinking I'd fall into such a deep sleep.

God, how strange to greet my children's father downstairs at the door with the memory of my own father so uncomfortably near.

Mike starts down the outside stairs with the children.

"Mike," I call him back. "How would it be if the children stay over with you tomorrow night?"

He looks puzzled.

"Let them sleep over. On Monday you can bring Christopher to school and drop Lizzie at Jessie's. That way there'll be one less session of passing them back and forth between us."

This idea just sprang into my mind.

"That sounds good. Yes, let's try it. When did you think of it?" he asks.

"Just now. I was dreaming . . ."

"Would you like me to take you to school Monday?" Mike asks Chris.

"Oh, yes," Chrissie answers.

"And me," Lizzie squeals, "take me too!"

"No nursery school for you yet, Punkin." Mike swoops her up in his arms. "*You* still go to your baby-sitter's."

"You could do the same thing on Wednesday," I say, inspired

by their enthusiasm. "Let them stay over, then take them to school Thursday morning." I smile. "I know how you must miss tucking them in."

"I do." Mike looks at me gratefully. "Thanks, Lou, it's a great-sounding plan. I should have thought of it myself."

"That doesn't matter. At least one of us did."

I watch from out the window upstairs as two happy children go off with their daddy.

Mike's new apartment is only a few blocks away. Things aren't nearly as bad as they were. We're close, but we're separated.

We both looked elsewhere for work, but we gave up the search. Mike couldn't find better pay than what he earns at the store with his overtime, and there was no job for me at five dollars an hour where I could work part-time and take time off when I needed it.

Jeannie and I make sure our schedules are totally different. Because the store is open every night, that isn't difficult. I haven't seen her once since I got the news.

I do see Mike at the store. It forces us to be civilized. It may even be good. It's getting less painful for me to see him. We talk about the kids in sort of the way that we used to—here and there, in between customers and work.

I don't want to hate him.

The kids need him too much.

Who am I kidding? I need him too.

"DeeDee still says our divorce will be senseless," I tell Dr. Mueller.

"And what do you think?"

"That it's better than living a lie."

I was fading away in my marriage. I don't feel that way now.

"You sound as though you feel things are worked out."

"In some ways, they are."

"Is it so easy?"

"You know that it isn't. It's just that I feel, by seeing you here, I have dual controls. Like in a driving school. The student can't crash."

Chapter Twelve

"I was afraid of that, Mike," I say, my guts churning, as he and I go over our finances.

"But, Lou, we're running two separate households. That takes extra money."

Mike always was the one who understood money.

When we lived together, I kept out of my paycheck what I needed each week for myself; the rest I gladly turned over to him. He paid the bills. Like clockwork, the first of each month. No more shut-off telephone, turned-off electricity, or cold home in winter. It was a more than fair deal.

Since our separation, Mike has been giving me one hundred dollars each week. I live in our house with the children. I keep the rent from the apartment, and that covers part of the mortgage, which is now mine to pay.

I've opened a checking account and put myself on a budget. Even so, ends don't quite meet. It all costs so much more than I thought it would. I don't want Mike to pay for Dr. Mueller, but I can't give *him* up.

"The store's busy now. I can work five short days each week—that is, if Lizzie starts nursery school."

"Isn't she a little too young?"

"Not really. Lots of kids start at two and a half. Anyway, the school is just two doors away, and she's been looking forward to it. She wants to go to 'big school' like Chris."

"Well . . ."

"I think we should give it a try."

"I think you're wrong about this."

"But, Mr. Napoli, why should Mike have to pay more?"

"Because he was the one who broke your marriage up."

"But he already works fifty-five hours a week. That's six days a week. I work only three."

"Doesn't matter. Let him go out and find himself another job."

"Then he'd have no time for our kids."

"You think he'll keep that up?"

"I know he will."

"He may have been a model father when you were married—"

"And he'll be a model father," I interrupt, "in our divorce. He's a *very* responsible person."

God, how I don't want my kids to go through what I did. These divorce arrangements precipitate unwanted flashbacks.

"Just who do you think you are, Lady Jane?" Aunt Tilly sneered.

"Big shot," Nana chimed in. "She see father and now she be big shot." They were united.

"We just went for pizza." I hid my excitement. "To the North End for pizza. That's all."

The North End. The Italian section of Boston. Pushcarts and stands. Friday-night bustle. I'd followed along after my father up Hanover Street, and in the restaurant the waiter had asked, "Is this your daughter, Ralph? Can't be, she's too pretty."

"And smart, too," my father said proudly. "She gets all A's in school."

The waiter served me my spumoni in claret sauce with a wink.

"I don't know why you hate Daddy so," I used to defend him to my aunt and my grandmother.

"He's a drunk and a bum. You'll see . . ." they both promised menacingly.

* * *

Now I *am* older. I *have* come to see that most of the time I'd spent with my father was when he was drunk. I made myself forget all the bad things about him—the waiting, the being stood up, the times he left me alone in the car in the dark while he went into some bar. I prefer remembering his rosy glow when we were together, but my dealings with Mr. Napoli have led me to search through old papers. I come upon a letter from Daddy to me. Black-and-white contradicts preferred memories. The rosy glows were exceptional—and I know it.

"Dearest Mary Lou," he wrote me in 1951 on letterhead from the Suffolk County House of Correction. I was sixteen.

As I agree with all that you wrote me, I'm sure I don't know what to say in this letter.

I have cried for the third time in my life.

No matter what I say, I won't be believed.

Despite whatever you may think, I love and always will love you and Sonny [Frank]. I know I haven't shown it but nevertheless the love is still there.

There is no use in blaming anyone. I have only myself to blame.

As for not writing you, what father wants to on this stationery?

Don't answer this letter as I'm being moved out Saturday morning and taken to court on Aunt Tilly's warrant.

My lawyer wants $200 to get me out. I told him that if I had that kind of money, I'd give it to you.

I've been told that I'm being sent back here for two years.

In view of that, you better forget all about me.

I will have no future when I get out. My only hope is to go away, change my name and start over.

If and when the time comes, you will probably have forgotten all about me anyway.

I don't know how deep they are going to bury me but you can rest assured you won't recognize me when you see me again.

All my love to you and Sonny.

                                                            Daddy

"Even now, I sometimes see my father as the victim, and other times I see him as the villain," I explain to Mr. Napoli as we review the agreement. "I want my children to have all the time they can with their father."

"But what does that have to do with whether or not you take the house?"

"It's not fair." I try to explain how I feel. "Mike owes the children and me a home. Not a house of my own. We bought the house with joint income. We own it together. And that's the way I want it to stay. I don't want to profit from our divorce."

"I'm warning you, from now on you have no guarantees."

"And a deed? What does that guarantee me?"

"The house. No judge would deny you—"

"And can a judge guarantee my children their father's love?"

"Of course not. I'm just trying to protect you and the children, and you won't let me do my job." He flails his hands on his desk.

"Your job, as I see it, is to help me walk away from this marriage with joint custody established and joint resources shared."

"But he's guilty." I can see that Mr. Napoli is exasperated.

"Of only one thing—falling in love with somebody else. And, may I remind you, his love for his children goes beyond his love for either Jeannie or me." Mr. Napoli's persistent vision of Mike as a villain prompts me to defend him even though I don't really want to. "You must not forget that Mike took in my brother and grandmother when we first were married. That's over. That's done. My grandmother lived with us until she died, and my brother's all grown. Mike always did the best that he could to right the wrongs of my childhood—and no one could ever really do that. I insist that you give him credit for being the person he is."

"I don't understand you at all." Mr. Napoli loosens his tie. "I've never been confronted with a situation like this. But if you're so sure it's what you want . . ."

"It's what I think will work. For *all* of us."

"All right then." He now tightens up his tie. "I'll have my

secretary type up this agreement. And," he adds, shaking my hand, "for your sake, I hope you're right."

"You're mine, aren't you?" Lizzie asks, curled up in my bed next to me.

"Yes."

"And Chrissie's too?"

"Yes."

"And Daddy's?"

"A little bit. But mostly yours and Chrissie's."

She frowns. "Do you love me?"

"Oh, yes."

"That's good."

Content at last, she wraps her body around mine and drops off to sleep.

Next to her, unable to drop off myself, I know I am coping, but I do not confuse coping with real peace of mind.

Chapter Thirteen

"I suppress angry feelings. I know I do," I tell Dr. Mueller, "not just with you."

"But don't you think there's more to it?"

"Such as?"

"The magical nature of your thinking. We usually see it in children. As a child, you probably believed you had to have no bad thoughts about your father at all, or he'd *never* come back."

"Are you really so sure?" I draw away from his interpretation.

"I think your own dream makes the point best. Yesterday I was fifteen minutes late because my car wouldn't start. When I arrived, I apologized. You said it didn't matter. That you were glad I was safe."

"But I was," I say in my own defense. "I was so relieved you showed up."

"My point exactly. By day, you remove yourself from your deeper feelings, which just proves how effective your defenses really are. That's why we *must* analyze your dream. It was later that night, while you were asleep, that your unconscious feelings emerged. And they tell another story."

"Me as a porcelain doll on a meathook, hung from the ceiling."

"And me?"

"The proprietor of an old curio shop . . ."

"Who makes a living by selling shrunken heads."

"That's not very flattering."

"Do you think every thought you have about me has to be good?"

"Sort of," I admit with reluctance. "You've been so good to me. It's crazy that on the one day you're late . . ."

"And in a bad storm."

". . . I have such a horrible dream."

The dream tells of rage and frustration I can't express otherwise. But that's how it is in psychoanalysis. Seemingly trivial events sometimes precipitate crucial insights.

"I'm ashamed to admit that I have any hostile feelings toward you."

"Because you do want to trust me, but you're afraid. After all," he says with compassion, "you've been hurt many times."

I nod. I'm embarrassed.

"Analyzing negative feelings can be very productive—*if* you do it here."

I laugh.

"What's funny?" he asks.

"I'm relieved."

Silence.

"You still accept me," I add.

The need for a father—once projected on Mike—is now projected full force on Dr. Mueller. Perhaps his fixed position in my life will enable me to explore my feelings toward all men.

Sometimes I confuse even him with my father, when I know Dr. Mueller is the least likely person to hurt me. As strange as it seems, I know that it's true: I don't fully trust him; I can't.

Just talking to him is an end in itself. I find it quite satisfying, but that's not the point. It's the work. It's the process. The ability to analyze is the one thing that can separate me from the feeling that, at birth, I was dealt a hand and ordained to play it. The fear that my life is a fixed game lies beneath each and every one of my anxieties. I need to develop belief in my own power to make choices.

"Save yourself," said my mother, "but stay away from deep water."

When I grew up, I came to accept the judgment that something was wrong with my mother. Now that I'm a wife and mother myself, an inner voice says: "Go *very* carefully."

If I can learn from my mother's life, I won't have to relive it. But I am more like my mother than I am not.

What happened to her could happen to me, and no assurances from anyone can persuade me to the contrary.

My mother so desperately needed my father. Time after time, he continued to fail her. A while back, my aunt Ruth gave me a letter that my mother had written to her. "Dear Ruth," my mother wrote to her sister-in-law:

> Do you ever see Ralph?
> When is he going to take me out?
> I'm nearly sick to death with worry where he is.
> Some say he's in jail.
> How true is it?
> I would love to come out.
> If you should see Ralph, please tell him to come out after me. Eighteen years is too long to be kept in the public welfare mental hospital.
> Please write to me, Ruth.
>
> Mary

No wonder I'm afraid to be without some man's protection. No wonder I want to stay on his good side.

Part Two

Star light, star bright,
First star I see tonight,
Wish I may,
Wish I might
Have the wish
I wish
Tonight.

Chapter Fourteen

I wake up with a start. March 10. My mother's birthday. How did I forget?

I force myself out from under warm covers and tiptoe to the window. Last night, when we arrived by train from Grand Central, it was too dark to see anything. And now, all this fog. I still can't make anything out. I curl up in the window seat under the dormer. The pre-dawn morning is quiet.

Abby's family's home. How my mother would love it.

Last night, before bedtime, a maid brought Abby and me milk and cookies on a scrolled silver tray—something I thought happened only in movies. And when we came up to bed, invisible hands had turned down our covers and hung up our clothes. The bed lamps were lit. The room was so cozy. In her bed across from me, Abby is fast asleep, so I don't make a sound.

Treetops. A slate roof on the eaves down below. The lawn. The woods. The receding fog leaves daylight behind.

So this is where Abby grew up. Pocantico Hills, the estate of the Rockefellers. This mansion we are in is one of several within the walled grounds, Abby had explained as we came up the driveway late last night.

My mother's illustrations. I think of them now. Did she used to imagine she'd grown up in a setting like this instead of in the frame house on Fort Hill in Roxbury?

The facts of my mother's childhood are pieced together from what she and my aunt and my grandmother told me.

My grandfather, called Pa, was the first one on my mother's side of the family ever to leave Latvia. In 1904, he came by boat from Riga to New York. He then took the train up to Boston to join some Latvian friends. He was lucky, Nana said, Pa found work right away. The Walworth Company took him on as a machinist. Then Pa found the apartment on Fort Hill; it had enough rooms for boarders. He soon sent for Nana. My mother was three when she and Nana joined Pa in Boston.

Nana took care of my mother and cooked and cleaned for the boarders. Then she had Jack, her only son, and a few years later came Tilly.

Pa worked for Walworth and played flute in the company's orchestra. He registered as a Communist and was a party organizer. The immigrants maintained old world ties at the Kenilworth Club in Roxbury; they held labor meetings there—and concerts and plays.

I used to love it when Nana and Pa took me to the club. There were other children my age, and once we all acted as peasants in an operetta the Latvians staged at the club. Nana made me a green skirt and a white blouse, and into my hair she braided long satin ribbons.

I remember my grandfather as very handsome—thick hair, blue eyes, and a big droopy mustache. He spoke softly in Latvian or thickly accented English which was not, as I recall, as broken as Nana's. I used to love to hear Pa play the flute for the family.

One night, when I was ten or eleven, Pa came down to see us in Atwood Square. Frank—or Sonny, as we called him then—was about two and he had the measles. "Hoopity-hop," Pa chanted as he gently bounced Sonny on his knee, "the horsey goes hoopity-hop." Sonny laughed, for he loved Pa and playing "hoopity."

We never saw Pa after that night.

Nana told us this story. She and Pa went to a concert at the club. They sat side by side. Nana felt Pa put his head on her shoulder. She thought he'd dropped off to sleep. When the concert was over, she could not wake him up. Their friends gathered around, and then everyone realized Pa had died of a heart attack.

At the Huggins Funeral Home, I saw no casket. There was a jar on a stand. "His ashes," Mummy explained. "Pa wanted to be cremated. It was his wish." The Walworth Company orchestra played. Tears streamed down the faces of the musicians. Lots of people were crying besides Mummy and Nana. Most of them talked to each other in Latvian, but I heard someone say in English to Mummy, "It was beautiful that he died listening to music."

Sonny cried. I did too. It was so hard to believe we'd never see Pa again, but somehow we knew it was true.

"Pa is gone," Nana said, "just like Jack." Before I was born, my uncle Jack went to Moscow—that was in 1933, and after one or two letters, Jack was never heard from again. No one ever found out whether he was dead or alive, but they spoke of him the way Catholics speak of a saint.

Pa's funeral was the second one I'd been to at the Huggins Funeral Home. The first one had been for Aunt Tilly's husband, my uncle Joe. "Will he come back soon?" I used to ask Tilly when she'd come home from the hospital. "We'll see," she used to answer—but he never did. It was cancer, and Joe died in the hospital. In his will, Uncle Joe left Tilly the house that Nana and Pa had been living in with Tilly and her son, my cousin, Joe Junior. My cousin was four years older than I, and he too was a saint—or, more precisely, was treated as one by the family.

"I was Pa's favorite," my mother told me at Pa's funeral. "Tilly is Nana's."

That did seem to me true.

Aunt Tilly used to make fun of my mother. "Mary thinks she's such a fine lady, she always was ashamed of her family." "She forget who she is," Nana would add. "You better know who you are," they both used to warn me. Their words come back to haunt me as I sit on the window seat in the splendor of Abby's family's home.

"But if I study and work hard, I'll grow up and write books," I used to argue. "Pshaw," Nana would say. "You grow up and have babies."

"But this is America," I'd say to my grandmother. "America!"

Nana would spit out the name. "Good country for millionaires. They crush all the workers."

I can still see my grandmother's hands. They'd spun and they'd woven. They'd worked in the fields. They'd gardened and stoked the coal furnace, made lye soap and crocheted. Nana's hands told her life story. They were strong, callused, and gnarled.

I knew I wasn't as strong as my grandmother was, so I grew up fearing "women's work." I fled to the library.

"Your mother," Nana warned, "she read books, go to school. Look at her!"

Yes, Nana thought Tilly at least had done something right— married a man who gave her a son and left her a house.

Had my mother been born into the wealth of the Rockefellers, how would her life have been different—or mine, for that matter?

Abby stirs in her bed.

I'll send my mother a Candygram, I think. I'll wire her chocolates—that way she'll have a present in hand when I call her up later.

My reaction to Abby's family's wealth surprises me. Many of my classmates at Radcliffe were rich, and I'd observed that their attitude toward the money that made their lives so impossibly easy was either blasé or scornful. Though I knew the "right" attitude, I was secretly thrilled at the chance to see for myself how the other half lives.

Abby wore jeans on the train; I wore a dress and high heels. The chauffeur met us in a sedan, not the limousine that I was expecting.

A butler opened the front door, and when I turned to close it, it was already shut. I knew I'd made a faux pas.

"Too bad your train wasn't just a bit earlier," said Abby's mother. "Uncle Nelson had us over for drinks with the Shah."

Abby did not look disappointed.

I followed her up the winding staircase. Look at those paintings. Three huge Monet water lilies—right *here*—in their front entrance hall! Incredible, I thought to myself. I tripped on the stairs up to Abby's room.

The walls to the third floor were lined with Daumiers. They couldn't be real, could they?

The first thing I noticed in our room was my suitcase.

At the table were just her mother and father and Abby and I.

"I was at a demonstration yesterday in Harvard Square," I tell Abby's father.

"Yes?" He looks interested.

"I saw a poster which read: 'David Rockefeller supports apartheid. Boycott Chase Manhattan.' "

Under the table, Abby kicks my foot.

"Were you there too, Abs?" David Rockefeller addresses his daughter.

She nods.

"How interesting." He dabs his lips delicately with his linen napkin.

"I just thought you might like to know," I murmur.

I've done it again. Another faux pas. Perhaps Abby does not feel obliged to tell her father every time his name comes up at a demonstration.

Then Abby's mother addresses us all. "Shall we have our dessert?"

Later on, from the adjacent study, Abby and I overhear her father on the telephone. "Hello, Charles. It's David. About that demonstration. I just heard about it. I'm told that negative things were said about the bank. . . .You don't? Oh, I see. That's too bad. You better find out then . . ."

"Who's that?" I whisper to Abby as we head up the stairs.

"Must be someone at Harvard. He's on the board, you know."

"I have to laugh at the irony," I say to Dr. Mueller Monday morning.

"What's that?"

"*Abby* is the Marxist!"

Not ironic, but troubling, is a dream I'd had on the weekend. Saturday night Abby and I slept in her family's New York City townhouse.

"I dreamed that Mike was seriously ill. I was trying to get to him." I recount the dream to Dr. Mueller. "I got trapped in an elevator."

"Hmm."

"There's more. When I was finally rescued, I got to the hospital to learn Mike was dead."

Is that a sigh I hear or did Dr. Mueller just take a breath?

"What comes to mind?" he asks.

"The sauna. There was one in the townhouse. I went in with Abby, but I felt very uncomfortable. I kept wondering what would happen to us if the door wouldn't open."

"And Mike?"

"He's in my dream because of our pending day in divorce court." My voice trails off.

"Yes?"

"Divorce feels like death."

Chapter Fifteen

It's Wednesday, my mother's day off from the nursing home where she works in the kitchen six days each week. It's also her first visit to Mead Street since I told her that Mike and I are getting a divorce. She is agitated.

"Shillitoers," my mother mutters as she paces back and forth in front of the bookshelves on my bedroom wall. "I don't suppose there's any point in talking to you until you're ready to give up these books."

Maybe she forgot to take her Thorazine. I think that would explain her foul mood.

"I gave up books"—she continues to pace—"and I lived happily ever after." She flashes me a sardonic grin. "Shillitoers. Goddamn Shillitoers."

In her paranoid outbursts, my mother uses names that sound real. Just who Shillitoers might be has never been clear to me, but I do know they're bad, and she speaks of them frequently.

"Don't pretend you don't know who they are." She glowers at me as though she'd been reading my mind. "And cover these books with a curtain. Then they'll be out of my sight."

Like mother, like daughter. The older I get, the more I find myself wondering how much my mother's failed expectations affect my own aspirations.

"I'm my baby's mother," Lizzie croons, walking into my bedroom, cradling her favorite doll in her arms.

"My name is Mary. Hers is Mary Louise." Then, seeing Lizzie's puzzled expression, my mother says sweetly, "Your mother's name is Mary Louise and my name is Mary."

"Lizzie,"—I give her a hug—"why don't you go play in your room. Grandmummy's upset but she'll be all right soon."

Lizzie does as I ask.

"You'll be cut down," my mother says when Lizzie is gone. "You're too big. You'll be cut down, and you better believe it." She sits on the edge of my bed, impatiently tapping her foot. "Nana used to tell me how much she hated living with you. She wanted to live with Joe Junior."

But Joe Junior lives in Virginia, has five kids of his own. He had no room for Nana.

"Nana told me how you didn't want me to live with you."

How can I even begin to explain?

No matter, my mother changes the subject.

Why is she so agitated?

"Do you trust Mike with the kids? Does he drink? Can you trust him not to fool around with the kids?"

"Shut up about Mike! Jesus!" I stomp out of the room. "Why don't you leave me alone?"

"I see I'm going to have to get tough with you." She follows me into the kitchen with her fists clenched.

Just as quickly as it had flared up, her anger dies down. "Please take Mike back," she says, her voice barely a whisper. "I hate to see your kids get it—the way you did."

I turn away so she won't see my tears.

"Life is disillusioning, isn't it?" She sits across from me at the table. "I went cracky-wacky over the reporter. He didn't want love. He wanted more women. And I cracked up over him."

"I won't crack up, Mummy. I'm all right, really I am."

"You're just heartbroken, huh?"

I get up to catch the coffee before it boils over.

"Do you miss Tilly and Nana?" she asks.

"Not really. How about you?"

"They bossed me the way they bossed you."

"Do you miss it?"

"Nah." My mother shrugs her shoulders. "I miss the attention."

I burst out laughing in spite of myself. I pour the coffee and cut my mother a big piece of pie.

"They were like your parents, you know."

I shake my head. "Never them. You were always my mother."

"But they took care of you."

"They didn't love me like you did."

My mother flips through a sketch pad forgotten by DeeDee. "A nice sense of color," she comments.

"She's an artist, like you."

My mother frowns. She does not like to be reminded of her artistic talent. To my mother, it was part of the reason she ended up in the hospital.

In Harvard Square Station, Lizzie, Chrissie, and I bid my mother farewell. From her seat on the train, she blows us all kisses.

I walk the kids up to the store and leave them with Mike.

Back home, I clear the cups from the table. Under my mother's saucer, I discover an envelope. Inside are three ten-dollar bills. "Buy the quilt we saw in the store," she writes, "I hope it's still there." Both my mother and I had admired the quilt. We respected the work some unknown woman had put into it. "I hope you can get it," she says in her note, "and I hope you enjoy it."

Chapter Sixteen

Please, Abby, be home, I think to myself.

May Day. Wednesday. My mother's day off.

"Hello." Abby answers as I'm about to hang up.

"Oh, Abby, I'm so glad you're home. I need to ask you a big favor."

"What is it, Lou?" Her voice is concerned.

"I just got a call. It's my mother. She's sick. It may be pneumonia. Mrs. Peretsky, my mother's supervisor, wants her to get to Mass General, but my mother refuses. She says they'll just lock her up again."

"In your mother's case, that fear is reasonable."

"If I can only persuade her to come with me to the hospital. I don't want to take her by taxi, and since I can't drive, I'd rather have someone she knows. I hate to ask . . ."

"Are you at the store?"

"Yes."

"I'll be there as soon as I can."

"Oh, Abby, thank you . . ."

But the buzz on the phone tells me she's already in motion.

Downstairs at the workbench, his hair and shirt covered with sawdust, Mike leans over a plank, the sander in his hand. He can't hear my footsteps over the noise.

When I enter his range of vision, he shuts down the sander and slips the red cotton bandanna from his face to his collar. He seems to know I'm upset.

Six months of legal separation hasn't changed the way we communicate. We both know certain things without really saying.

When I tell him the news, Mike shakes his head sadly. Were things normal between us, we'd embrace, but we don't. Besides, I'm just getting used to not touching him.

"I'm worried, Mike. She is sixty-five, and who knows the true state of her health?"

"But don't forget, she has Nana's constitution."

With no effort at all, I can see Nana as she was in the spring of 1953. She was seventy-six. The bank had foreclosed, so it was to be our last spring in Aunt Tilly's house. I was a senior at Jamaica Plain High. I came home from school to find Nana outside the house readying her plants for the new season: bushes of hydrangea, azalea, lilac, and rose; beds of marigold, tulip, lily of the valley, and Japanese iris. Nana was pruning and trimming as she always had done, as though we'd be there forever.

Her dress, sewn by hand, came down to her ankles and was bordered with rickrack. Around her head was tied a babushka, and on her feet she wore an old pair of my dead grandfather's leather slippers. Bending from the waist, her short, sturdy body made a forty-five-degree angle to the earth. Her legs, covered in brown cotton hose garter-rolled to the knee, stood stiff as posts. Her feet were set firmly apart. Her torso bobbed this way and that as she dug here and there with her small spade and clippers. I put down my books and worked alongside her, but in a short time I grew tired. "You be young girl," Nana scolded, "you ought to be shame." "Oh, Nana," I groaned, snatching up my books. Defiantly then, I stamped up the stairs to go do my homework, smug in the certainty that I could learn more from my books than from my old Russian grandmother.

"Do you remember how incredibly strong Nana was?" Mike asks.

"I do." I nod. "But what you're really asking is do I remember that my mother and Nana come from fine peasant stock."

"That's right," he says, a faint smile on his lips, "and you too."

Mike's mother had grown up on a farm, as had her mother before her. She raised Mike to respect farming and the hard work that goes with it. When Mike first brought me home to Ohio, I was embarrassed and nervous. "Don't be," he'd cautioned. "When she sees your broad shoulders my mother will love you. She'll tell you your shoulders are perfect for pulling a plow."

"You really think my mother is strong," I ask nervously, "despite fourteen years in state hospitals—and all that smoking?"

"Anyone not as strong as your mother could not have survived."

Mike reads my next thought.

"Don't worry about the kids. I'll pick them up early."

"I can't help it." My eyes meet the green-hazel of his.

When it comes to the children, Mike knows me better than anyone. He saw the change after Christopher's birth. I went from being a woman who could sleep through the ringing of telephones to a mother who woke up at any irregularity in her new baby's breathing.

As much as I hate to, I make myself leave them, for I know I'm a good mother only in my mind's eye. In fact, I'm cranky, short-tempered, though I try not to be. Jessie is placid and kind; she'd take care of my children if anything ever happened to me. She takes good care of my kids. She's raised three of her own.

"What would we have done all these years if we hadn't had Jessie for our baby-sitter?" I ask Mike.

"Not left the kids nearly so often—and worried much more."

"What will you tell them?"

"That Grandmummy is sick. I'll say that you're with her. I won't mention the hospital until we know what the matter is. And"—he smiles tenderly—"I'll do the May baskets."

Mike follows me up the stairs in time for us both to see Abby's green Volvo pull up to the hydrant in front of the store.

"Stay as calm as you can," Mike says, walking me to the car. "She'll pull through. And you'll help her." Mike squeezes my arm.

Chapter Seventeen

The prospect of having to take my mother to Mass General plays tricks with my mind, and I am mentally thrown back to 1963. It was a November day when I headed out to Met State at my mother's request. "I'll explain when I see you," she'd said on the phone.

I arrived at F-2 to find my mother dressed in her coat and hat, a cluster of shopping bags all around her. Together we made several trips up and down the back stairs. We left the bags outside at the rear of the building.

"Mrs. MacDonald has found me a job," said my mother when we were back outside, having made our last trip, "and I'm going to take it."

"That's wonderful, Mummy."

Because of her regular dosage of Thorazine, my mother's eyes glaze over hazily, but they weren't on that day. Her blue eyes were bright, her complexion was radiant.

"The job is kitchen work," she explained, "setting trays, clearing up, and running the dishwasher."

I winced. I'd hoped at least waitressing.

"The job's in East Boston in a nursing home," she continued. "Mrs. MacDonald took me over there yesterday. She showed me where you get the train to Harvard Square. I'll be able to see you on my day off."

"That's wonderful," I repeated. I think I was in shock.

"My boss is the nursing home supervisor, Mrs. Edith Peretsky. I met her yesterday, too. She liked me. I liked her. The nursing home's new. 'We'll be new together,' said Mrs. Peretsky." My mother was beaming. "Mary Louise, I'll be the only one on the staff who gets to live in." Her voice grew excited. "There's a spare room in the basement and it will be mine. The owner of the nursing home is a friend of my social worker's, so I really owe it to her—Mrs. MacDonald."

"She's a miracle worker."

"And the job pays real money," said my mother. "They'll take out room and board. The rest will be mine. What do you think of that?"

"It's a miracle, Mummy, the one we've been waiting for."

I looked down at the bags by our feet. "What's all this in here?" My mother had specifically asked me to bring wooden matches. I began to make the connection.

"Let's face it," my mother said, "it's a crazy idea to think I'll ever support myself with my artwork again. Most of the people who helped me are dead. I've lost all my contacts. I've been locked up too long."

"You don't mean this is all your artwork?" I looked down at the bags, then over to the rusted-out barrel, then up to my mother's face.

"Artwork's in the past." She nodded. "I have to destroy it."

I began frantically going through the bags. Sketchbooks and pads. Page after page of delicately drawn flowers. Rose-filled templates my mother had intended to transfer to walls. Hours and hours of her labor. "But, Mummy," I pleaded.

"I'm going to be a kitchen worker now." She spoke with pride and determination, no trace of ambivalence, not a hint of self-doubt. She bent down and began putting loose pages into the barrel.

"Please, Mummy." My mind raced for some way to stop her. "Let me go through them. Let me save some."

"No," she said firmly. "I used to make good money at drawing, but I can't do it now." She snatched a lush floral design from my hand and threw it into the barrel. "They must be destroyed. I want to start fresh."

"But—" I stammered.

"I may be a kitchen worker"—she pointed up to the ward— "but I'll be on the outside."

I could see that there was no stopping her. Reluctantly, I took the box of wooden matches out of my satchel, scanning the grounds to make sure no one was looking.

My mother filled the barrel three-quarters full. The day was a dry one. It took me only two matches to get a blaze going. I numbly looked on as Mummy fed her work to the flames. Sheet by sheet, page by page, one by one, she turned art to ashes.

A new reality came into my focus.

My mother was renouncing the notion that she would ever again be a successful commercial artist. She was giving up the idea that she would live with Nana and me. She was preparing to leave the hospital all on her own, and in so doing give up on the idea that my father would rescue her.

I had no way of knowing that day what would become one of the ironies of my mother's life: a menial job in a nursing home kitchen would bring her more genuine freedom than what she had known when she was a young, highly paid commercial illustrator.

True to her word, nurse Edith Peretsky delivered my mother the job.

Mummy worked parts of six days each week—breakfast, lunch, and dinner, with breaks in between. Wednesday was her day off.

For the first time in her life that I knew of, my mother had peace in relation to money. Room and board were taken out of her salary, so the leftover cash was "cigarette money." She spent it freely.

"I have no head for business," my mother told me, "that's why I want so much for you to take bookkeeping."

My mother, at that time, was sixty. She'd been on the outside for less than a month when Nana, who was still living with me at the time, made her long-postponed trip to Virginia to see her newest great-grandson, Joe Junior's fifth child.

"This morning, after she'd made pancakes for the children," Joe Junior had told me when he finally reached me to tell me the news, "she keeled over and fainted. I ran over to her and said, 'Nana, what's wrong?' 'I'm cold,' she said, so I covered her with a blanket. I called an ambulance. It came right away. The hospital's not very far, but when the ambulance got there, Nana was gone."

"What do we do now?" I'd asked my cousin. "How do we handle it?" I'd asked through chattering teeth.

My cousin had had time to think everything out. Nana had died close to noon of that Sunday, but because Mike and I were up in the country, Joe didn't reach me until nine-thirty that night. He'd been calling every half hour all day.

Mike brought me a chair and sat me down on it.

"There's no point in sending her back up to Boston. Her friends are all dead. Unless you object," he'd continued, "I think we should bury her here. I've found a plot on a hill near some trees in a very nice cemetery not far from the house. The winters aren't cold here. I think Nana would like it. . . ."

"That makes sense," I'd agreed, knowing in my heart that the most important thing about where Nana should be buried was that she be near the grandchild she loved best.

Joe Junior told me the plane schedules and where he would meet us.

When I hung up the phone, Mike drove me to my brother's and we made our plans.

The funeral would be Tuesday. Frank and I booked three seats on a Monday plane to Virginia.

That night I cried many hours. Mike said very little. He just held me in his arms. I couldn't stop shivering. I cried in anger and frustration, sadness and grief, and, yes, relief that Joe Junior was the one to be with Nana when she died. I was glad that the trauma of Nana's sudden death was one I hadn't had to deal with.

Monday morning, first thing, I went to the nursing home. I told my mother what Joe Junior had said. "She fainted. That was it. No pain and no suffering. The best way to go."

As, in some ways, my grandmother's life had been unreal to my mother, so was her death.

"You go, dear," she said softly, "you and Sonny, you go. I'm too old to fly. I better stay at my job."

"Are you sure?"

"I am," she said calmly.

Joe Junior had asked me what dress to lay Nana out in. Her most elegant one was black lace over crepe. Store-bought. Nana favored it. She wore it to funerals. But the dress that was most typically Nana she'd made herself for the trip to Virginia. Made on her ancient Singer sewing machine, it was a dark purple cotton in a rich paisley print with a crocheted collar. "Use that one," I'd told him, describing it.

Nana was simply laid out in a dignified funeral home. Aside from the staff, my cousin, his wife, my brother and I were her only mourners.

I stood alone next to Nana's casket. Now that she was at rest, I could face her. "I'm grateful you kept me alive, Nana, but how I so wish you could have loved me."

I took the chair next to my nineteen-year-old brother. He was openly weeping in unabashed grief. I held him in my arms.

Tuesday night, back in Cambridge, the first thing I did after putting Christopher to sleep was to go into Nana's room.

Most of her personal things I was able to fit into her old black steamer trunk. Mike helped me carry it down to the basement. When it got late, I insisted that Mike go to bed. I worked in a frenzy. I painted the walls, tiptoeing around, moving things this way and that. By dawn, I was finished.

When Mike and Christopher woke up, Mike and I disassembled Christopher's crib. We moved it out of our bedroom and set it up in the gleaming new room that, only hours before, had belonged to my grandmother.

All that remained of Nana's furniture was a dark mahogany bureau, Pa's second purchase when he came to America. It would now become Christopher's. There was plenty of space for the paraphernalia that the two-and-a-half-year-old had already accumulated.

When nine-thirty came on that Wednesday morning, Mike was getting dressed to go to the store. I was taking the day off to spend time with my mother. She was due in just a few hours.

"Why don't you let Jessie take Chris?" Mike suggested. "You have enough on your hands."

I went next door to find Jessie, who greeted me with "I was just on my way out to go see my sister. She adores Chris. Why don't I just take him along? And"—she patted my hand—"you take it easy. This one's on me. I'm doing this as a friend."

"But, Jessie . . ." I'd protested.

"Tsk tsk." She closed her front door and edged me over to mine. "Let's just get Chris bundled up. The day is quite chilly."

"Mike can drive you," I offered, "he's ready to leave."

"Let him go. I'll take Chris in the stroller. The fresh air will do us both good."

Mike left for work, and Jessie and I got Chris into his snowsuit. To Christopher, Nana was "still in Virginia." He could not comprehend "death."

From the window of our first-floor apartment I watched as outside Jessie reached down to make Christopher's mittened hand wave bye-bye.

Against the fading colors of autumn, Jessie was dressed in wine-red. Under the bulk of her thick woolen coat, her frame showed through heavyset, but her overall presence was girlish—far more youthful than her fifty-one years.

From the living room, I moved into the "new" room. The hand-hewn and hand-pegged cradle DeeDee had given us when Christopher was born. "As the godmother—my present," she'd said at the time. A dear friend had made it to DeeDee's specifications. Into it I put Christopher's many stuffed toys.

From out of the small bathroom I took the plastic-lined Dy-Dee hamper. Christopher was almost out of diapers, but the service was a continuing gift from Mike's mother and father.

Last of all, I set up a shelf and took from a basket all the wooden toys Mike had made for his son.

When my mother arrived, just past noon, she walked—as if magnet-pulled—straight to the back of the apartment. I stepped on her heels when she stopped short at the threshold.

"Where are Nana's things?" my mother gasped.

"In the basement," I answered.

She didn't go in. She just stood there and stared.

"I kind of hoped I could move into Nana's room, but," she said in a barely audible voice, "it isn't her room anymore."

I watched as she took in every detail with that fine eye that was both her gift and her curse. She took a few steps. She stopped at Christopher's crib. As she idly spun the mobile that hung just above it, I saw—through my mother's eyes—Nana's bed, which until last night had been in that very spot. It had been there on my mother's last visit, a bed that might now be hers, a trunk that my mother might use. Now they were gone. I could tell that my mother knew that I had done this on purpose: to make it clear that she would not be able to move in with us.

My mother turned to me, dazed. This new room was baby-boy blue. No more was it the room of my mother's mother, no more the room for my mother it might have become.

I looked away, too weak to confront that ferocious capacity to assess what was real that, on occasion, my mother could demonstrate.

She sighed.

I stood paralyzed.

She turned and walked past me into the tiny hall that led to the kitchen. "Do you have any coffee?" She stumbled into a chair and sat down at the table. Reaching for her purse, she began fumbling for cigarettes.

Like a robot, I went to the stove and put a flame to the coffee-pot.

Come move in with us, Mummy, I thought—agonizing over my own cruelty. I said nothing. I just bit my lip.

Nana had been an obligation I couldn't ignore. Of the two, I loved Mummy better, but I'd lived with my grandmother for most of my life, and something inside me told me that my mother and I couldn't manage if we lived together. We hadn't for twenty-one years.

For the first time in her life, I thought to myself, she can stand on her own. "Here," I said, setting the coffee in front of her.

The nursing home staff accepted my mother. She earns her keep. She's found a refuge, I told myself. She *can* stand on her own.

I sat down across from her and lighted a cigarette of my own. By the time I took a sip of the coffee, it had gone cold.

"I understand," my mother said quietly. "I remember when Daddy and I moved in with his mother. You were just a little younger than Chrissie." She spoke his name lovingly. "I hated living with Ralph's mother. I wanted a place of our own."

Tears rolled down my cheeks.

"You're not my baby girl Lullie anymore." How long had it been since she'd used that term of endearment? "You're a wife and a mother now. You have your own family."

I nodded dumbly and felt my face crumbling.

The absolution hurt more than any beating my mother had ever given me as a child.

"Oh, Mary Louise," said my mother, getting up to stand by my side. "Please don't cry."

"I can't help it."

"But there's nothing to cry about."

"That's not true." I buried my head in her bosom. The scent of her perfume was sweet to my nose.

"I know, dear." She stroked my hair. "But look on the bright side. I have my job. Kitchen work may be uglets and shitwits, but the money's not shit. The money is good. And," she added, with no trace of bitterness, "I'm very lucky."

I was sniffing and blowing my nose.

"Not every woman my age has such a beautiful son and daughter—and such a good son-in-law and a beautiful grandchild. I can still come and visit?"

"Anytime!"

And I started bawling all over again.

Chapter Eighteen

The Saratoga Nursing Home is hardly the castle of my mother's fantasy. For her to have considered the job in the nursing home's kitchen meant reckoning with a lifetime of dreams; for her to take it meant giving them up.

"Mrs. Shields?"

Mrs. Peretsky has come up behind me. A buxom brunette, she's smaller than I remembered, but that's probably because she occupies such a large place in my life and my mother's. Her starched uniform and cap lend her an air of efficiency.

"I'm glad you came quickly," says Mrs. Peretsky, "she's taken a turn for the worse. She was on her way to the bathroom when she fainted outside her door in the hall. One of the nurses found her there on the floor. She was delirious. Her sputum is rusty."

I follow Mrs. Peretsky down the stairs.

"I had no idea Mary was so sick." She talks as we walk. "I was off yesterday, but they tell me she worked the whole day. When I'd seen her on Monday, it seemed like a bad cold."

"What do you think it is now?" I catch up to her side.

"Pneumonia."

I can feel my knees weaken.

"Mary's got to go to the hospital. There's no other way. I'd care for her here if I could, but I can't. I have so many patients already under my care."

"I know. You've been so kind to my mother . . ."

"She needs medical help. Medicine. Bedrest. A sure diagnosis." The door to my mother's room is ajar. Mrs. Peretsky taps before we walk in.

On top of a pink chenille bedspread, my mother lies fully clothed. Her head is propped up on a pillow. She is pale and her hair is matted with sweat.

"She has fever and chills," whispers Mrs. Peretsky.

"Mary Louise," my mother moans, "have you and Mike come to take me home?"

"It's not possible, Mummy." I gulp. "You're sick, and Abby and I have come to take you to Mass General."

"Oh, no." My mother lets out a wail. "Not the hospital!" She sits straight up in bed.

I reach for her hand, which she clasps over mine.

"I'm all right, dear. It's just a bad cold. Ask Mrs. Peretsky. I did my work, didn't I?"

"Yes, Mary, you did do your work, but if anyone had known how sick you really were, they wouldn't have let you." She strokes my mother's head. "You should have been in bed all day yesterday."

"I was dressed up to come see you," my mother explains. " 'You look feverish,' she said." My mother points to Mrs. Peretsky. " 'Go to bed, Mary,' she told me, 'you're not going anywhere. Go right back to bed.' "

"But, Mummy." I strain for lightheartedness. "You're not *in* bed, you're on it."

With that sense of discretion good nurses have, Mrs. Peretsky says softly, "I'll leave you to talk." She closes the door behind her.

"Really, dear," says my mother as I sit down beside her on the edge of her bed, "with a few days of rest at your house, I'll be good as new."

"We can't do that," I say with a lump in my throat, "you're too sick. Mrs. Peretsky is a nurse and she says it might be pneumonia. If it is, it won't go away with just bedrest. If it would, she'd let you stay here."

My mother flinches.

"You need treatment," I continue, "more than you can get

here or than I can give you at home. Please let Abby and me take you to the hospital."

My mother looks sad.

"You remember Abby, don't you?"

"She's the one with the cute puppy?"

"Yes." I laugh. "She's the one with the cute puppy. She's outside in her car, grading papers and waiting. She wants to help. That's why she came over. She hates hospitals too. That's why she came. To make it as easy as possible . . . for you."

My mother's eyes widen in panic. New beads of sweat ooze from her brow. "Mary Louise, please don't do this to me."

"There's no other way. I wish I didn't have to. I won't let anyone lock you up," I say fiercely, "not this time. I promise you that." I squeeze her hand hard.

She seems to go limp. Stops resisting me.

"I'll stay with you. Abby will stay with us too. All they'll do at the hospital is take care of you medically."

My mother moves to get up from the bed.

I lend her my arm.

She goes to the mirror and begins combing her hair. I think: in this way, I am different from her—I wouldn't have cared.

"Trust me, Mummy, please."

I pray that it's a quiet day in Emergency. Mass General can be quite a zoo. God, how I hate hospitals too.

My mother peers in her mirror. She straightens her eyebrows with flicks of her fingers. She dabs on pink lipstick. She takes a tulle veil, the pink of the lipstick, and puts it over her hair. She looks very pretty. I look on in amazement—she looks frightened and wan, but really quite pretty.

She slips on her shoes. I help her with her faille coat. She steadies herself on my arm, and I can feel that she's shaky.

With one of my arms under hers, our hands tightly clasped, we make our way out of her room and up the stairs to the nursing station, where Mrs. Peretsky is waiting.

She looks relieved when she spots us.

A few nurses come forward to take my mother's hand. I move back. They embrace her with tenderness.

"You get well fast, Mary," says one.

"And let them take care of you at the hospital," says another.

Nurse May, big-bosomed and redheaded, hugs my mother with more fervor than I've ever seen anyone get away with. "You're a saint of a woman," she says to my mother, "God be with you."

"And, Mary,"—Mrs. Peretsky embraces my mother too— "your job will wait for you to get back. Keep that in mind. Your job will be waiting."

Outside, in the spring air, Abby leaves her car to come toward us. Reaching out to my mother, she asks, "How are you feeling, Mrs. Frazier?"

My mother says, "It's awfully kind of you to offer to drive us."

Abby helps my mother into the front seat, and I go around to get in the back from the driver's side.

Off we go, back through the tunnel over to Mass General, by the Charles River Basin. Abby and my mother chat the kind of usual chatter of people who are in more normal circumstances. My mother seems more relaxed.

I tune out their conversation and try to imagine how it will be at the hospital. As I think through my approach to the doctors, I decide I'd better be honest.

"You two get out here," Abby says at the main entrance. She gets out of the car and goes around to my mother's door. "I'll go park. Then I'll find you inside." She offers her arm to my mother and helps her out of the car.

"Thank you, dear," says my mother to Abby when she's up on her feet.

I come around and take my mother's arm.

I've been here so often, all those years that Nana came once a week to the clinic. I lead my mother toward the emergency room.

When Abby rejoins us, we've already registered and found ourselves seats. The others around us look as distressed as I feel.

Very soon, an impersonal staff diagnoses my mother as being in the early stages of pneumonia. The staff objects to my staying with my mother. "I can't leave her," I say.

"She must be admitted."

"Where?"

"The Intensive Care Unit."

Upstairs, in the corridor outside ICU, a nurse tells me, "This is as far as you go."

"That's where you're wrong."

I look down to the rolling bed. My mother, now dressed in a johnny, seems almost unconscious. "I'm not leaving her side."

"We have rules . . ."

"I don't care."

"We'll see about that." She turns on her heel and says over her shoulder, "I'm going to get Dr. Dineen."

"Good. You just do that."

She thinks I'm crazy. I muse on the irony. That's okay. Better me than my mother.

Dr. James L. Dineen is not very tall. I'd guess his age at less than thirty. He's the head of ICU. His demeanor is calm. He appears not to be angry with me.

I move us both a little away from my mother's bed. "Let me explain . . ."

In summary form, I tell Dr. Dineen my mother's hospital history. "Her new freedom is crucial, so you must understand that her terror here is because she's afraid she'll be locked up again."

"Mrs. Peretsky called Admitting and told them she'd suspended your mother's Thorazine."

"I know. I'm afraid that without it she'll be even more panicky."

"We can sedate her." Dr. Dineen has become quickly attuned to the complications my mother's anxiety might make in her treatment.

"If she panics, she might look crazy to your staff. She isn't. She's terrified."

"I think I know what to do." His expression is thoughtful. "I'll explain every phase of your mother's treatment—to her. We'll deal with it directly."

We approach my mother's bed. She's just coming to.

"Mrs. Frazier." He takes her hand in his. "I'm Dr. Dineen. I'm a medical doctor. You know you're sick, don't you?"

My mother nods.

"You have pains in your chest. Your sputum is bloody. You know that too?"

She nods again.

"I'm here to help you. I have the medicine you need and the staff to take care of you. Now, your daughter has just told me of your other hospital experience—"

"You didn't!" My mother glares at me.

At this flash of temper, I panic.

"She did the right thing," Dr. Dineen continues, unflustered. "I can't just treat your body. I need to know what's on your mind. The things that are troubling you might prevent you from getting well."

My mother relaxes. His tone of voice is plain-spoken, not tricky.

"You need all your strength to fight the pneumonia—not me and the hospital."

He looks to me, his eyebrows arched in unspoken question. I nod yes, wordlessly urging him to continue.

"You are very sick, but you have Mrs. Peretsky to thank for an early diagnosis. If you work very hard to get well, we can have you out soon—"

My mother interrupts him. "How soon is soon?"

"We'll know better when we've seen how you respond to the treatment."

"How soon is soon?" she repeats.

"Could be less than a week." He scratches his chin. "That is, if you respond and do what we tell you."

My mother sinks back on the pillow and sighs in relief.

"What do I have to do?" she wheezes.

"First, I'd like you to let your daughter go home."

She sits up and looks frightened again.

"But—" I start to talk.

Dr. Dineen waves his hand and goes, "Ssh."

"If you let your daughter go now, we can admit you to ICU and start up your treatment. She can come back tomorrow."

My mother looks at me anxiously, but I say nothing. I wait for Dr. Dineen to start talking again.

"I work until midnight." He fluffs her pillow. "I'll check on you every hour, see how you're feeling, see how the staff's treating you. I want you to tell me if you have any complaints."

I can't believe what I'm hearing.

"I'd like you to trust me." He takes her hand again. "That is, if you can. I'm here to help people, and all I want to do for you is to help you get well."

I cannot fully absorb the power of Dr. Dineen's words. He's so incredibly earnest.

"Does my daughter have to go right away?"

"Would it make you feel better if she stayed for a while?"

"Oh, yes, Doctor," she answers docilely.

I can tell that her trust is now with him.

He was right. She does know she's sick and that if there were any way humanly possible, Mrs. Peretsky would have cared for her there.

"Well then, she can stay," he continues. "She can go into ICU with you, but make the visit a brief one. I want my staff to start taking care of you." He presses her hand. "And I'll be back in an hour to see how you're doing."

My mother's smile is a grateful one.

We both watch as he heads down the corridor.

Grace under pressure. The best human virtue. Overworked, very tired, under all kinds of stress, Dr. Dineen wasn't so busy that he did not take the time to assure a sick woman that before he practices his medicine, he cares how she feels.

"He's a real gentleman," says my mother after he's gone.

"Yes, he is." I choke up when I speak.

"Isn't it lucky"—my mother is smiling—"that it's only pneumonia."

"*Only pneumonia!*" I burst out with laughter. "What did you think was wrong?"

"When I fainted . . . you know, the way Nana did . . . I thought it was death."

"Oh, you poor thing." I embrace her.

She pushes me back.

"We don't want *you* to get sick too," she says in a motherly tone. "Think of the children."

* * *

"Ice cream." I ask the attendant in the kitchen just off the ward. "It's for Frazier. It's allowed."

She goes to the refrigerator.

"Hang on," says a resident I'd seen in Emergency. "You hang on." He grips my shoulders affectionately, and for the first time all day I grow aware of myself, what I must look like. A glance in a wall mirror shows my face to be haggard and drawn. My God, I look older than my own mother!

Dr. Dineen keeps his promises, and after only three days my mother is well enough to be discharged. "She's covered by Medicare," says Dr. Dineen. Then he reports his conversation with Mrs. Peretsky. " 'We'll bring her the rest of the way back,' she told me, 'my own nursing staff has volunteered their days off to take care of her.' "

Saturday, Abby and I go get my mother. "You don't have to," I'd told her the previous night. "I know I don't have to," she'd answered. "I want to. Otherwise I won't feel the mission is completed."

"Mrs. Frazier!" A male voice calls to us from the lobby.

"Why, Doctor, I didn't know you were on." She greets Dr. Dineen.

"I'm not, but I didn't want to miss saying good-bye."

"I'm feeling so much better," my mother says.

"You look better, too," he says. "You're a very strong woman. I want you to take care of yourself. And if you have any problems, I want you to call me. Will you remember that?"

"I will," she says shyly.

"Thank you so much." I shake Dr. Dineen's hand.

"The pleasure was mine." He looks away from me to my mother. "And we'll see you back here in two weeks for a follow-up. Now go home and get well."

Go home.

He'd said, "Go home." And that's where my mother is going. Back to friends who will take very good care of her.

In the Volvo, my mother looks radiant. It's hard to believe she's still sick. She talks to Abby as though they were the oldest of friends.

"He sounds like a fine doctor," Abby agrees.

At the tunnel, Abby reaches into the pocket of her jeans for a coin.

"Oh, no, dear, we can't let you pay," says my mother, pressing a quarter into Abby's hand. "It's our ride"—she flashes me a broad smile—"isn't it, dear?"

This time at the nursing home, Abby comes in. She sees for herself how people care for my mother.

Mrs. Peretsky takes the bag and the letter Dr. Dineen sent along for her. A scan of its contents seems to reveal no surprises.

Downstairs, in my mother's room, someone has placed a huge bouquet of flowers on her bedside table. The touches of my mother's decorating now stand out. A lamp made of hobnailed milk glass in the shape of an old kerosene lantern, the pink chenille spread, and lots of fringed throw pillows. Pictures of me and the children are on her bureau, and one of my brother as a small boy—about the age he was when she was taken from us and sent to the hospital. Even now, my mother can't quite comprehend that Frank is grown up. She still calls him "Sonny," and she doesn't quite recognize him, so, through no fault of her own, she still searches out her "lost" baby, and this makes meetings with my mother very painful for Frank.

"There's ice cream for you," says Nurse May.

"Thank you." My mother looks radiant. "Thank you all for everything."

Mrs. Peretsky shoos them all from the room.

"You go home to the children now," says my mother to me. "Give them these presents." She takes a few packages out of her purse. "I bought them from the lady who came around every day with a cart."

"Oh, Mummy, you shouldn't have . . ."

"Go home to your children. You've spent enough time with your old mother. If I'm better at all, it's thanks to you and Dr. Dineen."

"You did it yourself." I stroke her brow gently. "You're a brave and strong woman."

When I bid farewell to the staff, Nurse May takes me aside. "Your mother's such a grand woman. She has lots of guts—and a very big heart."

"I know."

I give Nurse May a big hug.

Chapter Nineteen

"But I still don't feel ready," I tell DeeDee.

"Is anyone, ever? Don't we all get pushed into it?"

I tap the long ash from my cigarette.

"Look, Lou, you and Mike have been separated for more than six months. It's time. I just wish that you weren't so upset."

"And I just wish Donald hadn't told him anything about me."

"Donald told him you were both in the same boat. That's all." She takes my shoulders. My eyes meet hers. "Just come. Meet him. Who knows, you may even like him."

DeeDee's party is small. Low-key and comfortable. Mostly old friends of mine and of DeeDee's. Bob Lupus is a good friend of Donald's. He fits in with the group, and when I'm ready to go, he offers to give me a lift.

"It's on my way," he says, getting his coat. "I don't mind at all."

I accept, and the ride leads to an invitation for dinner the next Saturday night.

Dressing up for my date, I use makeup sparingly. Some eyeliner, a little mascara and eye shadow. I choose a dress of an Indian print I'd made from a bedspread. I zip up the back, put on a pair of brown pantyhose, and step into a pair of maroon pumps

that add a few inches of height. I stand close to six feet. I pinch
my cheeks pink and then twist up my hair into its usual bun.

When the doorbell rings, I take my coat and go down the stairs
to greet Bob.

"Good evening." The tall man on my front porch shyly smiles.

"Hi there, Bob." I extend my hand nervously.

Horn-rim glasses accentuate his long, angular face. His blond
hair is curly and recedes high back on his forehead. He wears a
blue blazer and slacks.

"How about French food?" he asks. "Have you been to Chez
Jean?"

"Once or twice. I like it a lot."

I step out onto the porch and close the front door behind
me.

Taking the hint that he's not to come up, Bob turns down the
stairs and opens the door on my side of his car.

Bob is a psychoanalyst, and our conversation seems to flow
easily. We share a bottle of wine. I tell him my mother's story,
and—though I try not to—I do lots of psychoanalytic name-
dropping to show off how well read I am.

With some encouragement from me, Bob speaks of the
breakup of his own marriage. "She fell in love with one of our
friends. She told me the day she asked me to move out."

"Neither one of us was prepared for rejection," I comment.

He seems to balk at my summary. "I wouldn't say that, exactly."

"But it's true all the same. I think I know how you feel."

I insist that he order another bottle of wine.

Why did I have to get drunk? I made a fool of myself. I'm sure
of it. My head pounds as I reach for the first coffee of the day. I
recall shaking his hand goodnight in his car. What a jerk he must
think I am.

The ring of the telephone interrupts my self-flagellation.

"How are you feeling?" Bob asks.

"Just awful. I'm sorry—"

He interrupts. "Have you had your breakfast yet?"

"I was about to make coffee."

"How about breakfast at my place? I'll come over and get you."

"I'm really hung over. I won't make very good company."

"I feel partly responsible. Let me help you get through the day."

I shower and try to make myself presentable. I can't seem to make any kind of decision, so I do the easy thing and wear the dress I wore last night.

When Bob picks me up, *The Boston Globe* and *The New York Times* are already in his car.

"Oh, good! The Sunday papers make life worth living." I set them on my lap.

"It's not Sunday papers that make life worth living," he answers matter-of-factly, "it's other people."

"I know that." I'm taken aback by his seriousness. "You have a way of commenting on casual things that's quite judgmental. It makes me nervous."

"I don't mean to do that."

"Perhaps it's an occupational hazard, but I feel as though you're categorizing me, and I don't like the feeling."

"I'm sorry if I make you feel as though I'm judging you. I'm not."

Bob's townhouse is impeccable. A large living room has walls lined with books, a few paintings, and a picture window overlooking the treetops of Beacon Street. Sunlight streams in. The room is a cozy retreat from the cold day outside.

"Would you like a fire?"

"I'd love one." I sit down on a rug by the fireplace and wrap my dress over my knees. "About last night—I'm sorry I showed off about psychoanalysis. I think I'm intimidated that it's what you do for a living. You're a little too much for me."

"I'm having a hard time myself," says Bob, on his knees arranging the kindling. "My divorce has sent me back to my own analyst to do some unfinished business."

I blew it last night. I don't want to do it again, but I give in to an impulse. "How well do you think you know yourself?"

"Fairly well." He sits down by the fire.

"Are you aware of what a restrained person you are?" I'm seated behind him and out of his sight. I bite my lip and continue. "Your silences. Last night they made me talk even more than I normally would have. I let down my defenses. I felt I had to explain myself. Did you do that deliberately?"

"Not consciously, anyway." He stands up. "Now that the fire's going, let me make us some breakfast."

Being here with Bob is better than being home all alone, but it's far from the intimacy I once felt with Mike.

How do people get not to be strangers? Bob and I should be able to find common ground. We've both been rejected in marriage. We're both in analysis. It's what he does for a living.

Last night, Bob told me how much he misses Susan, his wife, and Libby, his daughter. We both have voids in our lives. The need for affection does not diminish because the ones we love go.

How good it would be if Bob could share some of his feelings —not just his thoughts and ideas.

"Breakfast is ready." Bob's touch on my shoulder breaks my train of thought. He helps me to my feet, and, stockingfooted, I follow him into the kitchen. Bacon and eggs, bagels with jam. Café au lait. My stomach feels settled, and, over the last of our coffee, we thumb through the papers. I almost feel comfortable.

Back in the living room, Bob puts on a record of a string concerto. He sits down on the floor by my side and encircles me with his arms. I put my arms around him. I feel first the soft cashmere of his sweater, then the bony torso beneath. He kisses me tentatively.

"Oh, Lou, you'd be so easy to love." His voice is tender.

"I don't want love." I pull away from his arms. "I want a friendly relationship."

"You're kidding yourself. You want to be loved."

"What makes you so sure?"

"It's written all over your face. We're two lonely people. We don't even know each other. We're yearning for love," he says, stroking my hair, "and we're too old-fashioned to change."

I move up closer to the fireplace.

"You surely don't want a quick roll in the hay?" he asks.

I don't feel like fully confiding in him, so I ask, "Would that be so awful?"

"It would be settling for less than what both of us want."

His words and his tone indicate that the first sensual stirrings are over now. Clearly, we're not going to bed.

A slow anger bubbles inside me.

"You say 'settle for less.' I say 'take what you can.' My husband fell in love with another woman. Your wife left you for another man. We're the ones caught off guard. We weren't prepared."

I get to my feet and pace back and forth.

"Look at all these beautiful things. You're comfortable here in your bachelor digs, but you're lonely. Admit it."

I look down at him.

He does not look up.

"You miss your wife," I say softly. "Her. Not only the sex. You miss the loving, the intimacy . . . the comfort of having someone to feel close to."

Bob draws up his knees and huddles closer to the fire.

"I felt like experimenting. Clearly you don't. Sure we're strangers, but there's lots that we share. There was a chance we could have worked something out. Less than perfection, but more than the loneliness."

I sit down next to Bob. He stares into the fire.

"You may be too old-fashioned to change, but I'm not." I mask my hurt feelings with sarcasm. "If I can't get what I want one way, then I'll try another."

Bob's expression is hard for me to decipher. I vow not to speak again until he says something.

"You should have the ego strength to wait for someone who loves you," he says at last.

I shake my head no. "I might try something else."

"For now"—he gets to his feet—"how about a matinee with this here old fogey?"

"Movies in the daytime always feel slightly sinful." I'm grateful he's left us a way out. "Let's go."

I reach for my shoes, and we leave for the nearby movie theater.

Chapter Twenty

"I've been thinking about what you said."

"For two weeks, Bob?" I ask him over dinner.

"Not nonstop, obviously, but a lot." He sips his wine. "There's more to it than I told you the last time."

What can he be talking about? I wait and I listen.

"If we went on seeing each other, we'd end up in the sack."

I want to say, "So what?" but Bob is too serious, and something tells me that this is no time to be flip.

"I can't let myself make it with someone who's a control analysand at an Institute that I must deal with professionally."

Now that *is* a surprise. "Why ever not?" I ask.

"Bert Mueller, your analyst, is a colleague of mine."

"What difference does that make?"

"Psychoanalysts are the world's biggest gossips."

I must look confused, because he spells it out.

"If I sleep with you, all my colleagues will know."

"Dr. Mueller? Not him. He wouldn't gossip."

"Don't forget, he has a supervisor."

"I did forget that," I murmur, then hesitate. "Wait a minute, Bob, I just want to make sure I understand. Are you saying that you think we might have something together like what you've been missing since you split with your wife?"

He nods.

"And that you'll give up a chance for a friendly romance because you're afraid you would be professionally compromised?"

"Exactly."

"Then you're a damn fool."

"My work is all I have left, Lou. If my sex life became Institute scuttlebutt, I just couldn't stand it. Please try to understand."

"I'm trying."

I don't know whether I feel angry or sad. My thoughts are mixed up.

"I like you a lot," he says. "The other women that I go out with can't hold a candle to you. Perhaps we could be friends?"

I shake my head no. "I have enough friends, Bob. If I saw you anymore, I'd want us to be lovers. Take it or leave it."

He leaves it.

"Do you know Bob yourself?" I ask Dr. Mueller. "Is he someone you deal with on a regular basis?"

"We see each other at meetings occasionally and that's about it."

"Bob says we'd have no privacy, what with me telling you everything."

Dr. Mueller says nothing.

"I just want you to know," I say, after a long silence of my own, "that I trust you myself, even if Bob isn't able to."

"Well, that's pretty important." I hear Dr. Mueller shift in his chair.

"I think it is. The rest is Bob's problem. One thing he did say, though, still troubles me."

"What's that?"

"He thought that I didn't know him well enough to have any strong feelings for him . . . he suggested that he might be a 'stand-in' for *you*."

Silence.

"What do you think?" I ask Dr. Mueller.

"What do *you* think?" he asks me.

"I certainly suppress any sexual desire I might feel for you." I hesitate. "Could it be that my sudden attraction to Bob means that a real-life romance with an analyst would be easier than talking to you about how I feel?"

"There's a great deal we can talk about," Dr. Mueller replies, "when you are ready."

After our session, I walk down the hill pondering the vagueness of Dr. Mueller's final remark. Does he think Bob is right? *Could* Bob be a stand-in for my repressed sexual feelings toward Dr. Mueller? Is that why I was so willing to bed down so quickly?

Chapter Twenty-one

"I used to know the city very well, but only on foot," my mother tells me on the day that we return to Mass General for her checkup.

I take my mother's arm as we walk up from Park Street and through what used to be Scollay Square, now the new Government Center. "That's my favorite, too," I say, "coming to know a place by walking around."

"Grandmummy looks pretty," says Lizzie.

"Yes, she does." I admire my mother's print dress. It looks like a summer suit, pale pink flowers on beige. The same veil of pink tulle that she wore on the day that Abby and I took her to the hospital is wound around her hair and her forehead.

"A speedy recovery, Mrs. Frazier," says Dr. Dineen, "really amazing."

Relief is written all over my mother's face.

How different this is from all my trips to Mass General with Nana. One week we'd have a good doctor, only to find him gone by the next visit.

"Do you know how long you'll be at Mass General?" I ask Dr. Dineen.

"Not really. Perhaps a year. Perhaps three."

"What does it depend on?" asks my mother.

"Whether I want to be an academician or go into private practice."

"You make a very fine doctor," my mother tells him.

"I agree," I say, shaking his hand. "If you're taking a poll, register two votes for practice."

"That's nice to hear," says Dr. Dineen, smiling.

"What shall we do to celebrate?" I ask my mother and Lizzie outside in the glorious warm summer day.

"Swan boats!" Lizzie cries. "I want the swan boats."

"Oh, yes," says my mother.

I have fond memories of going on these same swan boats with my mother when I was a child.

The so-called swan boat is a sternwheeler, pedal-operated by a driver whose seat is concealed in the large wooden shape of a swan. The flat boat is rigged with several slat benches, on which passengers sit as the boat circles the small pond in the Public Garden. On the boat you hear the whoosh of the wheel in the water, but from a distance the swan appears to be gliding.

"The swan boats it is." I clasp the hand of my mother and my daughter on either side of me.

"That's an awfully cute little girl." A woman sitting on the bench next to us nudges my mother. "Is she your granddaughter?"

"She is." My mother beams as Lizzie snuggles up close.

From her end seat, Lizzie leans over the arm of the bench to feed popcorn to a passing mother duck and her ducklings.

"Is Mike coming back?" my mother whispers in my ear, so Lizzie won't hear.

I am caught off guard. My first reaction is hostile. "I don't want to talk about Mike."

"You mean you don't know if he's coming back?"

"We still have the same agreement as we had when Mike moved out of the house." My voice is controlled.

"It's like Ralph" She gazes off to the ducklings. "I want to like him but I can't. Not even if he came back. He wasn't there when I needed him, so I'd never take him back *now*."

My mother's not being critical of Mike—she's confusing him with my father. She's remembering how my father let her down. I relax my defenses.

"Oh, Mummy, Mike's not like Daddy at all. Our problems are different."

She looks at me skeptically.

"Don't you believe me?"

She shrugs her shoulders. "I feel good now," she says, changing the subject, "not my usual depression."

"I'm glad."

"But I'm getting so old." She touches her chin and her neck. "Are you still strong or are you getting weaker?"

"I'm tired, that's all." I rub my eyes with my hand.

"I worry that you'll get sick. I don't want *you* to get sick."

"I won't, Mum. Please don't worry about me. Just keep yourself well. I want *you* to stay well."

Lizzie's giggles interrupt our aside. The mother duck and the ducklings are following Lizzie's popcorn trail, and the sight of it all makes my mother and me laugh with the child.

Holding hands, the three of us walk from the Garden to the Common and make our way over to Park Street.

"She's a beautiful child," the lady from the swan boat calls after us, "she looks as though she'd been found in a temple."

Indeed, Lizzie does. Her little blue dress is hung from a yoke bordered in pink. Her golden hair curls, and her blue eyes look even bluer against her dress.

"You look very nice," I say to Lizzie.

"That's what I hoped." She squeezes my hand.

Downstairs in Park Street Station—that central artery of Boston's subway system where one can connect to almost anywhere —a sad look crosses my mother's face.

"What were you thinking just now?" I ask Mummy.

"Of Baby Sissa, our 'beautiful dreamer.' "

> Beautiful dreamer, awake unto me,
> Starlight and dew drops are waiting for thee.

I can't count the times that my mother hummed or sang that old ballad. Stephen Foster wrote it, she told me, for his dead baby daughter. It was at her drawing board that my mother most often sang its refrain.

"Our 'beautiful dreamer' lies in a cemetery, and . . ."

My mother's gay mood is gone. I can see *that*.

". . . The *next* school you go to," my mother says to me angrily, "better be Radcliffe *Business* School!"

"There isn't one, Mum," I laugh. "But maybe there should be."

Neither my attempt at lightheartedness nor Lizzie's loving hugs can restore my mother's good humor, and by the time her subway train comes, her mood is surly and mean.

Lizzie and I stand on the platform and wave until her train is out of sight.

✿

Chapter Twenty-two

✿

"We must not see each other again," she says.

"We *must* not see each other again," he repeats.

"We can't go on . . ."

"No, we can't . . ."

"No, we can't. But not yet."

"Yes . . . not yet."

Two dignified lovers—both betraying their spouses—agree to break off their affair.

At home, sitting in front of my television set, I am watching the English movie *Brief Encounter.*

When I walked into Mr. Napoli's office for the first time, he advised me not to act hastily. Eight months have passed, and some part of me still hopes Mike will stop loving Jeannie.

If Mike came back to me, I'd know I exist.

No, I don't want him back. I just want him to tell me that I was worth having.

The divorce was my idea. I'm burning my bridges behind me, but still I see nothing ahead. If I were a bridge builder, I could put up a sign: BRIDGE CLOSED FOR REPAIRS.

I stare at my television set.

"Not yet," I murmur, echoing the lovers' lament.

"There's no clinical, qualitative measure of aliveness."

Dr. Mueller is in the corridor talking to a doctor whose office is just down the hall.

"But, Bert," says the doctor, "what does it mean if a patient tells me 'I feel more alive'?"

"It means something to me."

"Come on. What if I tell you I feel more alive after two bourbons? What does that mean?"

I take my seat outside his office, and the two doctors finish their conversation out of my earshot.

Dr. Mueller is right, I think to myself, there are more feelings than any of us can ever put into words.

"Part of why I get so angry with my mother is she gets too close to the heart of things. She uses no tact."

I'm at ease on his couch.

"Yes?"

"Yesterday, when she asked me for the third time if Mike was coming back, I exploded: '*We* arrange. *We* agree. *We* make joint decisions, *and*,' I threw in, 'I *don't* want him back.' To all of this, my mother replied, 'Oh, I get it—*he* doesn't want you.' "

"Have you been taking your Thorazine?"

My mother's mood is still angry. She greets my question with a filthy look. She taps her spoon on her coffee cup as we sit at my kitchen table. With each tap of the spoon, her whole body twitches. Her lips are pressed tight. Her face is a frown.

We're into a new week of hostility.

"Rumnose. No wonder Nana ran away from you. You're no good." She eggs me on.

"Nana didn't run away." I try to be patient. I stop rubbing my nose. "She went to Virginia for a visit to Joe Junior. She'd have come home if she hadn't died."

"And *you*," she says haughtily, "will die in an asylum."

This toughness that comes on her—I used to see it more often when she was at Boston State. Occasionally I'd arrive and she would immediately vilify me. I'd hear all the accusations, even feel them. But somehow I knew that they weren't really directed at me. My mother was fighting back: at her phantoms, at her accusers, and at those who kept her locked up.

"Rumnose," she says again.

Now I feel angry. I touch my nose with my fingers. That same system of capillaries which causes my face to flush at the slightest embarrassment also reddens my nose. Especially in cold weather, but even in summer. And aside from biting my nails, one of my most steadfast nervous habits is rubbing my nose. My mother's is twisting strands from the front of her hair. She twists them now.

"You shouldn't talk that way to me, Mummy. I don't deserve it. You know I've had a red nose since I was a child."

"Rumnose. Shillitoer."

Please let her stop cursing me and those "Shillitoers"—whoever they are.

Why was my mother so angry today? I wonder later.

In those moods, she appears to hate me—but I know she doesn't. How I wish I understood more about her.

The day my mother burned her artwork she was in total command. She knew what she had to do, she seemed to know why. Will I ever grow to be so sure of any one thing?

Not yet.

Chapter Twenty-three

"Why not do what I do?"

"But with whom, Gloria, with whom?"

"I've met this guy at Harvard Summer School. I'm seeing someone on a regular basis, so I don't want to date, but this fellow is clearly available. He'd be perfect for you."

"Oh, Gloria, no."

"Oh, Mary Lou, yes," says my Radcliffe classmate, who's remained a friend all these years. "Let me bring him by. You can see for yourself."

"Not here," I gasp. "Not at the store."

"Why not? It's perfect. Dozens of people stop by to say hi in the course of a week."

I protest, but her idea interests me.

If she brings the guy by, I'll size him up for myself, decide whether or not I want to spend time with him. That beats a blind date.

"All right," I say.

"Good," Gloria says as we part.

Her confidence in this plan eases my doubt. I seem to need all the help I can get setting up some kind of a sex life.

Bizarre, one part of me thinks.

Realistic, thinks another.

For this new part of my life, I must learn to approach sex

differently. Sex will be a new way to redefine men . . . redefine my own needs—that is, if I'm up to it.

"My daughter's a hippie and a drug addict," my mother announces to no one in particular at the beginning of her new visit.

"Oh, God, Mummy." I laugh.

"Very funny." She sneers.

Is it me that she's talking to, or is she answering her voices?

"It *is* funny, Mummy, because it's not true."

"We'll see about that when the police arrive."

"What are you talking about?"

"I'm going to call the police and have them take the children away from you."

I collapse in the living-room chair and steel myself for the next round.

"I can't prove that you're an addict, but I'll tell them I think you are." She paces the floor, galvanized by that internal fury I've seen all my life. "Maybe Mike is an addict, too. Terrible. Terrible."

"Mummy," I plead.

"Don't 'Mummy' me."

"You better shut up about the police." My own rage takes over. I'll try drowning out hers. "You'd call them on me? You? Of all people?"

"Nana was right. She told me you didn't want her and that you didn't want me. That's what she died from in Virginia."

"What?" I shout. "Exactly what did she die from in Virginia?"

"From not being wanted."

My mother turns on her heel and goes into the kitchen.

I don't know how much longer I can stand these attacks.

"Shut your mouth." I follow her into the kitchen. "That's Chrissie downstairs at the door, and if you can't control yourself, you can damn well go back to East Boston. *Do you understand?*"

"Hi, Mum. Hi, Grandmummy." Chris comes upstairs and hugs my mother. From behind his back, I make a face at her, mouthing the words "Shut up!"

"Look what I have for you." My mother suddenly finds a new

sweet voice for Chris. She pulls out a box from her large leather handbag and gives it to him.

"Ooh," Chris says when he sees what's inside. "Vroom, vroom." Chris moves the small racing car with delight in circles down on the floor.

Christopher is happy, my mother's calmed down, but I have a headache.

I leave them alone and go into my bedroom.

How long will she keep it up? Will either of us live long enough to get to the bottom of it?

One thing is sure—I need some relief.

I lie down on my bed. Just getting off my feet feels terrific.

Lately, just living exhausts me. Flat out every day, I come home with no energy—or money—to keep in reserve for that proverbial rainy day.

DeeDee is worried, and she made no bones about why: "What will you do if you get sick?" "I have to rely on my health," I told her, "that's all there is to it." "Stored money is stored energy"— she waved her finger in front of me—"God, how I wish you could see that!"

I see it. I know what she means, but I'm nowhere near a point where saving is possible—I'm holding the line.

Is that why I find myself thinking about men and sex? Sex at least provides an outlet for nervous tension.

My friendships with women are nonsexual and comfortable. We seem to take turns being all things—mother, sister, and daughter—to each other. We nurture as crisis demands.

With my mother, I perceive circularity. Preprogrammed, almost. To see it doesn't mean I can break out of the circle. Perceiving is just the beginning.

Mike once nurtured me—and the children; he now nurtures them, and each day I learn more about managing within the money he gives me—and without all the love.

Dr. Mueller is "mind"; Mike is co-parent; my brother is my friend.

Until now, I have been so preoccupied with having love line up with sex, I denied my own sexual impulses. I don't let them surface.

"What's this, Mary Louise?" My mother barges into my bedroom and interrupts my train of thought. In her hand is a letter. She waves it in front of me, shoves it under my nose.

It's the letter written to me by the Boston Psychoanalytic Institute notifying me of Dr. Mueller's availability to interview prospective analysands. Where did she find it? I'm sure I hid it away in my papers.

"What does this mean?" She's toe-to-toe with me now, and I can feel her seething with rage. "Just what does this mean?"

"That I'm seeing a psychoanalyst." My defiant tone matches hers as I snatch the letter out of her hand. "That's what it means."

"Five? Ten? Two hundred and fifty? How much is it costing you?"

"Three dollars an hour, that's all. It's cheap. My doctor's in training."

"Wonderful." She is actually laughing. I don't get the joke. "That makes *two* of you who don't know what you're doing!"

"I'm not going to discuss this with you." I push past my mother. "I'm going to pick Lizzie up at nursery school, so you better calm down."

When we come in from the hot day outside, the first thing Lizzie does is take off her sunsuit.

"Don't go nude," my mother yells. "The police will take you away." She makes Lizzie step back into her sunsuit.

That does it.

"Come in here." I take my mother's arm and walk her into my bedroom. Lizzie is on the living-room floor playing with some Creative Playthings. I try to protect the children from my mother's rantings—if not always my own. Until now, Lizzie has never been the object of my mother's anger.

"I won't let you talk that way to her."

My mother breaks out of my grip. "You're unreal," she says. "You're the one who's out of it. Forget the unreal. Forget about Radcliffe. Go to a commercial course. Have something practical."

I can think of no way to stop her.

"Your little job," she whispers, "is housekeeping. Cook. Clean.

Sew. If you do those things, Mike will come back. That's where your attention belongs." She points to Lizzie, out in the living room. "On that sweet child. Not on the deep water." She slaps the spines of my books. "Give them up! Burn them alive!"

I sit down on my bed, weak in the knees. I should have told her about Dr. Mueller before, not let her find out. That's what brought all this on.

"Don't neglect your child. Look at her on the floor. She's a God-given Christian. No cloven hoof. No deformity. That's where your attention belongs." She blows Lizzie a kiss.

"We're different, you and I." I speak calmly, but inside I am trembling. "I need some psychiatric help right now in my life. I have a good doctor. I need him."

"That deep water—what for? And this stuff you bought for Lizzie." She picks up a Creative Plaything left behind on my bed. "That's an idea from Dr. Cuckoo. These toys are for the feeble-minded, not for redblooded normals like Lizzie."

I am not prepared for this outburst. I can feel myself shattering.

"My daughter's a damned intellectual. They don't know how to live. You're trapped by Harvard. It's not the best in the world. It isn't so hot."

She opens the door of my closet. "Come over here. Look in this miror with me."

"What for?"

"To see the destruction."

"Shit! God damn it to shit. Why are you acting like this?"

"My style hasn't changed. I'm the way I've always been."

"I don't think so." I sigh. "For weeks now, you've been on my case. I won't take it. I refuse to put up with it. I won't let you come here anymore to see the children—not until you stop this behavior."

"No mother in the world should have to listen to such a stinking child. People say you're no good."

"What people say that?"

"A countergirl in East Boston. Someone who sat next to me. She said you're no good."

It's the voices again.

"Why pay attention to them? Why not trust me?"

"Why should I?" Her tone is defiant.

"Why not?"

"Because," she says under her breath, "we're both hospital cases."

"Oh, God. I can't take much more of this. I'm telling you that."

"Hush. Don't say things like that."

"I?" I shake my head. "*I* shouldn't say things like that? What the hell's the matter with you? Do you hear what you're saying? Listen to yourself. Then tell me not to say things like that!"

Will there ever be any protection for me from my mother? Or for my mother from me? Beyond a point, I can't take it. I must draw a line. As it is, we move back and forth on a treadmill.

Chapter Twenty-four

"What's on your mind?" asks Dr. Mueller.

"My mother. She scares me with her talk. Whatever you call it that my mother suffers from—schizophrenia, psychosis, illness, or strategy—she shuts me out. She's been through so much. She doesn't really mean me. I know that. . . ."

"Yes?"

"All the same, it's hard to forgive. I blew up at her yesterday."

"Do you remember the time you blew up at me?"

"Not exactly."

"You accused me of not caring about your psychoanalysis. Said it was my job . . . what I had to do for my certification."

"I didn't mean . . ."

" 'I'm holding on by the skin of my teeth' is what you told me at the time."

I flush with embarrassment.

"It sounds to me as though you think you have to make some kind of a leap," he continues, "and that there's no turning back."

"I'm not leaping. I'm falling."

"Do you think nobody cares? Nobody sees?"

"All I know is that I miss Mike. His love. The closeness. The consolation of sex. Without him, I feel so alone."

Dr. Mueller says nothing.

"With you, we shake hands occasionally. Our minds are in

touch, but that's all. If you did touch my body, I'd be terrified, but sex made me feel real. Without it, I'm not sure I exist."

Is it a coincidence that the longing for sex comes at a time when my mother's so hostile?

"You haven't brought me up to date on your arrangements with Mike."

"That's because nothing's changed. We're going through with the divorce."

"There's something else you haven't discussed with me."

"What's that?"

"My vacation. It's already June, and you've known for some time I'll be gone for part of August and on into late September. It will be our longest separation since we began the analysis. Don't you think we should talk about it?"

"I'll try. You know how hard it is for me . . . but I promise . . . I'll try."

Chapter Twenty-five

I have the dimmest perception of self, a self with some dignity, some part of me that lies free—free of domestication and socialization, free of family myth and society's role. Perhaps that dim self is my psyche's essential element, the protoplasm with which to rebuild a new me, move beyond Suzy Homemaker, become who I am.

My mother and I live within two shared circles. I coexist with her rise and fall. In relation to me she is constant, but I must always translate double images, synthesize many voices. I must also remember that much of my mother's "circle" exists only for her—and is closed to me.

Before I was born, my mother had her own mother to deal with. What I know about Mummy and Nana is information hard won.

I think back to the time that I was pregnant with Christopher.

At the time, newly married, Mike and I lived with Nana and Frank, who then was sixteen. Throughout the pregnancy, I worked six days each week at the store, an arrangement I liked because my job left me tired and able to sleep, with no leftover energy to turn into anxiety about what was going on in my body.

One Sunday, I dragged myself into the kitchen to make morning coffee.

"You go see mother today," Nana said, handing me a brown paper bag.

"What?" I asked, barely awake.

"You go see mother today," she repeated matter-of-factly.

I stared at my grandmother.

Into my focus came a very strong woman, strong-willed and headstrong. She was then eighty-five, but the curly wisps at her temples were all that was gray of her chestnut-brown hair neatly pulled back in a bun. Her belly was grotesquely distended by the hernia she'd carried for years. Each month at Mass General, they monitored Nana's high blood pressure. From time to time, a new resident would recommend surgery to restore Nana's body to its normal shape. The prospect scared both of us, so first she, and then I, would ask about the strain of surgery on a woman her age weighing close to two hundred pounds. Even the most enthusiastic novice had to admit the odds weren't in her favor. Their prescriptions were always the same: "Here's a diet, low-salt and low-calorie. Come back next month."

As I stared at my grandmother that morning, into my focus came this woman whose strong will dominated my own. "Iron these," she would say on a Saturday, handing me my cousin Joe Junior's shirts. Joe was free to go off with his friends. I was the one who ran the countless errands that kept our household going, but it was Joe and my brother Nana worried about—did they have enough meat? I ate lots of eggs.

As I stared at Nana that morning, I realized that a lifetime of effort had failed to earn me the grace she showered on my brother and cousin. Her favors to them were a birthright. They were born male.

"Nana,"—I chose my words carefully that day—"if you want to bring what's in that bag to your daughter, you can. Mike"—I gestured toward our bedroom—"can drive you to Met State, or you can call a taxi yourself. Keegan Taxi will pick you up, and when they let you off, you can tell them what time to come back for you. The only time you see Mummy is when she comes here to visit. If she can manage by bus, surely you can manage by taxi."

Nana's mouth drooped in its perpetual sulk. She slumped down in a chair, the bag on the table in front of her.

"I'm tired, Nana." My eyes wandered to the drizzle outside the window. "If I felt like going out to the hospital, I'd have gone. If Mummy felt like coming out here, she'd have called." I moved toward the door which led out of the kitchen. I could feel my heart pounding. If I couldn't earn her respect, I'd have to demand it. Nana was living with me, as I'd lived with her when I was a child, but no longer was I the little girl she once ordered around —I was a mother-to-be.

"I need this day to rest up," I continued. "You can either go to the hospital or not go at all. I don't care which . . . but stop telling me what to do!" I went into the bedroom and got under the covers next to the still-asleep Mike.

"I never see daughter like that," Nana had muttered under her breath as I left the kitchen, but later that morning, she called her own taxi and she went out to visit my mother for the whole afternoon—the first such visit I could remember in years.

That day marked a turning point, because after that Nana avoided confrontations with me. When she desperately wanted me to do things her way, she'd make her wishes known to Mike. I found it fascinating that she used him as a go-between. He, of course, always confided in me.

I am meeting my mother in Harvard Square, so I hurry. From the kiosk I can see her waiting under the marquee, but it takes a few minutes for the traffic to clear before I can cross. I arrive out of breath.

"Hello, slut." The venomous tone in her voice stops me in my tracks. She glowers and gives me a menacing once-over.

I bite my tongue lest I say something cruel. "Let's have lunch at Chez Dreyfus."

Uncertainty was a big factor in my decision to meet my mother away from the house; if she was in a bad mood, I didn't want the children around.

As we turn the corner to Church Street, I can feel my mother's bristling hostility.

Drawn velvet drapes shut out the daylight, and the Dreyfus is dimly lit with small lanterns. Booths line the walls. I head for the one farthest back. Please don't make a scene, I silently pray. As we walk past the dozens of diners, I keep my head lowered to avoid making eye contact with any acquaintances.

"Don't we look nice today."

Thank God it's Marie who greets us. She's worked here for years. She's one of the nicest waitresses in all Harvard Square.

"Where did you get such a wonderful hat?" Marie asks my mother.

"It's just a little something I made up myself with a piece of black veil from the five-and-ten." My mother seems to melt with the compliment.

Maybe we'll make it through after all. I glance at the menu. Calves' liver sliced paper-thin served with onions and bacon is the house specialty.

"Would you like a drink before lunch?" Marie asks.

"I never touch the stuff," says my mother, directing a tinge of hostility in Marie's direction. "I'll have coffee."

"Me too." I give Marie my best smile.

In my whole life, I've never seen my mother take a sip or a taste of anything alcoholic, but—from my aunt and my grandmother and my mother herself—I know she was drunk when they locked her up the first time, back in the Twenties. A broken love affair with a reporter led to a binge, and the combined trauma precipitated my mother's first nervous breakdown. Ironic, I think, that, years later, Aunt Tilly could have my mother committed and declared insane, yet when Aunt Tilly died, it wasn't clear whether cancer or cirrhosis dealt the death blow.

My mother eats her lunch heartily while I pick at mine.

"Anything wrong?" asks Marie, clearing the table.

"Not with the food, Marie."

For dessert, my mother orders apple pie à la mode.

"Are you sure?" I ask. "Did you forget they have a pastry tray?"

"The pastry tray." My mother oohs like a child. "I remember the first time I saw one in Schrafft's, I thought it was the most beautiful sight in the world."

She chooses a big, fluffy cream puff.

We're almost through with no scene. I order a pastry myself.

Marie pours us more coffee. When she's around, my mother smiles graciously, but when she leaves, my mother returns to her glowering. "Nana always said you were no good."

"You better stop now," I whisper fiercely under my breath. "You better stop it right now. You *can* control this kind of talk. I know you can. You did it just now when Marie was here."

My mother's lips purse in a mocking smile. Her expression is cold.

"Mummy, I'm telling you now, I won't let you near the children. You won't set one foot in my house until you begin to treat me with respect."

My mother jerks back in the booth. "What are you talking about?"

"You know what I'm talking about. You had your own problems with Nana. Be honest. You fought with her the way you're trying to fight with me now." I search her face for some sign she acknowledges what I've just said, but there is no such sign. I use my trump card. "Nana used to tell me that *you* were no good."

"She *never* said that about me!" My mother raises her hand in a fist. "She never said that about her own daughter."

"If you hit me now," I hiss through clenched teeth, "if you make a scene here"—I gasp for breath—"I'll never again go out in public with you as long as I live."

"What did you say?" She looks hurt. "What did you say to your own mother?"

"You heard what I said. I won't let you see the children. No more swan boats. No circus. No more lunches at Schrafft's. Nothing. I mean it!"

"Little bitch," says my mother.

The hum of diners' voices and the clatter of dishes are sounds I am grateful for, because somehow we've remained inconspicuous. Though I can't make out what she's muttering under her breath, I can see that my mother has dropped her clenched fist.

"Mummy, Nana used us against each other. Behind your back, she told me you were crazy, no good—a spendthrift. Not a good mother. She wanted me to be grateful she took me in—and I was—but I never loved Nana the way I love you." Still in a whisper, I go on, grateful that Marie now leaves us alone. I must remember to leave her a generous tip. "When she was alive, Nana couldn't control Pa or Tilly or her miserable life in America. She didn't mean to, but she had to feel she had control over something. So much of her life was one disappointment after another. She felt that she *had* to try to control you and me. I'm not sure that she knew—after all, she was an immigrant—that she held the power to sign you out of the hospital, and she sure kept me in line right up to the end. She even tried using my own husband against me."

The glistening in my mother's eyes tells me that I've struck a nerve. "Nana has been dead for five years now. Do you really want to pick up where she left off?" I shake my head. "I think you love me. I think you know my own children love you and I love you too. You don't need to bully me. You don't need to imitate Nana." Her head drops toward her chest, so I bend my own to try to catch her eye. When I can't, I dare to reach over and lift up her chin so our eyes can meet. "We were both Nana's victims"—I speak tenderly now—"but she suffered too. She had very few choices, but we *can* choose to treat each other with love and respect. If you treat me fairly, I'll be fair to you."

I can tell by the way she now holds her head high that my mother understands what I've said. She resumes her genteel, lady-like manner, and we drink our coffee in silence.

"What is it?" asks Dr. Mueller from over my shoulder. His voice sounds concerned. "What's the matter today?"

I tell him about the scene with my mother.

"And what do you make of it?" he asks when I finish.

"I won't let anyone bully me anymore. Even my mother, after all that she's gone through. I used to see myself as a victim, not having choices. I saw her that way, too."

"How have you changed?"

"I'm not sure exactly, but as long as I saw my mother and me as two circles, overlapping, our destinies were tied. If she was mad, so was I. It was that simple. Yesterday, I insisted—for the first time in my life—that she had a will of her own. She was in charge—not her voices, not her dead mother, not her dead sister.

She, she alone, was in charge of herself. I don't think I can explain any better than that."

I leave Dr. Mueller's office hiding behind my dark glasses, but I feel a renewed sense of my own possibilities, a new measure of freedom.

My mother and I are linked, we're not bound. Our futures are open, and although parts of my mother are forever destroyed, there's much that remains.

❁

Chapter Twenty-six

❁

The more I think about it, the more I know I need a whole new approach to sex. I must learn to have a lighthearted affair. For a woman to have casual sex is no longer the scandal it once was. I need new experience. There's no doubt in my mind.

Intellectually, I know an affair is the answer if I'm to move on from Mike. Can I do it emotionally?

I'm lonely and desperate. I feel it inside. Sexually, Mike's rejection has left me feeling no longer attractive to men. I've grown comfortable in asexual roles. I can't say I feel trapped, but I suspect that I might be. I repress sexual memories, and I can't seem to masturbate.

With Bob, I'd been honest. I let myself feel some desire. I was willing to bed down with him without even knowing him, but underneath my cavalier attitude, I was scared. Had we begun an affair, perhaps I would have become obsessive. Could he have seen through me? Was he right to decline?

If thoughts about having sex with a man I barely know scare me, something else scares me more—the emptiness I feel with no sex life at all. I feel alone, not just in my bed, but alone in the world. A lifetime of little rejections come back to haunt me. I relive nights of waiting for Daddy. I relive days of missing a mother who was out of my reach. When all that loneliness catches up with me, it's not in the form of lust or desire, but when I was living with Mike, his caresses would make the feelings subside. Sex was a great consolation.

When the children are with me, I'm defined as "the mother," so I come up with unnatural strength to meet all their needs. But on the nights they're with Mike, I can't stay home alone. I have to go out and be with people—even if only at a movie. I need to feel caught up in other lives.

I can't let the children fill the void in my life. To let them give my life its meaning isn't fair. I could smother them. I'm glad they have Mike. He was always a natural nurturer; I had to work at it. When I would cry from exhaustion because the new baby Chris wouldn't sleep, Mike would hold both of us. When Elizabeth came, I grew even more tired, because then there were two. Chris would nap while Lizzie was up, and she seemed to sleep whenever I couldn't. Many a night I nursed her in the rocker, wearily waiting for her to drop off. Mike would appear, take her out of my arms, and send me to bed. In those days, we had so much love for each other. Now he has Jeannie.

When Mike recently asked me if I objected to his bringing them over to Jeannie's, I'd answered, "Not really."

But in my heart I did object.

I felt left out.

I forced myself to remember that, as much as Mike and Jeannie have hurt me, they do love each other. I believe in love as a force that can heal. Jeannie's two children are sweet and adorable. Maybe having each other will help all the kids adjust to this new lifestyle we seem to be set upon.

My needs are separate from the children's and—at this point— from Mike's. When the emptiness comes over me, no man can help me, no stranger, no friend. I've taken to drinking wine on the nights I'm alone. It helps sleep to come.

If sex with a stranger is fraught with all kinds of danger, so is being alone. I'm too injured to love, and too vulnerable to live long without it. If I don't work out some plan to alleviate my frustration, I'm doomed to remain vulnerable to men—all men. The prospect that one might show real affection makes me prey to the ones after sex only. I can't wait for the right man to come along, which means, in my own way, I'm out after sex.

How frightening.

* * *

"The better I get to know him, the more ideal I know he'll be for you, so I'm going to bring him by the store and introduce both of you. He's just too good to pass up," says the relentlessly matchmaking Gloria as she climbs my front stairs on this hot July day. "His name is Yoshi. He's Japanese and an assistant professor of political science at the University of Michigan. And"—she smiles mischievously—"he returns there when summer school ends."

Gloria reads the puzzlement which must be on my face.

"When he goes home, your romance will stay what it is. . . ."

"I don't understand."

She laughs. "A summer romance, silly."

"But what did you tell him?" I'm impatient to know.

We pour iced coffee and move from the kitchen to the back porch. A breeze makes its way through the trees in the vacant lot between the house and the train tracks. Gloria slips off her sandals and slides into an orange canvas folding chair. "Let me tell you about him," she says, putting her feet up on the railing. "He's clearly a flirt, but that's good. You don't want someone who's going to fall head over heels in love with you." She sips her coffee.

I try to grasp the new criteria. Gloria has been divorced a long time, dated dozens of men.

"You do understand?" she asks.

"Sort of."

"There's no 'sort of' about it. If you want a lighthearted affair, you don't begin with someone who's serious, now do you?"

"No."

I do see her point, and I feel my feet getting cold.

According to Gloria, Yoshi is clever, good-looking, and nice. He has savoir faire, and—best of all—a built-in expiration date: the last day of summer school.

It sounds as though Yoshi does fill the bill, but what about me? Can I handle him?

I'd like to experiment with carnal knowledge. I want to stop needing love and romance. I want sex, pure and simple. Is there any such thing?

* * *

As Gloria predicted, the meeting in the store passes unnoticed by anyone. When Yoshi calls me later for a date, I say yes. We meet in the Square.

"Gloria calls you Lou. What kind of name is that?"

"Short for Mary Lou."

"Hmm, neither suits you, I think." He pauses. "May I call you Maria Louisa?"

"That's very close to what my mother calls me. I like it."

"Good," he says, pleased, "Maria Louisa it is."

Yoshi is part Japanese, part Formosan. He grew up speaking both languages, and he learned English in high school. During Chiang Kai-shek's reign of terror, Yoshi witnessed the murders of many young men. He is a revolutionary and belongs to a group who want to see Formosa (Taiwan) free for Formosans. "Just as Americans don't think of themselves as British, most Formosans don't see themselves as Chinese," he explains.

When he speaks of politics, Yoshi sounds idealistic. When he speaks of women, he sounds cocky. Why not? After all, I'm not planning anything serious.

I try saying goodnight to Yoshi at his dorm in Harvard Yard, but he insists on walking me home. On the porch, he looks as though he expects to be asked up. He knows the children aren't there, but I continue to sit on the railing and make no invitation.

"I have work to do," I finally say, getting up to go in.

"How about next Saturday night? Would you like to go to a movie?"

"Yes," I answer, relieved that he makes no move to come toward me.

"In the Square?"

"About eight?"

Yes, Yoshi nods. He bows and turns to go down the stairs. "Goodnight, Maria Louisa."

"See you next week."

From Christopher's window, I watch Yoshi disappear around the corner past the school.

I'm not ready yet, I think to myself.

It's only eleven. I begin cleaning the house. On hands and knees, the way Nana did, I scrub the kitchen linoleum. I dust the oak floors of the bedrooms and living room. I clean kitchen counters and scour the sink. One chore after the other until the house looks all clean.

Sunday-morning sunrise streams in the window as I get into my bed and under clean sheets. My thoughts are of Yoshi as I drift off to sleep.

"Take a bath," I tell Lizzie on Thursday night. "It will cool you off." The evening temperature remains in the nineties.

"I don't want to," she says stubbornly, although I can see that her hair is matted with sweat.

Tomorrow Mike takes them for a week's vacation to Ohio. As much as the children are looking forward to flying, they're cranky as well.

"Why are you mad at us?" asks Christopher.

"Because you fight all the time." I hear the harshness in my voice and see the hurt in his eyes. "Why don't the two of you just play in your room? I'll lie down and read, okay?"

"Okay," he says.

It's not very long before I hear "It's mine." "No, it's mine," Lizzie wails. "It's mine," Chrissie shouts, "and you broke it!"

I leap from the bed. "Goddammit," I shout on the way to their room. "I told you kids not to fight. That does it." I swoop Lizzie into my arms, flinging the broken toy in the air. "You're going right into the bathtub and then straight to bed. As for you, Christopher, you better clean up this room."

I run the tub for Lizzie and slam things around in the kitchen. I lift up a Dorchester pottery mug, my freshman welcome to Radcliffe. I smash it into the wall.

"What was that noise?" Chris runs into the kitchen. Seeing the shards on the floor, he bends down and says, "Oh, Mum, your favorite mug. How did it fall?"

"It didn't."

He looks from me to the broken pieces of pottery. "It didn't?"

"I threw it."

"But why?"

"So I wouldn't hit you." I burst into tears. "Or Elizabeth."

He comes into my arms and strokes my hair. "Oh, Mum, why didn't you tell us you were so depressed? We would have been good."

Would it have been so simple? I marvel at my son's perceptiveness as I sob on his slim shoulder.

"What's going on?" Lizzie shouts from the bathroom. Her water's stopped running.

"Ssh, Lizzie," says Chris, "Mummy's upset. Let's be good."

Chris takes a bath. I take one too. "Can we all go to bed early? You don't have to sleep right away. Just be quiet."

As I lie in my bed, the only sounds are outside—kids next door in the schoolyard, traffic on Walden Street, and an occasional train in the back. I doze off a few times before going to check on the children.

Lizzie is asleep in one of her favorite positions, bottom up in the air. I smile and kiss her small face. I turn out the light.

Chris, on his stomach, lies on the lower bunk of the bed Mike built for him. I switch off his light before going over to kiss him.

"Everything will be all right," he whispers.

"I know." I hug him. "You have pleasant dreams. Tomorrow you'll be in Ohio."

Separations bring out the worst in me.

I want the children to go. I want time for myself, but I'm not sure I can cope. Being "mother" at least gives me an identity, and the demands cut down on the time left over in which to worry.

Friday night, I arrive home in time for the phone call that says they've safely arrived. I lie down on my bed to find a note on my pillow.

A torn sheet of lined notebook paper has Christopher's scrawl on it:

Mary Lou is the nicest mother and persen. I love her more than anything but my father is very nice too and I shall help both of them.

Being a mother is hard, but Christopher's pledge reminds me of how painful it is to be a child. Adult behavior confuses. Why can't I be more understanding?

"When you come home, I'll try harder," I promise my far-away children before I fall asleep.

The store fills with browsers.

Because Mike is away, I'm taking his place on the Saturday sales floor. I'd forgotten how nerve-wracking the family shoppers can be. "Don't touch that, Laurie." A harried mother with a baby in her arms issues an order to her toddler, who's danger-ously close to the marble slabs.

Through the store's plate glass window. I see Jeannie across the street. She stands waiting for the light to change. Even from here, she cuts a fine figure. Her blond hair is pulled back in a twist, and she wears a short A-line dress. The abstract print flat-ters her tan arms and legs. Why does she have to be so very pretty?

Run to the basement. That's my first impulse. No, that won't do. It would embarrass the others. I'm lucky to be waiting on a husband and wife who are taking forever to map out a shelf system.

When Jeannie walks through the door, I nod hello. She does the same.

My customers need to see a shelf not on the floor, so I en-courage them to come down to the basement with me.

Somehow I get through the day by making lots of sales in the basement.

"Good evening, Maria Louisa."

I look up from the magazine I'm reading at the kiosk to see Yoshi standing there with a warm smile.

He wears a khaki safari jacket over a white shirt. His black hair is shiny. He looks very cool.

How will we ever get from here into bed?

"How about tea?" Yoshi asks after the movie.

"My place?"

"I'd like that." He looks surprised.

Good, I think, *that's* out of the way.

When he follows me up my front stairs, we haven't yet touched—even hands.

"Yoshi, we both know we're going to bed, but I'd like to talk about it."

"I've never known a woman who wants to talk before making love." Yoshi laughs.

"But you do sleep around?"

"Certainly."

"What do women do? Fall into your arms?"

"If you give me a chance, you might do that too."

"I'm serious, Yoshi. Please don't make fun of me. How do you do it?"

He shrugs his shoulders and gestures off toward the bedroom.

"I didn't ask *where*, I asked how. Don't you arrive at some understanding?"

"I never have. . . ."

"But what if a girl thinks you're in love with her? Doesn't know it's just sexual? Wouldn't you want her to know?"

"Maria Louisa." He touches my bare shoulder, the sensation a shock. "You are too formal. Words kill the spirit."

"Words free the spirit." I speak with a confidence which belies my self-doubt. "We're ruled by our minds. Without words, there can be no sexual freedom. I want to know what to expect."

He has no answer.

"And if you've had so many lovers, why do words make *you* feel so uncomfortable?"

I put on the water for tea and take some cups from the pantry.

"I can't do without words, Yoshi. I'm sorry."

"But why?"

"By relying on love in my marriage, I got myself hurt. Now . . . with just sex . . . I don't want to find myself hurt in some new

way I don't understand. I think rules—understanding the game—
make things awkward at first. . . ."

He seems concerned and confused.

He's twenty-seven. I'm thirty-three. I feel like the novice.

"Yoshi, have you ever been in love?"

"Only once."

"Who was she?"

"An American girl. Last summer in Michigan," he says, "and
I'd rather not talk about it." Yoshi shows his first sign of nervous-
ness.

"I know about sex where there's love, but you and I don't want
to get emotionally involved. With a few rules," I tell him, "we'd
both be protected. We could make limitations."

Give it up, I think. The more you say, the dumber you sound.

Don't give it up, says another part of myself. If you're going to
survive, you've got to have rules.

"Is it really so strange to talk first?" I ask Yoshi.

"Sitting out here when we could be in there." He gestures
again to the bedroom.

"You know my children are away. If you and I get along, I'll
have time for a fling. Do you know the word 'fling'?"

He looks as though he feels patronized. "Yes," he answers, "I
do."

"That's what I want. No commitment beyond that."

"Then we are agreed?" He brightens up.

"Not quite. If we get along and want to see each other, fine.
But if either of us doesn't want to get together, he or she should
be able to decline and not have the other ask questions."

He nods in eager agreement.

"When my children return, my time won't be my own."

"Of course."

"You must put no pressure on me."

"These are your rules then?"

"All I can think of right now."

He rises. "Shall we go into your bedroom?"

I hesitate. "Yes. Now we can go."

I turn off the tea water and accept the hand that he offers.

In the warm dark of my bedroom, a shiver runs through me. I

did not allow my body to feel any desire when we were in the kitchen. I trust it will come to me.

I turn my back, remove all my clothes, and get under the covers, kicking the quilt to the floor to avoid standing up and exposing my nudity to the lights from the street.

Before he joins me in bed, I catch a long glimpse of Yoshi's lean, hairless torso.

His body feels silkily smooth.

He reaches for me. I assume the position I used to for Mike.

Yoshi takes me by surprise.

My body responds, but my circuits feel jammed. Yoshi, patiently, skillfully, brings me to climax. Still unaccustomed to this new intimacy, I fall asleep—not in his arms, but on my own side of the bed.

I wake up to the sound of footsteps. Yoshi tiptoes to the bed with a tray. A pot of tea and two mugs. The cups he has chosen were brought by Abby to me from Kentucky. The black glaze of the finely spun clay is as luminous as Yoshi's straight hair.

He sits next to me, naked.

I wrap myself in the sheet.

The hot tea is smoky.

When the last of the tea is drained, Yoshi reaches for me.

I go to him easily, let him unwrap the sheet. I want more of last night.

Will I really be able to give up this mesmerizing sex when the time comes?

Chapter Twenty-seven

Fantastic sex with Yoshi has stirred up old memories, there's no doubt in my mind. Two vivid scenes from the past, both involving my father, come to mind now.

"Who is this 'other man'?" my father complained one night during my sophomore year at Radcliffe. It hadn't been that long since I'd broken up with my first boyfriend, Wally.

"You don't mean Benson, do you?" I'd asked my father. "He's no 'other man,' he's my new boyfriend."

"So," my father had sneered, "my little girl's got hot pants. She sleeps around like a tramp."

I went red with embarrassment.

But wait—where had I first heard those terrible words?

I was a child, tucked into my bed in Atwood Square. Someone slid into bed next to me while I was asleep. I smelled tobacco and whiskey and felt someone rubbing my back. I moved to turn, but his strong hand restrained me. "So," said my daddy, reaching down into my pajama bottoms, "my little girl has hot pants."

* * *

"Why so oblique?" asks Dr. Mueller, when I try to explain what's going on with Yoshi toward the end of the children's vacation.

"You've got to help me. Obliqueness makes a place where an idea need not be spelled out. I can say it before it gets fixed."

"You once told me," he says, "that if you can't say it to me, you sometimes can't say it to yourself."

"I need to get close to an idea before I can say it right out."

"Sex with Wally and Benson caught your father's attention."

"Yes." I try to recall. "When he knew I had a boyfriend, he brought me to meet his mistress. Del was her name. She told me what my father was like—in bed and out. We drank muscatel. She told me my father told her that I had hot pants. I got drunk, then I walked down the hill to the subway. I never saw her again."

"Do you think it's a coincidence that you've begun your affair with Yoshi just before I go on my vacation?"

"Does everything I do have to revolve around you?"

"We must consider the meaning of everything." He takes my cue and pushes my own idea into clearer focus. "Is your affair with Yoshi an attempt to get a reaction from me?"

My throat tightens up. I go dry in the mouth. Images. Flashes. I can't bear to speak.

Daddy. A ladies' man. Yoshi. A ladies' man too. A sexual acrobat. When Del tried to tell me about Daddy and sex, I got drunk. I didn't want to hear what she had to say.

As a kid, I fought Daddy off. What he wanted from me—I knew it was "dirty."

"Strange what I'm thinking." I finally can speak to Dr. Mueller. I rub my chest as if to slow down my heartbeat. "No. Too much to say."

"We must try to speak the unspeakable."

"I feel guilty," I murmur.

"What for?"

"I'm not sure. Even in college, I wanted my father back. No matter how much trouble he'd been the last time, each new time I believed he'd stop drinking. Take care of Sonny and me." I press my hands to my forehead. "But why is all this coming up now?"

"Perhaps," he says gently, "because I am going away."

I sigh. "I think I feel guilty about *not* having had sex with my father when I was a child. As though my refusal drove him away from our family. And . . ." I hesitate. "This new sexiness I feel with Yoshi . . ."

"Yes?"

"I think . . ." I can feel myself turning red. "It will attract you . . . to me."

"That's what it does sound like," he says very gently.

"Which doesn't make sense. You've never made an untoward move. I'd die if you did. To this day, I hate my father for that."

And I thought I was so smart.

New sex. Without permanence. No emotional ties.

But what if Yoshi is a stand-in for Daddy, a way to allow me to "sleep" with my father?

If that's so, then sex as a means to love has merely assumed a new form.

The good Dr. Mueller. Straightforward. Reliable. Not at all like my father.

And what's my response?

Play the vamp.

Little Miss Hot Pants.

As though that's what Dr. Mueller wants.

Not Dr. Mueller . . .

Chapter Twenty-eight

In the summer of 1955, between my sophomore and junior year, I discovered that Nana and Sonny were eligible for Child Welfare and Old Age Assistance not just in Sharon, where they were living with friends, but anywhere in the Commonwealth of Massachusetts—so I found us an apartment on Cambridge Street only a few blocks from Harvard Yard, where I had most of my classes.

We were the second-floor apartment in a three-story duplex. The five other groups of renters were all extraordinary. We became an extended family of sorts.

On one side lived the Gordons, John and Madge. John was at Harvard Medical School, and Madge, his southern wife, stayed home with their babies. Since the house was always teeming with people, eleven-year-old Sonny was permitted to baby-sit. He liked the money and the feeling of being needed.

On our side, downstairs, lived Jeffrey and George. They were both at Harvard Law School. They taught my brother how to play chess.

Upstairs lived Annie and Gwen. Gwen was a potter and poet. Annie taught the piano and was home most of the time. Except when her students were there, she always made Sonny welcome.

I relied on them all.

Our second-floor apartment opened into the living room. I slept there on the couch.

To the left of the living room, toward the front of the house, was Nana's room, the biggest one in the flat. Off hers was the smallest. It had just enough space for a four-poster bed and the small table on which Sonny built his model airplanes.

To the right of the living room, a step led down to the kitchen, off of which was a little hall to the bathroom.

Our scant furnishings were those taken from my aunt's house for Nana and Sonny when they moved out to Sharon. When the bank foreclosed, everything else was put into storage and eventually lost. The company refused to release any part unless the whole bill was paid. Gone are most of the family pictures that were in Tilly's desk. Gone is my mother's trunk which had been stored in the basement.

That first summer on Cambridge Street, I worked in a Boston department store. Thanks to Nana's good sense about money, we were able to manage.

Thanks to my sponsor, I had no financial problem with school. When my scholarship expired my freshman year, Miss Hargreve agreed to pay my tuition and books until I graduated. She bought me some wonderful clothes. Had I wanted to, she would have paid for the dorm, but I preferred living back with Nana and Sonny. In short, Miss Hargreve was my fairy godmother.

By September, we were all settled in. My shy little brother went off to the Longfellow School, and I began junior year.

It was Nana for whom the move to Cambridge proved difficult. Although she'd complained she was isolated in Sharon, she refused to learn how to use the bus into Harvard Square even though the stop was two doors from the house. She had no inspiration to garden. The yard was down a flight of rickety stairs off our back porch, and we had to use the kitchen window to get in and get out. It was too much for her seventy-eight-year-old arthritic joints. Nana talked to her friends on the telephone, and she took to crocheting in front of the television set. She'd either watch soaps or look out her front window, where we'd set up her sewing machine. The high school was down the street and Holy Ghost Hospital was just across from us, so there was always lots of activity.

That summer I broke up with Wally, and in the fall I began seeing Benson. Nights I waitressed at the Capriccio, and days I had to work hard to get passing grades.

One night in November, the bell rang in our apartment and I went down to answer the front door.

"Can I come up?"

There he was. Badly dressed for the weather in a gabardine coat with no hat or scarf, Daddy stood shifting from one foot to the other. "Well, can I?"

He looked thin. The coat hung on his five-foot-nine frame. Somehow he always looked better in work clothes, overalls, jackets. When he smiled, he was careful not to expose his rotted-out teeth.

It wasn't in me to turn my father away.

Upstairs, he explained to the three of us that he'd been out of jail for a week. He was looking for work. His friends were no good. They were a bad influence. He wanted to give Sonny a father, make a home for us, perhaps get my mother out soon.

What was odd was that Nana herself didn't protest.

Like me, she seemed caught up in his vow to reform.

No more drinking, no more hanging out with cheap crooks—Daddy was going straight. He just needed a chance.

I forgot all the unfilled promises, all the last chances—all the things I should have remembered.

I gave up the living-room couch and moved in with Nana.

When each job fell through, we were sympathetic—ex-cons have a hard time finding work, we knew that.

My father spent a lot of time in the house, and he could, on occasion, be good for a laugh. One day when the heat went off and the apartment was freezing, I came home to find him at the kitchen table with Nana. "Join us in the solarium," Daddy said, pulling my chair into the sunlight.

Nana, in those days, spent hours with my father. They watched television, played cards, and gossiped. Our women neighbors had tried befriending Nana, but she had been standoffish, critical, cold and rejecting. She still preferred a man's company to that of a woman—but my *father?*

＊　＊　＊

I think back to my high-school years. At that time, Nana loathed my father. Whenever he'd stop by to take me out for pizza, we'd say goodnight downstairs at Aunt Tilly's house. "I don't want to be raked over the coals," Daddy would say, and since I heard what Tilly and Nana said about him behind his back, I never questioned him.

When I'd get upstairs, Nana would say, "I know what you do, little tramp, with your father downstairs in hall."

Since I'd repressed childhood memories, I really could not understand what she was talking about.

Another time, when I was still in high school, I had to take a day off and go to the big courthouse in Boston. Two men brought Daddy into the courtroom. He wore a black turtleneck and black work pants. He was in handcuffs.

I sat a few rows back. From where I sat, I could see his bald pate.

When the judge sentenced Daddy to three years in Norfolk for petty larceny, I had to go to the ladies' room, where I leaned my head up against the cold marble wall of the cubicle until I was able to vomit.

Only days before that Boston courtroom scene, I'd been out to Boston State Hospital to visit my mother.

"Daddy's joined the Alcoholics Anonymous club," Mummy had told me happily, "and that's good. If they can help him, we'll have our own home and a happy life together. It's time that we did. I hope I can work again when we have our own house. Oh, Mary Louise, we'll have such a *nice* place—better than we ever had. I'm hoping. I'm wishing . . ."

I think I was sixteen at the time. Anyway, I was old enough to know better. Who said dreams die hard?

In a way, I was relieved to have Daddy sent off to jail. At least I'd know where he was.

That day in Boston was the second time he'd been sent up; I think I was twelve when he first got sent away to Deer Island for nonsupport, and that same year Mummy went back to the hospital. With both Mummy and Daddy certified wards of the state, Aunt Tilly could collect welfare for Sonny and me.

Daddy's last trips to jail were done on his own. He'd become a hustler and con man. He was sent up for forging, passing, and uttering—petty-larceny crimes.

Daddy had written from prison:

> I have so many things to ask you and yet when I start to write, I'll be darned if I can remember what they were.
>
> I'm writing to mother tonite and hope she will be able to come home this weekend.
>
> Try not to aggravate her and keep her off Aunt Tilly's ear.
>
> It will not be much longer before I am out and I'm sure of going to work right away, if things go right and I'm sure that they will. It will only take a month or so for us to find someplace and perhaps things will go smoother and happier for us. Let's hope so. . . .

I answered his letter, but I was afraid to go see him. Cousin Jane persuaded me to go with her. Daddy had asked her to ask me. It was Jane who went regularly to visit him with candy and cigarettes from my father's sister, my aunt Ruth.

Along with the grown-ups, we were searched. We were let in by a steel door, to face another door in a space like a corridor. Boxed in glass, up above, stood a policeman with a gun—a rifle, I think. What if they shot us by accident?

I never went back.

My dream of graduating from Radcliffe wasn't so much to find a career or a job: I was looking for answers to my family riddle, and some force within me had determined that all that had happened to my mother, my father, my brother, and me was comprehensible. Once I understood everything, I could solve all our problems.

I imagined owning a big house, one with Greek columns like the ones down by the Arborway. There would be rooms for everyone, and I'd take care of us all because people would pay lots of money for my stories. In my fantasy, I didn't see myself out on a job but at home, writing books, the way Louisa May Alcott supported her family when she was my age. And my mother would have her own studio.

Radcliffe was the key to it all.

I would learn about paranoid schizophrenia, dementia praecox, and delirium tremens. Armed with knowledge, I would turn the family's fortunes around.

Meanwhile, back in 1955—in that real world of my junior year at Radcliffe—no jobs materialized for my father. He was drinking, and I couldn't figure out where he was getting the money for booze.

My brother stayed away from my father. When I asked why, Sonny said, "He's a stranger. Besides, I don't like him."

Sonny was about three when my father deserted us, so my young brother was unaffected by any nostalgia.

It was less than a month before I regretted having opened the door.

The first warning sign was the rosy glow. As a teenager, I'd seen that stage in Tilly. After the glow came the outright hostility.

"What's this I hear about you running around with boys?" he asked me after dinner one night.

Not long after that, I woke up from a nap in my brother's bed to feel my father's hand on my breast. I knew I had to get him out of the house—but how?

The next day, a Friday, I had a long day of classes. A friend from the Capriccio drove me home so I could change clothes for my long night of work at the coffeehouse. I had him wait downstairs in his car.

The apartment was empty. Nana, as planned, was with her friends in Sharon. They'd drive her home on Sunday. Sonny was babysitting. My father was out. I put on a black sweater and skirt that Miss Hargreve had given me. In front of Nana's big mirror, I ran a comb through my short hair. I added a long string of fake pearls.

I heard footsteps.

The door to the living room opened, and there in the doorway stood my father—dead drunk.

"Who's that outside?" he slurred. "A new boyfriend?"

"None of your business." I picked up my coat.

"No you don't," said my father, blocking the door. "You're not going anywhere."

"That's what you think." I faced him defiantly. "Are you going to get out of my way, or am I going to call the police?"

He lunged and wrestled me to the couch. His hands pulled on my breasts. I wriggled loose, but he grabbed at my pearls. With a deft motion, he knotted them at my neck. The string snapped. I ran for the door. I pushed him aside and into a chair. They both fell over. Down the stairs I ran, as fast as I could—down the stairs in a shower of pearls.

"What's the matter?" asked my friend as I flung myself into his car.

"Just get me out of here."

From work, I called Sonny. Told him Daddy was drunk. "Don't go home. Stay the night with Madge and John. I'll go to DeeDee's."

Later, when I asked Sonny how he'd feel if I kicked Daddy out, he said that he wouldn't mind. "He hit me once. I never told you."

"What did you do?" I asked.

"Told him I'd kill him if he ever touched me again."

"Oh, Sonny, I'm sorry. Having Daddy back with us hasn't worked out the way I thought it would."

DeeDee agreed my father had to go.

"You were crazy to let him back in the first place."

When I got home on Saturday, my father was docile. His mood made my job easier. I put his belongings in grocery bags. "Give me the keys," I ordered. "Now go."

Downstairs at the door, I told him how much Sonny and I liked this house. "We're fond of the neighbors. They don't know you're a drunk. They don't know you set fires in couches with cigarettes, and if you ever come back I'll tell them everything and we'll all call the police."

Hanging his head, he walked to the stop, and I watched until the bus came by and took him away.

The next few weeks were nerve-wracking.

What with Christmas coming, I was sure he'd show up again,

full of self-pity. One cold night in mid-December, when the doorbell rang, I was sure it was Daddy.

"I'll go," said my brother.

"Can you send him away?"

Sonny nodded and went downstairs to the door.

"It was Daddy," he told Nana and me when he came back upstairs.

"What did you tell him?"

"We don't know him here."

What word I ever had from my father after that incident came indirectly—through Jane. The message I always gave her to relay to him was the same: "Stay away, or I'll do what I can to destroy you."

"There's been a bad fire," Jane said over the phone one night in 1967. "Uncle Ralph is at Boston City. He asked me to call you."

"Poor Jane," I sighed, "all these years and you're still making visits. I know you think I'm a monster, but I still can't cope with my father."

Jane didn't answer, nor did she preach.

"How bad was the fire?" I asked. "Where was it?"

"My sister's." Jane's voice cracked. "I couldn't take him in here what with four kids of my own." Her tone was defensive.

"Oh, Jane. Do you think I would ever criticize *you?*"

"Dolly was letting him sleep on her couch. He was trying to find a place of his own."

Oh Lord, the place he's been looking for since Atwood Square. Twenty years now.

"Dolly went to bed. Uncle Ralph was already asleep on the couch. The next thing she knows, she's trying to get out through the smoke. She can't reach the baby." Jane began crying. "Her baby died in the fire. My father says if Uncle Ralph doesn't die in the hospital, he'll kill him himself."

"Then they know how it started?" I hold my breath and wait for the answer I already know.

"The couch. It started in the couch. Uncle Ralph must have got up for a cigarette."

The hairs on my arms and my neck prickle my sleeves and my collar. How often, as a child, had I dreamed of a fire only to wake up and find I wasn't dreaming?

Smoldering fires in Daddy's bed were something I'd grown accustomed to. More than once, I outwaited him, and when he'd fallen asleep, I took a burning cigarette out of his hand.

"Oh, Jane, how awful for Dolly. How is she?"

"Crazy with grief." Jane sighed. "The doctors say she'll be all right after a while. It takes time . . . I haven't told you the rest."

"The rest?"

"They had to amputate Uncle Ralph's right arm. They say he'll never work again."

A little close to hysteria myself, I felt like laughing. "What's new about his not working?"—but I said nothing so flip to my cousin.

Then I felt faint, and was *sure* I could smell burning flesh.

"He wants to see you."

"I can't."

"What should I say?"

"That I'll *never* forgive him. For what he did to my mother and to Sonny and me—and now to Dolly."

Jane didn't call back.

Chapter Twenty-nine

The affair with Yoshi produces rarefied sex—and a new set of anxieties. My expedition into "casual sex" has unearthed appetites in me I hadn't known existed.

Yoshi's skills are almost professional, so detached are they from any emotion. The thrill for him is to push me past my own thresholds. For me, the experiment is very illuminating.

I let myself be pushed when it comes to the sex. It's what I signed up for.

"You always keep something back," he says to me one night, in a petulant mood. "There's always some part of you that you keep back from me."

"You know my appetites, Yoshi," I angrily answer. "You do not know me."

For all his claims that he's the one who's sexually free, I can tell that Yoshi is unhappy that I'm not falling in love with him.

Is it, I wonder, because he's a man and he can't take me, a woman, at her word? We hammered out an agreement. I know I'm within it, but Yoshi seems to want it both ways—he wants me under his spell and he wants to be free to go.

When he speaks of Formosa, Yoshi sees politics clearly, so I ask him, "Why don't you carry your liberal politics over to women?"

"Sex and politics are unrelated, and," he chides, "please remember that I, and not you, hold the Ph.D. in political science."

"But, Yoshi, if a Don Juan like yourself wants every woman he sleeps with to fall under his sexual spell, can't you be called a colonizer of sorts? A sexual imperialist?"

"What a ridiculous notion."

I sense that I'm in a political struggle I don't understand. By sleeping with Yoshi, I'm confronting my fears, facing my lust, but somewhere in it all, my father haunts me.

Yoshi speaks candidly with me. Most of the many women he's slept with are younger than thirty. That information leads me to suspect that I may be the one in a better position to make some comparisons. My affairs have been ones of the heart. Might I know something he doesn't?

Yoshi reminds me of a famous actor I heard on a talk show. When he was a young virgin on vacation in France, an older woman took him to bed. When the sex proved fantastic, the young actor assumed all was as it should be. When his vacation was over, he bade the woman adieu. "I've never had sex like that again in my life," said the actor, a man in his sixties. "Some people are sexually talented. Had I known then what I now know about sex, I don't think I'd have ever been able to give her up. My whole life would have been different."

Unlike the actor and Yoshi and perhaps even the girls Yoshi has slept with, I view high-powered sex with a questioning eye. From my own experience, I know that when deep emotion fuels sex, the physical act goes beyond mere calisthenics and lends sex a dimension it doesn't otherwise have, a dimension which cannot be measured. Since I have no emotion to give to a man at this point in my life, counting orgasms seems harmless, and "calisthenics" feel good.

But what if sex is like heroin?

I confide these fears to DeeDee. "You better go carefully," she warns.

The early-August return of the children restores my life to its normalcy. Once again mother-defined, I relax about Yoshi. I assume he'll be off running around, but he surprises me. He asks if he can have a few of his activist friends over to dinner. He'll do the cooking.

I go shopping with Yoshi down in Chinatown. We buy smoked duck, wood ear, and a gallon of soy sauce. In another store, he chooses large dried mushrooms, finely spun bean thread, and sea-weed from Japan. He invites his friends, and I invite Ramona, Abby, and Ben. The talk is of politics, the cuisine a mix of three cultures. The children are there, so I don't let Yoshi stay over, and we begin the wind-down of our passionate sex.

Only one more weekend remains. I let him sleep over. I feel subdued, and I'm grateful. It will make parting easier. I cancel Monday's appointment with Dr. Mueller and spend the whole day with Yoshi.

"You mean you won't miss me?" asks Yoshi. "Not at all?"

"I'll miss you, but not in the ways that you think."

He looks disappointed.

I'm lying, of course. I shall miss him precisely that way.

"Why won't you come to the airport with me?"

"Because I want to say good-bye here." I stand at my front door. "I must pick Lizzie up soon."

He leans toward me seductively.

"No, Yoshi, please." *Let it stay what it is*, I can hear Gloria saying, *a summer romance*. "It's better this way."

With a bow and a flourish, Yoshi runs down to the cab.

In bed, later that evening, I let the realization come—I have one more farewell. Dr. Mueller will be gone for almost five weeks, until September 23. He leaves in the morning.

I can't fall asleep.

Yoshi is back in Michigan already. He's gone. Mike got me through some bad years and gave me some good ones, but now he has Jeannie.

My father, in fantasy, gave me someone to cling to. My brother, nine years my junior, stands by me now.

I'm so dependent on men.

Tomorrow—the clock says 4:00 A.M.—no, today—Dr. Mueller goes, too.

"It's your *job*," I tell him in the morning, "it's what you do for a living."

Outside his office are none of the usual sounds—the footsteps, the voices, the traffic in the hall. Most of the other doctors are already gone.

Do I really exist?

"This intimacy is not what it appears," I continue. "You are free to go. Last summer I didn't have to face such a long time without you. I liked that much better."

"It sounds as though you think I plan my vacations around you and how you feel."

"That's not it." My words are faltering. "Last year I felt that I had a place in your life. I want that feeling back."

"What feeling?"

"The fantasy. I want to believe that you have no life of your own. No wife and no family. I want to feel I'm the important one. This departure feels brutal."

"Well." I hear him take a deep breath. "You better get used to my comings and goings, because I *will* leave again."

Can psychoanalysis be worth all this pain and embarrassment?

"What about Yoshi?" he asks.

"He's gone," I answer.

"And what were your feelings about that?"

"I was prepared. I spent lots of time thinking about how I would manage . . ."

"Without him?"

"Yes. Without Yoshi."

"Instead of thinking about how you'd manage without me?"

"Why are you being so pushy?" I ask him peevishly.

"You speak only of Yoshi. You were late twice this week. You canceled Monday's appointment."

"I called."

"But you didn't show up."

"Frankly, Dr. Mueller, I figured that my last day of sex with Yoshi would be more memorable than anything you and I could conceivably discuss. We have lots of time. You always say so yourself. I decided not to get out of bed—and isn't one of the goals of analysis to help people learn to make their own decisions?" My tone is decidedly flip.

"It is," he replies solemnly, "and, as you just said, *you* made the decision, so we have no time left to discuss what it means for you to have me go away."

When I wake up the next morning, I can't remember my dreams, but my knuckles are white from clenching my fists.

Chapter Thirty

"Mary Lou Shields?"

"Yes."

Who can be calling at this hour of night?

"This is Dr. Larkin."

"Dr. Larkin?"

"From the Long Island Hospital."

"Oh. Dr. Larkin. What's the matter?"

"Your father is dead. . . . Mrs. Shields? Are you there?"

"Yes, Dr. Larkin, I'm here."

"I need to know the arrangements."

"Arrangements?"

"Your plans for a funeral."

"I have none."

"Arrangements *must* be made."

"His sister can make them."

"Mrs. Reynaud?"

"Yes. Ruth Reynaud."

"There's a problem with that."

"What is it?"

"Your father named you as his next of kin."

"I see." I reach for a chair and a cigarette. "Does that mean the law requires me to make the arrangements?"

"Not if you don't want to." His tone sounds icy.

How can I explain how I feel to a stranger?

"I don't want to." That's all that I can think of to say.

"Who would then?"

"His sister. I told you. She really *is* his next of kin."

"Mrs. Reynaud visits regularly with her daughter, Jane."

"My father was Mrs. Reynaud's only sibling."

"There's still a problem with that."

"Why?"

"You'll have to assign your father's body to his sister."

"Assign his body?"

I don't want anything to do with my father's body. I never have.

"How do I do that?" I ask.

"By telegram."

"Assign a body by telegram? Forgive me, Dr. Larkin, but this all sounds ghoulish."

"It's standard procedure."

"Where does it go?"

"The telegram?"

"Yes."

"To the Medical Examiner for the Commonwealth."

"How do I word it?"

" 'I release the body of my father to his sister, Ruth Reynaud.' "

"What's the Examiner's name?"

"Michael Luongo."

I don't want to hang up, but what more is there to say? When Dr. Larkin last called, he told me my father "doesn't have long." I told him to let me know when he died.

"Dr. Larkin?"

"Yes."

"How was it for him at the end?"

"He lost consciousness for a few days. He never woke up."
Sleep. Coma. Unconscious death.

"I just wanted to know. I guess that's all then. Thank you for taking care of him. He needed somebody."

"Should I discuss the arrangements with Mrs. Reynaud?"

"Does she know yet?"

"She won't be surprised. She was here the day before yesterday with her daughter, Jane."

"Please tell her I'll call."

"Goodnight, Mrs. Shields."

"Goodnight, Dr. Larkin."

I'd rehearsed for this call. Told myself hundreds of times that Daddy "died" long ago. Real death is irrelevant.

Then why can't I move?

Thank God Dr. Mueller is back.

I saw him for the first time today, and I can see him tomorrow.

"Hello." Frank answers after only three rings.

"I'm so glad you're home."

"What's wrong, Lou? It's late. What's the matter?"

"It's Daddy. They called from the hospital. He died in his sleep tonight."

"Well," Frank says after a while, "we can't say we're surprised."

"No, we can't."

"We knew this moment would come when we refused to go out to see him."

"Yes, we did."

I imagine my brother's face. I know his expressions almost as well as my own.

"We're not changing our minds?" I put the question to my brother.

"About having anything to do with the funeral?"

"That's what I mean." My tone of voice leaves Frank an opening to say yes or no.

"We've come this far." His tone was resolute. "I think we should go all the way."

"I just wasn't sure . . ."

"Why don't I come over."

"Please, Frank, please do."

The next day, Dr. Mueller's second day back, I arrive a half hour early.

"What would I have done if you hadn't come back from your vacation yesterday?" I am more than relieved to be back on the couch in his office.

"What will you do about your father's funeral?" asks Dr. Mueller.

"Not go." I shudder involuntarily. "Do you think I sound awful?"

"How do you think you sound?"

"Like a daughter whose father died a long time ago."

"There's one thing you've left out of all that you've told me."

"What's that?"

"You haven't yet told me how you feel."

"Feel?" I touch my hand to my shoulders. "I feel . . . nothing."

"You know, Mary Lou, you and I were never that close. You were always closer to Jane. Please don't take me wrong, but I don't think you know what you're doing."

Ruth wants to arrange the wake for tonight and the funeral for tomorrow.

A sweet Catholic woman, Ruth believes in forgiveness.

"It doesn't seem right, you and Sonny not going to your own father's funeral. And"—she pauses—"what about Mary?"

My mother! I forgot about her. Frank and I never discussed it. Whether or not *she* should go to the funeral.

My mind clicks along like a train on a track. "We're not telling her, Ruth." I think it out as I speak. "She doesn't need to go to his funeral. My God, she hasn't seen him for almost twenty years. Ralph wasn't *always* in jail. He knew where she was. He could have come out to see her."

"Poor woman, your mother, I always wished Ralph had treated her better."

"Me too, Ruth. Me too."

"Well, dear, if your mind is made up . . ."

"My mind is made up. So is Frank's."

"It will seem strange not to have his own children. And I guess this is good-bye."

My father's death does sever this family tie.

"Good-bye, Ruth, and please tell Jane I'm sorry—for her sake."

One more call to make. Western Union.

"Release the body of my father . . ."

"I beg your pardon?"

I explain the situation to the operator and begin my message again.

Mike takes the children. I'll think about what I tell them tomorrow. It's my mother I'm worried about.

I'll take the decision out of her hands and tell her the day after tomorrow—when the funeral is over.

She chose not to go to Nana's funeral. Maybe Daddy's death will be as unreal. It's been so many years since she's even laid eyes on him. She hardly mentions him anymore.

That's the right thing to do. Take the decision out of her hands, then she won't have to agonize over what she should do. What if his death throws her over the edge?

I don't know about Mummy, but I know *I* can't deal with that.

I do things in a trance.

Frank has class tonight, and together we decided to go about living. Do things we were supposed to. My brother is very smart, but schoolwork comes hard for him. Better for him not to miss his class.

Maybe I should go out? Where? Not a movie. *That* would be obscene. Go to a movie when my father's being waked? No, can't do that.

I pace around the house in an acute state of restlessness.

The phone rings.

There's no one I want to talk to. But what if it's Frank?

"Okay, I'm coming." I reach for the phone.

"Lou Shields?" says the male voice.

"Yes?"

"Hi. I'm Lon Williams, a friend of Marge's from New York. Did she tell you about me?"

"Yes, she did." Is that my voice? Sounds so bouncy. "What can I do for you?"

"I'm here in Boston. At the Parker House. I wonder if I can take you to dinner."

"Not tonight, Lon."

"Aw, come on."

"I can't. You don't understand."

"Try me."

"You wouldn't believe it. Maybe some other time. Call me again, will you?"

I hang up the phone.

Marge did tell me about Lon. He's in television. Too bad, I think to myself. He's probably interesting.

The phone rings again.

Maybe *this* is my brother.

"Hello."

"Hi."

"Not *you* again."

"You told me to call."

I laugh in spite of myself. Some men don't take no for an answer. "Look, Lon, I'm not trying to give you a hard time, but I have a real problem. What if I told you my father died yesterday?"

"I'd say I was sorry."

I explain the whole situation.

"I'm not coming on," he says, "but this sounds like no time for you to be all alone. Why don't you come over here? I'll take you to dinner."

"I . . ."

"You'll have someone to talk to," he coaxes.

Is it sex that he's after or is he just lonely? I wonder under the shower. Doesn't matter. I want to get out of the house.

The Parker House, just up from Park Street. It's one of my favorite hotels. Memories of finer days linger in threadbare old carpets. I go through the revolving doors and ring up to Lon's room.

"Come on up," he says cheerfully.

It's hard to bury the dead without ceremony. Somewhere in Boston, I don't even know where, my father is being waked in some funeral home. And I'm in an elevator on my way to meet a strange man. Hot pants? Oh, what the hell. My father's dead now. I don't have to worry.

The door opens. In front of me stands a black man with a

muscular build and a radiant smile. The smile is literally dazzling. Must be caps—or all those years on the tube. His white shirt is unbuttoned at the neck. His trousers are chino, loose-fitting and casual. Looks about thirty. How old is he anyway? Marge didn't say.

"Sorry about the room," he says, closing the door. "There's a salesmen's convention. It's the best I could get."

"I like it." The room is perfectly fine, if on the small side. A bed, a couple of easy chairs, and a television set.

"Want some music?" He goes to the radio.

I shake my head no.

On the bureau, he's set up a bucket of ice next to bottles of soda, bourbon, and Scotch.

"You didn't say what you drink. If you want something else, I'll send down for it."

"Bourbon is fine."

"Mixer?"

"On the rocks."

I go for one of the easy chairs, drop off my sandals, and tuck my bare legs under me. I straighten my dress. "So"—I lean back in the chair—"you don't think it's strange that my father is being waked and I'm here with you?"

"People do different things with their grief."

"I'm not grieving." I take a big swallow.

He looks at me skeptically.

"Since they told me he died, I haven't shed a single tear."

It sounds like I'm bragging.

Lon takes his own drink, leans against the bed's headboard.

I wish he hadn't chosen the bed.

"Take it easy," he says, "that's hard liquor."

"That's why I'm drinking it."

"Whatever you need," he says softly.

I can sense he doesn't know what to say. "I really should explain . . ."

"You don't have to—unless you want to. I told you I'd try to help out and I meant what I said. I can handle anything you want to do."

I avoid his frank gaze.

I'm pretending to myself that this whole scene is normal when I know what I'm doing is crazy.

"I think I want to get drunk."

"That's okay with me."

"I think I may want to stay."

"I've got nothing but time."

"I have an appointment in the morning. It's my analyst. I can't miss it."

He points to the phone.

"I don't get it."

"Wake-up. One of the beauties of a hotel. They wake you up. What time should I say?"

We're so close to Park Street. Then the Waverly bus. "Seven-thirty. That leaves plenty of time."

"This is room 307. I'd like to leave a wake-up call for seven-thirty."

He puts down the phone, I hold up my glass.

"I guess you meant what you said."

"What's that?"

"You want to get drunk."

"I just don't want to feel."

He makes me a new drink. "You're safe here," he says, giving it to me, "don't be so uptight."

"I don't want to leave. . . ."

"No dinner?"

"No dinner."

"There's room service."

"I don't want to see anyone—except you." I hear my speech slur. "You're very nice. Really you are. I bet you've seen your own share of hard times."

"When you see this color black"—he points to his bare arm—"you know you're looking at someone who's no stranger to trouble."

"I want you to know I'm glad that I came . . . whatever happens tonight."

"And what is it you want to happen?"

The thrill of the touch of his hand on the nape of my neck tells me to be honest. I cover his hand with mine. "I think you know."

"O-kayyy." He pulls me to my feet, reaching down to switch on the radio.

"I don't dance."

"You don't have to. Just move with the music."

I follow his orders, move when he moves, sway when he sways. Just having someone to hold on to is soothing.

"You've got to let it out," he whispers, "you can't keep it in."

The booze is doing its thing. I feel woozy already. "Can't cry anymore." I hold on to him to keep steady. "I'm dizzy. Can't stand up anymore." I slide to the bed.

The bourbon has loosened a knot deep inside. My purpose is his, but some part of my brain wants to renege on this just-made commitment. The "prescription" for my release is more than this heat. My "answers" are all based on reason.

I move to get up. "Want another drink."

He pushes me back. "Hey, don't get blown away."

"Sex. Nothing to do with you . . . nothing at all." I try shifting his weight off my body.

"Some things just *are*. We're together. I *am*. I *feel*. You do too. Don't mess with it." He kisses me gently and slips off my dress. I watch as he strips off his clothes.

"Lay back, baby, just you lay back. I got what you need to forget."

I yield to his confidence.

His tongued nudgings speak to my senses and coax my reactions, but his "oh baby" seems automatic.

The warmth of his body hypnotically rocking, kneading, and probing loosens old hunger.

To his feverish inquiry, my body cries "more." I can't get enough of him.

His "ooh ba-by" finally moans honest.

"Well," says Dr. Mueller the next morning, "don't you think this is very unusual?"

"He was tender and kind. It was a stroke of good luck that he called when he did. I'm going back when I leave here. I want to see him"—I rub my throbbing temples—"in daylight."

"But what about your father?"

"I'm a lot like him," I say, matter-of-factly, "and I've got a lot to work out here—but not today."

I come up from the dark subway into bright sunshine. Dozens of Plexiglas phone booths ring the station. I dial the nursing home.

"Mary Louise," says my mother. "I was so worried that you were angry with me. Please don't be. We're in this together, whatever it is."

Outside my booth, a grim hurdy-gurdy man angrily cranks out his music. His monkey holds out a cup.

"Mummy, I have something to tell you."

"What is it?"

"I . . . I love you very much."

"And I love you too, dear, remember that—always."

Not yet, I think, coming out of the phone booth, I can't tell her yet.

Chapter Thirty-one

"But," asks Dr. Mueller, "is it coincidence that you choose this style now?"

"I'm slipping away. Sex kills the pain."

"But why now?"

"You mean while my father hovers between life and death?"

"Hovers?"

"No, I'm the one hovering. My father is dead. I know that—and I know that talk here is what will save me."

I hear the sound of his pen scratching on paper.

"My father's death seems to have thrown me into limbo. He died without my consent. Isn't that crazy? But that's how I feel. I wasn't ready."

"And?"

"I'm not ready yet." I brush my hair back from my eyes. "Dr. Mueller, do you think this abandoned-little-girl part of me will ever grow up?"

"That's what we're here for, but what more are you getting at?"

"It feels good to give my body contingent on nothing but the shared moment."

"Can you be sure that this kind of indulgence won't hurt your analysis?"

"How could it?"

"By distracting you from your internal conflict."

"You think I'm running away?"

"I didn't say that."

"But it's what you're thinking. Dr. Mueller, the times are changing, and if I'm to change, I must change along with them."

"It's not your right to grow that I'm questioning, Mrs. Shields. I'm concerned that this new mode of behavior will disrupt your analysis."

"I'm living my life the best way I can."

"Here we must look at everything."

"But, Dr. Mueller, I can't analyze every goddamned thing I do."

"Some things are more important than others."

"Such as?"

"Men."

"What about them?"

"Are you reminding yourself that you can still love?"

"You've missed the whole point, Dr. Mueller, I'm proving that love has nothing to do with it."

"I'm worried about you, Lou. Ever since Yoshi, you've been as high as a kite. You're out of touch with yourself."

"Oh, DeeDee, don't be so old-fashioned." It's DeeDee I'm out of touch with. We haven't been spending much time together.

"I hate this cockamamie sex business. Men in hotel rooms."

"One man. One hotel. Don't make it sound tawdry."

"The depression you mentioned. *That's* how you really feel. The sex is just a distraction."

I have no rebuttal for DeeDee.

"Lou," she says gently, "you've got to start using your time with Dr. Mueller to figure out why you feel unworthy without a man in your life."

Chapter Thirty-two

"Mary Louise, you look very tired," says my mother on her next visit. "Is anything wrong?"

"The store has been busy. You know how it gets in the fall." I lie to my mother about what's really the matter.

"Why don't you take a nap? I'll read to the children."

It's late afternoon, but in my body it feels like the end of the day. "Okay, Mum, I'll lie down for a while, then I'll make us all dinner."

I draw the shades and get into bed under the new quilt. Maybe I should take a nap.

I hear the door open. I close my eyes in case it's one of the children. I feel hands tuck the quilt under my feet.

"You're my flesh-and-blood daughter," I hear her whisper. "I look at you. I can't see behind your eyes. I don't know what you know."

I keep up my game of pretending to sleep.

"You've been to hell and back," she continues. "I don't even know what you've been through." She pulls the quilt up around my shoulders. Her hand brushes my hair. I hear her tiptoe out of my room, closing the door behind her.

"I just don't know how to tell her!" I beat my fists on the couch. "I feel so rotten. I'm in some kind of pain but I don't know what it is."

"Can you explain how the sex fits in?" asks Dr. Mueller.

I make an X over my rib cage. "It's like emotional surgery . . . a way to get at the pain which is deep inside . . . like a tumor."

"To hear you describe it that way reminds me of how you described yourself the day *before* your father died—the day I came back from vacation."

"What did I say?"

"That you were in a 'deep freeze.' "

"You're right. I did say that. And it *was* the day before my father died."

What can it mean?

"It sounds as though you haven't taken me back," says Dr. Mueller.

"Taken you back?" Preposterous, I think to myself. Am I some child playing peek-a-boo? Hiding its face only to say "you can't see me now"?

"You think that's what's the matter?" I ask him.

"It's just a guess."

"And I guess I'll have to think about it."

My period is late. I've missed a few pills. What if I'm pregnant?

My calendar is still turned to August—when Dr. Mueller went away. I move to turn the pages to October, then stop. I'm not ready to move forward in time.

"Turn out the light," says Anna Karenina (as played by Vivien Leigh) in the darkened movie theater where I am alone. "How much that seemed splendid and out of my reach has become worthless," mourns Anna, "while what I once had is gone forever. Turn out the light," Anna says just before she throws herself under the train, "there's no point in going on in the dark."

Ahead of the house lights, I run down to the ladies' room. My dress feels clammy and wet. Blood runs down my legs.

I grab some paper towels and close myself into a cubicle. I mop myself up, discard the towels in a bin, and buy a pad from the machine, which I pin to my underpants. Lucky I'm wearing black tights, I think as I pull my coat over my dress. It's night, but I put on my dark glasses and head for the subway.

On my way down to the bus level, the light of a train coming in from Boston mesmerizes me in the tunnel.

"Everything in me wanted to die," I tell Dr. Mueller.

"Not everything," he says gently, "or you wouldn't be here. Can you try to tell me what you were feeling that night?"

"Anna couldn't make sense of her life."

"Mrs. Shields?"

Dr. Mueller sounds a light-year away.

"Yes."

"Did you say something?" he asks.

"I said 'yes.'"

"There is one requirement to psychoanalysis that we never discussed."

"What's that?" I ask.

"You must go on living."

"I see," I whisper.

"For the next few days, I think you should sit up and face me—starting now."

It's been so long since I've seen his face. Can his sad expression be reflecting my own? I scan the fine lines that etch his character. I know him by the sound of his voice, an occasional clearing of throat, and any irregularity of his breathing. But mostly I know him by the force of his mind.

"Hello." It's a relief to see his face.

"Can you tell me a little more about why you felt suicidal Saturday night?"

Suicide? The word comes as a shock. "I didn't think of it that way. Had I fallen under the train, it would have been accidental."

"Would it have been?"

"I had to go home to shower. I was a mess from my period."

"What about your period?"

"Life . . . my life was flowing out." I hold out my palms. "I must take my life"—I clasp them—"or I must take my life"—I make a slashing gesture. "But I must take my life soon."

"What do you feel now?" Dr. Mueller leans closer.

"That I . . . that my . . . father is dead."

"What did you say?" he asks forcefully.

"My father is dead. Daddy. Oh, Dr. Mueller, he's gone . . ." I put my head in my hands and start to sob. "I can't talk . . ."

"That's all right." He hands me a box of tissues.

I don't know how much time passes before I can speak again. "Dr. Mueller,"—I bend my head down so I don't have to face him —"I can't stop this crying. What shall I do?"

"Cry some more, Mrs. Shields. Cry some more."

Part Three

A tisket
A tasket
A green-and-yellow basket
I wrote a letter to my mother
And on the way I lost it.

Chapter Thirty-three

"What a cruel thing to say, Dr. Mueller." Sitting up in the chair means I can smoke, so I light up a cigarette. I glare at him angrily. "If I were a man, you'd think nothing of my carousing around."

"You're throwing yourself away," Dr. Mueller repeats.

I'm hung over and in no shape to argue, so I try to make light of my situation. "It's a wonder I even got here at all." I point to the heavy downpour outside his window. "I woke up in Boston this morning. When I told the guy I had spent the night with where I wanted to be dropped off, he thought I really *was* crazy, but he drove me here anyway"—I break into laughter—"in a little red sports car."

No smile from Old Stoneface.

Why did I bother to come? Dr. Mueller is so disapproving. God damn him anyway. Who does he think he is?

I continue to glare.

His expression turns pained. I flush with embarrassment. Dr. Mueller is organized, punctual, kind, and considerate. Are such virtues ever easily come by, or are they always hard won? "I was rude, Dr. Mueller, I'm sorry. If I were a man, you *would* disapprove, wouldn't you?"

He nods.

"But why?"

"Because it's such a terrible waste."

His words take my breath away. I see now that his expression is not disapproval but shock at the sight of me, rumpled and wrinkled and reeking of whiskey. I see what he sees—I am making myself a "bad girl"; I am living out my father's negative image of me.

Above and beyond social mores for women, promiscuous sex, for me, has meanings untold.

A terrible waste. That's what Dr. Mueller had said. And how else would I describe my father's life?

One Saturday afternoon—it was springtime, I think—I was on my way home from the Children's Museum. There was a crowd on the corner right next to my school, and a paddy wagon was parked not far from the crowd. "Come on, fella,"—I heard a man's voice—"we're going to take you over to City." When I got closer, I saw two policemen helping a man to his feet. The man's head was all bloodied, and on the ground next to him, in a pool of blood, was a crushed Easter lily. Steadied by the two cops, the man reached out toward me. The sight of his head sickened me, because part of it was caked with blackening blood. I stepped back in fright.

Gone was the good mood I'd been in when I left the museum. I cursed my own curiosity. Had I walked around the crowd, I'd have been spared this nightmarish spectacle.

"Mary Lou," the man cried out, "please don't leave me alone."

When he spoke, and only then, I realized that the man was my father.

"Daddy!" I gasped, under my breath.

"Do you know him?" asked one cop.

I shook my head no. That man *was* a stranger.

"She's my daughter." My father again lurched toward me.

"You can ride to the hospital with him in the paddy wagon." The cop extended his arm.

"No. No, I can't." I backed into the iron fence of my schoolyard.

"Two guys beat up that one, then ran when the wagon came," I overheard one neighbor explain to a new arrival. "No one saw how it started. The guys got away."

"That's my little girl," said my father again, and the crowd turned toward me.

I felt faint . . . very woozy. I was gasping for air.

"We're taking you to Boston City for stitches." Both cops took his arms and moved him toward the wagon. "Come along now. We're not going to hurt you."

"Come with me," my father pleaded once more.

And I turned and ran—away from him.

"Can you talk about what's on your mind?" asks Dr. Mueller.

"Derelicts. They roam through my dreams, ragged and shabby and smelling of piss." Just the thought makes me nauseous. "And, in real life, I'm never sure when one of them will turn out to be Daddy."

"*Will* turn out?"

"Used to—of course, I mean used to. They sometimes 'used to' turn out to be Daddy—that is, when he was alive."

My father has been dead for almost two months, but I still can't seem to stop running away from him.

Daddy isn't my problem—at least not nowadays. Mr. Napoli and I are hammering away at the separation agreement between Mike and myself, which will also act as the instrument for our divorce.

"You have the custody. Mike has visitation rights." Mr. Napoli speaks firmly to me.

"Why can't it read 'joint custody'?" I look up from my typed copy of the separation agreement.

"Because it's almost unheard of." Mr. Napoli looks up from his, too. "If you're after such a—as you call it, 'cooperative divorce,' I honestly can't understand why you don't just take him back."

Mr. Napoli's plea is born of frustration.

"We've been through that already. I told you I can't."

"And *I* can't say I'm happy about having drawn this agreement up to *your* specifications. As your lawyer, it makes me very unhappy."

"Just tell me why the custody can't be joint."

"Legally, it's better for one parent to have the last word. If you and Mike come to disagree over what's best for the children, your view should be the final one."

"That situation isn't likely to come up."

"You'd be amazed at what comes up after a divorce."

"But the separation has worked out so smoothly."

"You're not the first woman to sit here in my office and predict how her husband will act after the divorce." Mr. Napoli's eyes wander over to his huge double filing cabinets. "Nor would you be the first ex-wife to return in a year and tell me your husband's new wife is expecting a baby and you're afraid for your own children's security. It happens all the time."

"Mike told me they wouldn't . . ."

"And, as your lawyer, I'm telling you that you can no longer trust what he says about the future." Mr. Napoli says this in front of a photograph of his own smiling children.

"You mean well, I know you do, but I barely know you and I don't understand the law. I'm forced to believe that Mike means what he says when he promises that he'll always take care of Christopher and Elizabeth. I know him too well not to."

"Okay, okay. Then Mike will have to trust you too. *You* have the custody. Now can we move on?"

"All right. Let's move on."

The husband and wife agree that the property in said Cambridge shall be and remain in both names as tenants in common whether or not a decree of divorce is entered as between the said parties.

"You still want to go on sharing the ownership? It's not too late to change. My secretary can retype it."

"No. That part is fine."

"Now, about the alimony . . ."

"Here we go again." I sigh.

"When it's money for child support that Mike will be giving you, why do you insist that we call it sixty percent alimony and forty percent child support? It's one hundred percent child support!"

"I'll try explaining once more." I maintain my calm in the face of Mr. Napoli's open dismay. "*You* know it's child support and *I* know it's child support, but that one hundred dollars that Mike will give us each week is more than half of all the money he makes—including his overtime."

"So?"

"That leaves him barely nothing to live on!"

"You do understand"—Mr. Napoli now swivels his chair toward the view from his window, and away from my line of vision—"that if it's a deduction for Mike, *you* must pay taxes on it?"

"But I earn so much less than he does, it will cost me almost nothing."

He taps his fingers on the arms of his chair.

"Mr. Napoli." I hear the pleading tone in my voice. "Please try to look at it as a matter of distribution. If you do as I ask, there's more money for me *and* my family. Only the Internal Revenue Service gets a little less than it might otherwise have received."

"Mrs. Shields, may I ask you why you're being so conscientious about Mike?"

"I'm trying to think of what's good for *all* of us. We'll be in this together for some time to come."

"I hope you're right about Mike." Mr. Napoli shakes his head.

"I know I am. I'll come back in a year and make you rethink the way you counsel women to proceed in divorce."

"That will be a new one on me." He bursts out laughing. "I'd like nothing better than to have you prove me wrong." He gets up from his desk and reaches over to give me a warm handshake. "I think we've covered everything. Now all that's left is to have the judge accept this as both your intentions. Will Mike have counsel in court?"

"He's leaving it up to you and me."

"Nine-thirty then. Thursday morning—by the side door of the courthouse."

"I'll see you then."

"Either fish or cut bait, Lou."

"DeeDee, you're not being fair."

"Either make up with Mike and go back together or get a real divorce and make plans to live your own life. Now *that's* good advice."

Outside the courtroom, DeeDee, my reluctant witness, grows suddenly nervous.

"Dr. Mueller told me just this morning that he sees nothing to disagree with about this arrangement."

"What did you expect him to say?"

"DeeDee, be reasonable. If anyone is going to tell me I'm crazy, don't you think it would be Dr. Mueller?"

"You're so pigheaded that Dr. Mueller can see for himself that you're going to do exactly what you want to do, whether your lawyer recommends it or not. Why bother paying Mr. Napoli if you won't take his advice?"

"There's Mr. Napoli now, DeeDee. Drop it, please, will you? What we've worked out is something Mike and I can both live with. The thought of raising the kids without Mike gives me the creeps."

Mr. Napoli opens the door, and we follow him into the courtroom.

In less than a half hour, we're finished. I'll be legally "free" next April, 1969.

With the divorce arrangements behind me, I try to bring new concentration back to my analysis.

"I've been back for two months and you have yet to speak of how you felt while I was away," Dr. Mueller says—rather aggressively.

"There's been so much going on—"

"And," Dr. Mueller interrupts me, "the more energy you've put into acting out, the less you've had for your analysis. As long as you won't talk about how you felt in my absence, you are demonstrating to me that you don't see me as separate. Mrs. Shields, I can—and I will—go away again."

"I don't want to think about it."

"You've made that very clear, and your refusal to think keeps your analysis at a standstill. Perhaps it would be better for you to go into therapy . . ."

"No!"

"Not everyone can do psychoanalysis."

"I can do it. I can." My mind races to recall last night's dream. "I had a dream that I went on a trip."

"Hmm."

"An ocean liner. I think it was the *Queen Elizabeth*. See," I say peevishly, "the dream shows that I'm moving."

"Did you see last night's news?"

"You mean about the *Queen Elizabeth* being retired?"

"Going to her 'final resting place' was the way that I heard it."

In my dreams, I'm on the run. An ocean liner on its way to a permanent standstill. A train with no engine. And in all of my nightmares, I search for a "passport."

Before Dr. Mueller went on vacation—and before my father died—I was doing analysis as though I had choices. Now I feel trapped, and ever since Daddy died, I've become a female Don Juan of sorts, as though sex can substitute for the things I believe I can't have.

"How do I find my way back to the couch?" I ask Dr. Mueller.

"The answer is in you. You can stop or go forward."

Shazam.

Open Sesame.

I must find the right words.

Chapter Thirty-four

"But I can't give up the analysis."

"This is *not* analysis, Mrs. Shields, nor has it been for some time. It's the middle work to see if analysis can continue."

"I still need your help." I usually avoid biting my nails right in front of him, but today I bite one down to the quick.

"If you will not or cannot discuss your feelings, then we will have to terminate, but perhaps in therapy . . ."

"Why don't you just admit it, Dr. Mueller? It's the sex. You disapprove of it, and I don't know why. It brings me relief."

"Such relief that it's brought your analysis to a standstill." Dr. Mueller's tone is sarcastic, but his eyes reflect deep concern. "Can't you see that I am not the one stopping our work?"

"Are you trying to tell me that I've gone as far as I can?" I press a butt out in the ashtray and hold my breath until he responds.

"You and I must work out the answer to that question together."

That's a relief! How can I tell Dr. Mueller that what for him seems to be normal behavior feels to me like a miracle? He does what he says he will. He always shows up. He's what I want out of life—someone to rely on.

"I feel a sense of oneness with you, Dr. Mueller. It's spiritual and intellectual."

"And the sex?"

"There's oneness there, too . . . but I lose my identity."

"Mrs. Shields, if you should prove to be unanalyzable . . ."

"Stop. Don't finish that sentence."

Unanalyzable. Sounds like the end of the world.

"Last night I dreamt I was in an old house. Someone was chasing me. I ran up the stairs, one flight after the other."

"Who was chasing you?"

"A soldier. And by the end of the dream I'd disarmed him. We met face-to-face . . ."

"Disarmed?" asks Dr. Mueller.

"He . . ." I close my eyes to recapture the dream memory. "He had no penis."

Face-to-face. As he and I are now. Disarmed. With no penis. Can Dr. Mueller be the dream rapist?

Dr. Mueller's expression tells me that he's made the connection, so I feel forced to keep analyzing this unpleasant dream. "I guess you are the soldier, and the house might be psychoanalysis," I say, flushing.

"In the first part of the dream you are running. In the second part, you're in control." He pauses. "And the man has no penis."

I hate it when sex comes up in our sessions. I find it hard to admit to Dr. Mueller that when I take control in the sex act, I feel that the men are "disarmed." They have no power to hurt me. But why dream that I "disarmed" Dr. Mueller?

"What are you thinking?" he asks.

"I have trouble saying."

"Do you think you're in this alone? I can help you, but it's up to you to help me find a way. If we're to get past this point, you can't shut me out."

"The night after my father died"—I take a deep breath—"when I was in bed with Lon, he asked me to suckle his breasts." My voice drops to a whisper. "I thought of my father. I wanted love from him—not sex." I swallow hard and try to keep talking. "When you went away for your vacation, I was ashamed of how 'hungry' I felt. You left me to cope."

"I pushed you away from the breast."

"My father was always seductive, so I never showed any signs of being a sexual person—whether he was around or he wasn't, since I never knew when he'd show up. I was afraid that any expressed sensuality on my part could be construed by my father to be a turn-on for him. Most men, when they meet me, think I'm a teacher or a librarian. Even now—and I like that."

"But I know you have hot pants," he adds. "You've told me so."

He's deliberately used the words that I gave him. I know that. All the same, it's a shock to hear them come out of his mouth. I feel myself turning crimson. I hear myself gasp.

"You dream me with no penis because then you will be safe." He speaks with authority.

"Oh, no! You're so different."

"You want to believe that, but your own father used his sex as a weapon over you. How can you ever be sure?"

I blush in silent embarrassment.

"Perhaps you dream of me with no penis because you want me to play 'mother' here."

"In some bizarre way, the sex with the strangers does feel as though I'm being mothered, but I can't explain why."

"Could the pure physicality evoke the time at your mother's breast?"

"Could be . . . I'm not sure."

"Let's look at the pattern. Before I went away you perceived me as good, but because I was a man, you were always a little mistrustful. I'm gone for five weeks, and on my first day back your father dies. Somewhere in your mind, do you suppose you were afraid I'd take your father's place?"

"I was angry with my father and angry with you. I was hurt . . ."

"Dreaming of a man with no penis is a way to guarantee not being hurt."

"It's also a way"—the dawn comes quickly now—"to express anger at men."

"Go on." He encourages me.

"I was afraid to express direct anger toward you because I might drive you away. Then I wouldn't have anyone—no father, no husband, no you."

"So?"

"I 'terminated' the analysis as a way to get back at you. And that was childish, because I just hurt myself. Stopping my work hurt me more than you, but it felt as though you were the one being punished."

"And?"

"I guess you could call it passive aggression."

"I think we could." He nods sympathetically.

"We can." I smiled, relieved to have all this sex stuff out in the open. "I went straight from the deep freeze into passionate sex with men who are strangers as a way to deny that *you* can go away, as a way to deny that my father is dead, and as a way to deny that soon Mike and I will be divorced. Sex became a way to deny separation and loss."

Dr. Mueller nods in agreement.

"Do you remember that dream I once had of Aunt Tilly's house when I went back to find it all boarded up?"

"I remember."

"Well, last night I dreamt I went back again, and this time I found the windows unboarded. They were all clean. I wanted to look into them."

"What comes to mind?"

"I'd like to 'go back' to see how it was."

"Do you think you have to 'go back' alone?"

"I hope not."

"If you have any hope, any wish . . ." He gestures toward the couch, as he had done that very first time.

Shazam.

Open Sesame.

Chapter Thirty-five

I feel stronger and safer now that I'm back on the couch doing analysis again. I summon the courage to do what I've postponed far too long.

"You look troubled, Mary Louise. What's the matter?"

My mother is quick to pick up on my apprehensiveness as we stroll arm in arm through the Boston Common. The day is like spring, that kind of miraculous weather that can sometimes happen in January. I'd planned to tell my mother the news at home, but the unexpected thaw makes us want to stay outdoors, and my mother enjoys feeding peanuts to every pigeon we come upon.

"Let's rest for a while." She guides me to a bench by the frog pond. "Poor thing, I should have brought bread from the kitchen," my mother says sadly as a scrawny squirrel snatches the last of the nuts.

"Mummy." I take her hand in mine. "I have something to tell you, and it's hard."

"Not the children." Her eyes widen in panic. "Nothing's happened to them?"

"Not to them. They're all right. It's Daddy."

She lets out a deep sigh. "Did you hear from him?"

"Not from him . . . from the hospital." I'd better just say it straight out. "The hospital called to say that Daddy was dead."

"Poor Ralph."

I watch her face closely.

"Was anyone with him?" She reaches into her handbag for a Pall Mall.

"He died in his sleep."

"When?" She lights up the cigarette.

"That's what's so hard. Oh, Mum, he died last September."

"September?" She shakes her head. "I don't understand."

"Sonny and I didn't know how to tell you."

"You poor dear." My mother takes my face in her hands. "To think that you've carried this around in your heart all this time. I knew something was wrong with the two of you."

"You mean you're not upset that we didn't tell you?" I find it incredible that my mother's first response is concern for my brother and me.

"If I'd known, I might have gone to see him laid out. How did he look?"

"We didn't go. That's why it's all so unreal."

"Then who ran the funeral?"

"Ruth. And Jane, too."

She nods. "Ruth would always take care of him." She relaxes. "At least he had someone." She stares off at the pond. "You saw more of him than I ever did," my mother says softly.

"Life has been so hard on you, Mummy." I can't fight back my tears.

"You're my little girl. Always remember that." She holds my face in her hands and smudges the tears from my eyes with her thumbs. "And I know what you've been through . . . better than anyone."

Her compassion shakes my composure, and I sob in her arms, no longer caring that passersby stare at us there on the bench by the frog pond.

"There, there," she whispers in my ear. "He never took care of us. It's not the same as losing someone who's close to you."

"Now light the match," Abby says, getting into position six feet away from me.

The furniture is pushed to the wall in both her living and dining rooms, giving Abby one long space to work in. Her cotton uniform is tied with the white belt of the novice. Abby seems to be in a state of deep concentration, and her manner is serious.

I light the match.

Abby moves sideways. Snap. She extends her leg. Out and up. Close to my face and inches short of the match. The wind from her kick puts the match out.

"How wonderful, Abby." I jump up and down. "Do it again!" And she does.

"You should take it up too, Lou."

"What's it called again?"

"Tae kwon do. A form of Korean karate. It changes how you feel about yourself and your body. It would be so good for you."

I shake my head no. "I'm too out of shape." I stand alongside Abby and try to make my feet do what hers do. "Besides, I don't think I could stand being taught in a class full of men."

"They do give us trouble. There are only four women in the class, and it's pretty clear that the men would drive us out if they could. One of them 'accidentally' kicked me in the shoulder yesterday."

"I couldn't stand it." I wince.

"It makes me try harder."

"Maybe that's one of the differences between having been born rich and having been born poor."

Abby frowns. "What is?"

"Having nerve."

"Until women can control their own destinies, we will all be politically powerless—rich women and poor. Controlling one's body is just the first step."

From behind, Abby corrects my primitive pose. "This way," she murmurs, "hold your shoulders this way." Her touch is gentle but firm.

In her full-length mirror, I can see that I'm a long way from Abby's posture, but, all in all, I look better than I thought I would.

"You've got it," she says. "There, that's riding-horse stance."

"It's time for your meeting."

Abby checks her watch. "I better get changed."

Abby's group, Cell 16, has closed its membership, but all over Cambridge and Boston, new groups form every day, and Abby has agreed to accompany me to a general meeting about women's liberation.

"Thanks for coming," I tell her as we walk the long MIT corridors in search of the meeting room. "I'm really nervous."

WOMEN, reads the scrawl on the blackboard, LIFT UP YOUR SKIRTS AND PULL DOWN YOUR PANTS.

The classroom begins to fill up with women and the sounds of indignation and anger. "Jesus Christ, aren't women respected anywhere?" says one woman. "Impudent bastards," I hear another say as a copper-haired woman in a striped shirt and jeans goes up to the board, erases the slur, and carefully prints:

SISTERHOOD IS POWERFUL!

Abby and I join the others in cheers and applause. "Right on!" cries the woman standing next to me. "Right on!" resounds through the room.

"But, Abby," I say when we're on our way home, "it's not enough for me to be told I'm as good as everyone else when I know I'm not. You're equipped, so is Jayne. You both have what it takes. I don't have the stuff 'liberation' will have to be made of."

"Don't give up before you even begin, Lou. Jayne and I are roommates, we take tae kwon do together. We work on the journal. Compared to us, you're so isolated. Why don't you go to the next meeting of the consciousness-raising group you were in? At least give c-r a try."

"I guess I've got nothing to lose, have I? And, who knows, I might become liberated."

Just as psychoanalysis has given me Dr. Mueller to confide in, so the women's liberation movement promises "sisters" with whom I can share my life's experience. I can't yet see where I fit in, but perhaps it will be enough to just go and try.

Chapter Thirty-six

Where am I?

Dry mouth, great thirst, and pounding pain in my head are the first sensations I feel as I open my eyes to see where I am.

The room is neat and orderly, small and cozy. Sloped ceilings make tiny alcoves, the windows have small panes, and the walls are creamy white. A white coffee table next to a blue-corduroy-covered easy chair makes me think it's a living room. I'm on a sofa bed. Next to me is a man, and he's sound asleep.

Who can he be? My mind strains to bring back last night. The movie with Gloria. The Casablanca afterward. Ken. Gerry. Don. They were there, all my old friends.

How did the evening end? Why didn't I go home with Gloria? Or Ken? Or Don? I'll have to call Gloria.

What time is it? No clock in sight. From the light, it appears to be early morning. Of what day? Let's see. Mike took the kids early last night. Good, today's Sunday.

Come to think of it, I remember Gloria asking me if I was sure I wanted to stay when she left, and I promised her I'd go home with Ken or Don.

I was drunk when she left. I got drunker later. I guess I knocked myself out.

His shoulders are bare. Next to him, I am naked. Can there be any doubt that we two had sex?

Thank God for the pill.

He's German. I remember now. He has an unusual name. I can't get it back.

The room is so warm. I can't stand this thirst. Careful not to disturb him, I slowly move out from under the covers.

I peek out the window and recognize what has to be Boston's Bay Village, the unmistakable row houses and gaslights of probably Melrose or Fayette Street. Good. It's a nice part of town, and close to the subway.

Blacking out. I've done it before, but always with friends and in places where I knew I'd be safe.

I remember the movie. It was sad. The Casablanca brought back old memories. Piaf love laments on the jukebox. I was drinking compulsively. Usually I give myself some kind of warning when I go off the deep end. Not so last night.

On a bright red director's chair are my brown corduroy pants with the rest of my clothes, all in a pile. Just last week, in Central Surplus, Abby talked me into trying out pants. The first ones I've ever worn in my life. Good thing, too. This morning they'll look a whole lot better than a wrinkled-up dress would. Picking up my turtleneck jersey and underwear along with the pants, I tiptoe out to the kitchen in search of the bathroom. A closet. The only other door has a latch. Can the john be outside? I undo the latch slowly so as not to make noise. There is the bathroom—out in the hall. No other apartment up here. Must be the top floor. Just stairs going down to a landing. The whole building is quiet.

I close the bathroom door very gently. A glance in the medicine-chest mirror reveals what I knew would be there. Bloodshot eyes. Flaking skin. I long for a toothbrush, but settle for a rinse with Lavoris. I stand under the shower in a spotless porcelain tub. I feel a little more human as I rub myself down with one of the towels from the neat pile of bright colors. I borrow his comb, twist my hair in a bun, and use a little Sea & Ski as cream for my face.

I tiptoe back into the studio.

Should I just slip away? Leave him a note? Dear Sir? To whom it may concern?

In the bed, the man rolls into the spot that I had just occupied. He opens his eyes. They are blue.

"Good morning," he says, rubbing his eyes.

"Good morning." I blush.

"How are you feeling?" He speaks in a way that accents every syllable.

"Not very well. I had too much to drink."

"I tried to stop you, but you were not to be stopped."

"How did we get back here?"

"My Volkswagen."

"I mean how did we happen to come here?"

"You don't remember?"

"Not really."

"When the bar was closing, you wanted not to stop drinking." There's no doubt about it, his accent is German. "You asked me if I had liquor at my place. I said some beers. You said 'let's go back to your place.'"

"I did?"

"Your friends, Ken, and the other chap . . ."

"Gerry."

"Yes, Gerry. They tried to insist that they drive you home, but you said no, that you preferred coming with me."

"And?" I nod toward the bed.

"You don't remember that either?" His tone is one of astonishment.

I shake my head no.

"Well." He blushes himself. "I made you scrambled eggs. You had eaten no dinner. You ate the eggs, drank a beer, and then asked me if I wanted to go to bed." He clears his throat, and I think I detect his face getting redder. "I told you that it would be very nice to go to bed. You stood right over there." He points to the empty director's chair. "You undressed right in front of me."

"I didn't!" I feel the heat rush to my face.

"You did. Then you got into bed." He sits up and wraps the top sheet around his bare midriff. "I knew you were drunk. I didn't want to take advantage. I must tell you that it was what you wanted to do. I don't think I could have stopped you—not that I wanted to."

"Oh, dear." I cover my face to hide my embarrassment. It does sound like the truth. Almost a verbatim report from the sound of it. "I've got to go home now. I hope you don't mind. I don't feel very well."

"Let me drive you." He gets out of bed, wrapping the sheet like a toga. His body has an athlete's lean muscularity, and he seems to feel as self-conscious as I do.

"What street is this?"

"Fayette."

"I thought so." I get up to go. "You don't have to drive me. Honestly. This is so close to the subway."

He disappears behind a folding screen. "It would be my pleasure."

"I have a confession to make," I say when he's out of my sight. "I don't remember your name."

"Many people who know me longer than you have and who have not had nearly so much to drink as you drank cannot remember my name." He reappears in dark trousers and a black turtleneck. "I am Zygmunt." He laughs. We shake hands.

In the same instant, we both see the humor of our situation. We break into belly laughs.

"I am Mary Lou." I bow. "You are Zygmunt." My tongue seems to remember having pronounced his name, although before last night I had never heard such a name.

"I don't usually do this sort of thing" is what I really want to tell him. What does it matter? The damage is done and I just won't see him ever again. He's seen a side of me I hide from myself.

"May I treat you to the Sunday papers?" I ask when we pull up to the kiosk.

"I'll see them tonight at work."

"You work nights?"

"Don't you remember? I told you I work a night shift as a typographer."

"I don't," I murmur, embarrassed at yet another lapse.

Mead Street is deserted. I reach for the car door handle as Zygmunt asks for my number.

"I'd like to see you again."

I start to protest, then give in.

Upstairs, in the kitchen, I nibble on a roll before taking three aspirin. Could I go back to sleep? I doubt it. Too much anxiety. I start cleaning the house.

Can it be coincidental that I pull such a stunt just as I'm beginning to explore my female identity in my consciousness-raising group?

Chapter Thirty-seven

"But nowadays, it's *all* that you talk about."

"Haven't I always?"

"Yes, but freedom for blacks and the poor. And liberation for Vietnam and for Formosa."

"Dr. Mueller, it's females of all races who make up more than half the world's population. Until *we* are free, there can be liberation for no one."

"Why this sudden change in philosophy?"

"It may seem sudden to you, but the questions we discuss in my group have been in my mind for a lifetime, and it's such a relief to have someplace to talk."

"Can't you talk here?"

"It's not the same."

"Why?"

"You're not a woman." I don't want to hurt his feelings, but I don't want to lie. "Having Abby and my group is a way to put these questions in perspective. I compare my life to the lives of all women."

"And how does this help you?"

"Suzy Homemaker, for instance. She wasn't such an aberration. To some degree, all women are confined to a role—mother, wife, consumer, sex object."

"And that is why you feel that you must carry into your

analysis the discussions you have in your women's group?" Dr. Mueller sounds like he's trying hard to understand.

"Do you mind?"

"Perhaps bringing it here will help focus the rest." He pauses, considering. "It's been nearly two years now, and you still speak of yourself as an abstraction. You still see yourself as acted upon by the outside forces which you feel define you, but then, you're aware of that, aren't you?"

"I am," I whisper. "I'm frightened of liberation and I'm frightened of men. I say I don't want a man but I don't seem to last long without one. I'd like to try a new way to relate to men. Not the old-fashioned love and marriage, but more than one-night stands with men I don't want in my life."

Another Wednesday evening rolls around. It's rainy, but I promised Mike I'd deliver the kids, so I pull a slicker on Lizzie and help Chris with his boots. We take the bus into the Square. Mike welcomes them at the store, and I kiss them goodnight. Pulling the collar of my trench coat up, I head into the drizzle to go the few doors down to the Wursthaus.

I pause before pushing open the inner door to the restaurant. The clock over the bar shows the time to be seven, the time we agreed to over the telephone.

On the deli side of the restaurant, in front of a glass case filled with cold cuts and cheeses, people, two rows deep, are waiting for takeout. Straight ahead, rain-soaked students queue up to be seated for dinner. Should I queue up too, or should I go look for him? The absurdity hits me—I'm meeting a man with whom I've already gone to bed and I'm not sure I can remember his face.

"I'm looking for someone," I say to the hostess.

She waves me on by.

Hanging from rafters are Bavarian beer steins and ads in German for beer. I make way for a waitress carrying an oversized tray of weiner schnitzel, bratwurst, red cabbage, and sauerkraut. The jukebox is blaring a polka. There, in the last booth, I recognize Zygmunt.

"Over here." He stands up and waves.

"Good evening," he says, pronouncing "evening" as though there were three syllables. He hangs my coat on the end of the booth, and I slide in across from him.

He's better-looking than I had remembered. Sandy hair, intelligent face, and very nice eyes. His plaid shirt and beige trousers appear to be European and are cut from good wool.

"So." He smiles across from me.

"So," I repeat, somewhat at a loss. I look into his face as though for the first time.

"I am happy you accepted my invitation to dinner."

"Zygmunt, let's get something straight. I said yes to dinner, but I'd like to pay my own way."

"You won't accept my hospitality?" He looks genuinely offended.

"Men shouldn't buy women dinners. It makes the women beholden and it gives the men funny ideas." Oops. We've been to bed already, and even if I don't remember, he does.

"I have never thought that by buying the dinner, I was 'buying' the woman—if that's what you mean."

"If I were a man and we had just met, would you buy me dinner or expect me to pay my own way?" I hear the self-righteous tone in my voice.

"Well . . ."

"You see. It *is* a way to get a woman indebted."

"Perhaps." He backs off.

Zygmunt seems tongue-tied. His persistent politeness and equally persistent hurt feelings force me to see he's confused by my free-floating resentment. And I know that underneath my assertiveness, I'm as insecure as he is, perhaps even more so.

We both retreat to the menu.

"Do you know how the food is here?" he asks.

"But you're the German," I laugh. "Isn't the menu familiar?"

"Yes, but I don't know how well they prepare here."

He is so self-effacing. Next to him I feel like a brute.

"What did we talk about that night back at your place?"

"You asked a lot about me," he replies.

"Such as?"

"If I had a girlfriend."

"Do you?"

"Not since last summer."

"You mean you broke up with her last summer?"

"Yes. But also I have gone out with no woman since last summer."

"You mean you hadn't slept with anyone"—I quickly compute—"for six or seven months until that night you went to bed with me?" I lean back against the booth in disbelief.

"That is true," he says simply.

"But why? I mean, why me if it had been so long?"

"Somehow I felt we were communicating."

"But, Zygmunt, I was drunk . . . out of my mind."

"And I was stoned."

"You were stoned?" I'd been so obsessed with my own condition, it never dawned on me to question his. "You were stoned?" I start to laugh.

"On pot. I had been with some friends smoking very good grass. They seemed very close to each other and not to me, so I became paranoid. I had been driving around for some time before I came to the Casablanca. I was desperate to talk. You and your friends took me in." His side of the evening pours out. "You were all very friendly, but you were the friendliest. I could see you were drunk, of course, but I could also see you had the art of talk. I felt it very strongly. You spoke seriously with me about what I was feeling and how it was for my life."

"Zygmunt, wait a minute." His unabashed sincerity moves me to kindness. "I'm glad for your sake that you found someone to talk to that night, but you must see that the whole thing is crazy and it's nothing to base anything on—except that single night."

"But there was truth there—not for one time only."

I shake my head. "I'd have never had dinner with you tonight if you hadn't called so many times. I gave in because I hoped that when we were together, we could reason things out."

"Since last summer"—he looks at me with the most sincere expression—"I believed no close relationship for me would be possible. Not with a woman. You changed that. You took me, and I gave you what I could from my deepest feelings."

"You don't mean you have expectations based on that night?

Can't you see I don't even remember it?" I look away from his gaze and fidget with the silverware.

"I can see that you are afraid because I am a man. I am Zygmunt. I would like very much to keep seeing you, because I think we could be friends."

"Oh, God." I look up to the ceiling. "I don't believe this is happening."

"What don't you believe?"

"You. I don't believe you."

"You think I lie?" He looks hurt. He's taken me literally.

"Oh, no." I reach for his hand. "Not that. I mean I can't believe your sincerity. It's just an expression. I don't mean at all that I think you are lying."

He relaxes but keeps holding my hand.

I gently remove it from under his. "What is it you expect from a woman? Do you know?"

"To be understood. To be taken for a whole person."

"I'm not the right one, Zygmunt. I've just gone through a painful divorce. I have two young children. I can't take anyone seriously at this time in my life." His stare is intense. It breaks through my defenses. "What went wrong in your own romance?"

"She was a student like myself. She wanted to marry. She was American. She could not understand that I am a journeyman, an immigrant, not yet sure I can make my way here in America."

"It's very hard what you're doing." I look at him with new respect. "Even if you were American, going to school full-time and working full-time is terribly hard. How old are you anyway?"

"I came here at twenty-five. I am now twenty-seven."

"Who broke it off, you or the girl?"

"She did, and I must tell you that I have never hurt so much in my life. Since then, I have gone out with no woman until you."

"I've been hurt too," I say softly. "I go out with men, but I don't let them get personal. I came here tonight to tell you that I couldn't see you again. . . ."

"Yes?" He leans forward expectantly.

"Now I don't know." I let my eyes meet his.

The waitress brings us two steins of beer and sets them down on paper placemats.

"How do you see the relationships between men and women?" I ask Zygmunt.

"As circles." He makes a sketch on the mat. Two circles. Separate. Just their edges touch. "Men and women are joined," he answers, "but there is an inseparable wall between them. And you? How do you see them?"

I borrow his pencil and draw two circles that overlap. "When I was married to Mike"—I point to the large overlap—"that's what we shared. It was a great deal. That's why he was so hard to give up."

"Do you know what you want now from a man?"

"I'm not sure. Sex—without roles. I don't know if it's possible. And you? What do you want from a woman?"

"To be loved by someone not myself."

"Zygmunt." I swallow hard and try to ignore the butterflies in my stomach. "I think you are sincere and straightforward. I respect you for that, but I must warn you that I'm not an easy person to be with. I don't think you should stake any hopes on me."

"You are a very nice woman, and my only hope is that you will agree to see me again."

He's more than I bargained for.

Were I looking for love and marriage, a man who sees an inseparable wall between men and women might be off-putting. For now, a man who sees distance between himself and a woman might be ideal.

"To ask more," Zygmunt had said, when he was drawing the circles, "would lead to frustration."

Chapter Thirty-eight

" 'Mind your own business,' that's what it sometimes sounds like you're saying to me." Dr. Mueller sounds the least bit petulant.

"But when?" I ask him indignantly.

"Mostly when you go on about women's liberation."

"I'm sorry. Really, I am. I don't mean to tell you to mind your own business, I just get terribly frightened that you can't understand how I feel because you're a man."

"Can you give me an example of where you feel this has happened?"

"Mike. Remember you told me I had to analyze major moves?"

"Yes."

"And the next day I asked Mike to move out?"

"I recall very well. You never analyzed your behavior. You acted impulsively."

"I had to let go at the right moment."

"Was there only *one* right moment?"

"Yes—*the* moment when I found the strength. Can't you see that I was so locked into gratitude toward Mike that if I hadn't acted impulsively I'd be with him today, and on his terms, not mine?"

"Do you think I was asking you to be passive?"

"No. You couldn't have known that to express one drop of anger, I had to reach into my soul and renounce an ocean of gratitude. How could you know that?"

"You could have told me."

"Not then, but perhaps now. I have the same problem with you. I'm so overwhelmed with gratitude toward you, I find it difficult to express anger."

"Why?"

"I'm afraid we won't survive."

"We can," he says, no trace of doubt in his voice. "Your existence does not threaten me."

"When I first heard of 'penis envy' "—I reach into my past to try to convey my fear of psychology to my own psycho-analyst—"I was in college. I couldn't imagine what the theory could possibly mean, so my professor explained it. Don't forget, I was the poor little girl who got into Radcliffe, and there I was facing a big Harvard expert who was explaining to me that my ambition was a 'denial of femininity.' "

"What did you do?"

"I wasn't smart enough to argue with him and I was too shy to answer in terms of my own life, so I sat down and took notes."

"How did you feel?"

"Rotten . . . no, angry. I'm still angry today. In my group, we talk a lot about how destructive Freudian theory is to women, and I'm afraid some of that anger is going to have spillover to you."

"I'm a stand-in for Freud?"

"Sort of."

"So women's liberation will tell *me* that having a penis is not where it's at."

"That's right." I have to laugh in spite of myself. The words sound so funny coming out of his mouth. "You've got the point, Dr. Mueller. For centuries, women have had to survive in the face of society's view that we are inferior. Women's liberation will change all that. Men will have to survive the knowledge that they are not superior."

"Female revenge?"

"Justice, I'd say."

"I'm not sure how this affects your analysis."

"Even at Radcliffe, the message came through that it was im-portant to marry a man whose career you admired. Abby got the same message at home. I thought the obstacles between me and my ambition were education and money. Abby didn't have those disadvantages, but she faces obstacles too—*because* she's a female. Can't you see, Dr. Mueller, that it's feminism, not femininity, that will give us both a new chance?"

"Yes," he answers thoughtfully, "I do see what you're getting at."

"In women's liberation, we're calling it 'sexism.' "

"The 'it' being . . . ?"

"An age-old condition for which no word has been coined."

"Sexism?"

"Some feminists want to call it 'male chauvinism,' but the term is too clumsy. 'Sexism' is clearer."

"Like 'racism'?"

"Exactly."

Chapter Thirty-nine

"How was it when women got the vote?" I ask my mother.

"Very exciting. Suffragists marched right down Tremont Street carrying banners." My mother's eyes sparkle. "They were a wonderful sight. We thought the vote would change everything, but it didn't. Not really." Her expression grew sad.

"Don't ever forget for a moment," wrote my father from jail when I was sixteen, "your mother was smart. In fact, her trouble is that she is so far ahead of us, some things sound funny. But, in reality, had she done other things in her youth, she today would be a famous lady. Her marriage to me didn't help, but then I gather you're aware of these things."

I recall my mother's newspaper illustrations. The women she drew were not only fancifully beautiful but independent as well. An aviatrix stood on the wing of her plane, a few golden curls escaping from her helmet as she waved farewell to an attractive young man. An Olympic swimmer was sketched in a tank suit which revealed her lean, muscled body. A second sketch showed the swimmer in frills with a boyfriend in tow. In my mother's drawings, women were shown enjoying work *and* romance.

How would my mother's life have been different if she'd had "sisters" the way I do? In my group, we affirm one another and our female experiences: as straight women and gay; as lovers and wives; as mothers and daughters; and as housewives and revolutionaries. Women's History—the research that I am doing at Radcliffe's Schlesinger Library—is becoming a great consolation to me. The more I read, the more clearly I see that the road that those of us in the women's liberation movement travel is the same unpaved highway traveled by feminists over history and time; it was—and continues to be—a very rough road.

"I'm sorry I'm late," I say, out of breath, as I close both doors to Dr. Mueller's office behind me. I hang my coat next to his in the closet.

"Dr. Mueller sets aside the journal he has been reading. His clipboard rests on the arm of his chair and is set with a fresh piece of lined paper.

"I overslept." I lie down.

He makes no comment.

"I'm worried." I take a deep breath and try to compose what I want to tell him.

"What's on your mind?"

"I have to talk to you about things going on in my group, and I'm afraid you'll think it threatens our work, yours and mine."

"Have I ever so indicated?"

"No."

"Then what do you fear I'll object to?"

"Perhaps"—I laugh, seeing the irony—"I'm worried because my group is pressuring me to explain why I'm still in analysis."

"Psychoanalysis doesn't mesh with feminist consciousness-raising?"

"To many feminists, psychoanalysis is directly *opposed* to feminist goals because its theories are so riddled with outmoded sexism. Feminist psychologists are challenging all of psychoanalytic theory from a new social and historical perspective. I'm sure you can see why Freud's the main target. For him to have confused female ambition with a wish for the male organ was an outrageous mistake. Even in Freud's day, women didn't envy the penis, they envied the freedom conferred by society on those who happened to have been born with them."

"But why is what Freud thought so relevant?"

"Because his antifemale theories thrive in the offices of countless male therapists all over America—and those men are in the unique position of being able to make their female patients believe they are 'sick' to want more than the traditional roles."

"Aren't you exaggerating?"

"If anything, I'm understating the case. Gloria's group has a woman whose analyst initiated sex. He carried on the affair during their sessions and had the nerve to bill her for the time," I say angrily. "Are you going to deny having heard such tales yourself?"

"What I want to know is where I fit into all of this."

"I try to explain to my group that you've proven yourself, but it comes out all wrong and I end up sounding like the women who say, 'Oh yes, all men are chauvinists, but my man is *the* exception.' "

"So?"

"I end up defending Freud!"

"And how do you do that?"

"By defending his process. Freud brought his technique as far as he could—always aware that his era was *very* repressive. He envisioned a more open society in which others would be free to take his ideas and develop them. It's not his fault they've stagnated." I can feel myself blushing. "I don't mean to tell you your business, but didn't Freud write that if psychoanalysis *did* survive beyond his death, it would not be as therapy, but as an invaluable tool for research into the unconscious mind?"

"He said that in one of his lectures. I can't recall which one."

I wait for Dr. Mueller to continue, but it's clear he's waiting for me.

"Since most patients are female and most therapists are male, it's in the doctors' best interest to reinforce the status quo. After all, like other men, they have wives at home and mistresses outside them."

"Are you saying that no one has worked through the issue of feminist consciousness?" His tone is incredulous. "Even though they have been professionally trained?"

"Damn right. Analysts least of all. The field of psychology is probably even more sexist than society at large."

"How so?" He sounds curious.

"DeeDee says analysts are the worst, precisely because of those long years of training. She says penis envy is sexism taken to its furthest extreme."

I hear him sigh and shift in his chair, but he makes no rebuttal to my accusation.

"How old are you anyway?"

"Forty," he answers. "Why do you ask?"

"I'm thirty-three. That means that the first wave of feminism in America and Germany occurred before either of us was born. No amount of training before this very time can possibly incorporate what's happening now . . . for that very reason. It's happening *now*."

"That's a pretty big generalization."

"But it's one that I stand by, and, come to think of it, I bet your wife does too. What does she do, if I may ask?"

"She's a doctor."

"What kind?"

"A child psychiatrist."

"I see."

"What do you see?"

"That, even though she's a professional woman, your being an analyst would qualify you as the 'superior'—professionally, I mean. Being a doctor, your wife is more liberated than a lot of women, but back home she's your subordinate."

"Ahem." Dr. Mueller clears his throat. "You don't think a few of us might have worked *some* things out?"

I shake my head vehemently.

"What makes you so sure?"

"The world hasn't worked it out. Historically, the question is just now being raised."

I tell Dr. Mueller of a dream. I was on a bus filled with women. When the driver lets me off at McLean, she wishes me luck. I stumble my way up a steep, rocky path. At the top, a man gives me a hand. No ridicule, no fuss, just a helping hand. From there, I continue alone.

"It's so clear to you?" Dr. Mueller asks when I've told him the dream.

"No matter how contradictory some things I tell you may

seem, the dream sums up how I feel about you and my group. It's a clear demonstration that I need you all, and did you notice, neither Zygmunt nor Mike is in the dream?"

"I did."

"That means I'd like to channel my dependence on men in general and place it onto just you. You, as my analyst. Not on some man who wants to marry and have children."

"Are you saying it's neurotic to want to have children?"

"Most women don't 'choose.' "

"Contraception is readily available."

"Readily available? I don't think so. Now Coca-Cola, *that's* readily available! All over the world. Until birth control is as available as Coca-Cola, we can *never* know how many women and girls 'choose' to be mothers."

"Have you answered my question?"

"Not really, so I'll leave you with a question instead: can you honestly say—to me *or* to yourself—that it's perfectly all right for a woman *not* to want to ever have children?"

Chapter Forty

"Beer and sandwiches! I'm starved." I tear open the bag to see what he's brought. Pastrami and cheese on pumpernickel. Pickles and chips. "Wonderful, Zygmunt." I give him a hug. "Let's call it midnight supper."

Zygmunt has just returned from work.

"I do not want food." He leers lasciviously, lunging toward me playfully. "My hunger is for something else." He embraces me in his strong arms, and his long kiss is no joke.

"I can't." I push him back gently, gasping for breath. "I'm sorry, Zygmunt, I can't."

"Then let us eat, shall we?" he says, pretending not to be hurt.

"May I have a Heineken?" I ask, pretending not to notice my own behavior.

"We talked until dawn," I report to Dr. Mueller on Monday, "and by the time we went to bed, I felt very close to him. We made love easily."

"And then you dreamed of building a house out of rubble?"

"Yes. It was then that I dreamed it."

"What do you make of it?"

"The man in the dream, the one who tells me that my house won't be strong unless I do it his way, must be Zygmunt."

"But you've told me that he's very nice."

"And he is. Don't get me wrong about that. It's just that when we talk, Zygmunt agrees our affair should be light; then, when we make love, his passion scares me. I think his feelings go deeper than he can express, and they frighten me. That's why I pushed him away."

"What about the sex?"

"I enjoy it. It's just that I'm not used to having such intense pleasure with a man I don't love. Intellectually, I know I'm supposed to be free enough to have sex without a lasting commitment, but inside . . ."

"You're afraid he'll knock your house down."

"By eroding my defenses. I want to *expect* less from men, and with Zygmunt it seems to mean *accepting* less than his full passion. Less than his full confidence. It's all so new, I'm not sure I can do it."

"So what *do* you do?"

"Tell him over and over that I have no intentions to marry again. I get him to talk, too. About Laura, his former girlfriend. He says I'm more mature than she was, and I warn him not to focus his lost love for Laura on me, and that's why I sometimes experience trouble letting myself get fully aroused." I can feel sweat on my brow.

"Why are you so anxious?"

"I don't really know."

"It's hard for you to believe men . . . to trust them. I mean us." He catches himself.

"And I try."

"I guess I don't feel that women *should* fight," I tell Abby, "that's all." I feel under attack.

"But, Lou, are you saying that if a woman is attacked by a rapist at knifepoint, it's more honorable to die or be raped?" Abby is adamant.

"That's not what we're talking about."

"Oh, yes it is," Abby says fervently, "we're talking about women's right to defend themselves."

"Aren't women special? Shouldn't we help men to become more like ourselves?"

"Women aren't learning martial arts so they can go around attacking men. The men who rape and beat women are cowards. Don't you imagine they'd think twice if they thought the women could defend themselves?"

I smile. "Three or four times."

"My point exactly."

"I don't want to argue with you, Abby. The simple truth is that I could not learn tae kwon do in your class because learning with men would freak me right out. I can't bear the thought of being hit, even accidentally, the way you already have been. You'd have to take me home in a basket."

I resist Abby's urgings to take up self-defense. I resist even as I admire her growing competence.

What feelings are tapped? Old ones, I suspect.

Yet another repressed family scene moves center stage in my mind.

"Get out of here, Ralph," I heard Mummy shout, "go back to the barroom and leave us alone."

I woke up in my bed to the smell of whiskey, Daddy's face close to mine. I could feel his stubble on my face and shoulders.

Over my body, they scuffled.

"She's my little girl," Daddy groaned.

"You're stinking drunk," Mummy screamed. "Get out of here now! Go back to McBride's where you belong."

The only light in the room came from the kitchen. I made out Mummy's small form shoving my father through the door out into the kitchen.

I slid out from under the covers and scrunched into the corner. No, better hide under the bed, I thought.

Back into the room they stumbled. "Where is she?" I heard Daddy yell. His work shoes were within my hand's reach from under the bed. I saw Mummy's bare feet. I tried not to breathe.

"Get out, Ralph."

More scuffling. More screaming. The feet disappeared. A door slammed. No more voices.

I crawled out from under the bed and went toward the door to the kitchen. My mother stood by the door to the bathroom. There was the sound of a flush.

"Get back," Mummy hissed, but not before Daddy opened the door. He staggered out, a knife in his hand.

"Let me by." Daddy shoved Mummy aside. "I want Mary Lou."

I stood rooted in terror.

"I won't let you touch one hair on her head," my mother said fiercely.

Daddy lunged. Mummy grabbed for the broom. I jumped back. She banged the broom into his knees.

I ran back into the bedroom.

From where I hid behind the door, I heard the sounds of their combat.

"She's my little girl. I want her."

"Filthy animal, you can't have her! Go back to your barroom or I swear I'll kill you first."

More terrible sounds.

Why does my father want to kill Mummy or me? I can't understand. What if he hurts my mother? I peered out from behind the door to see Mummy backing Daddy into the wall between the bathroom door and the kitchen sink. Holding the broom, she gave him a kick in the shins.

"Oww!" Daddy groaned. "Why did you do *that?*"

Once more, Mummy kicked, this time to the groin. The knife fell out of Daddy's hands, and he let out a roar. Using the broom as a harpoon, she jabbed him hard in the stomach. His glasses fell to the floor. "Jesus Christ, you're trying to kill me!" He doubled over.

Stabbing him again with the broom, Mummy backed him out the kitchen door, out into the hall, out of my sight.

Thud. Screams. A body falling downstairs.

Oh, my God, what if it's Mummy?

I ran to the door. Mummy stood, gasping for breath. The hallway was dark. There never were any lights. By the light from the kitchen, I saw no blood on my mother.

"If you come back here, I'll kill you!" Mummy shouted from the top of the stairs.

"Goddamned son of a bitch!" I heard Daddy curse from the second-floor landing. Then all we heard was the sound of his breathing.

A foot on the stair.

Coming up?

No. Going down. Down the whole flight. Daddy's body banged the walls as he stomped. Bang and slam. The front door slammed shut.

Mummy led me back into the kitchen and bolted our door. I ran to the front window to see my father staggering up the alley.

What was wrong? What had just happened?

I slumped down onto my mother's trunk and began sobbing.

"There, there." Mummy came toward me. I fell into her arms.

"I'll put up with anything but not that! I told him I'd kill him if he ever laid a hand on you." She stroked my hair. "I won't take that from anyone. *No one* beats you or beats me. There, there, Mary Louise, don't you cry. We're safe now. He won't come back here."

And she held me.

"How old were you?" asks Dr. Mueller when I tell him the memory.

"Under nine is all I know for sure, because my brother wasn't born. I might have been five or six, but I don't really remember."

"Do you know why you remember it now?"

"Abby has been encouraging me to take up self-defense. I'm afraid. I hate violence. I don't want to be like a man. But . . ."

"But?" He prompts me.

"I can't help but wonder what my father might have done that night if my mother hadn't been able to fight him off. As small as she was, my mother fought like a tiger and beat him off both of us."

"What do you make of it?"

"I've never let any man hit me. Mike did only once, that night I banged my head into the wall, and I can still hear him pleading.

'Hit me, Lou. Please don't hurt yourself.' That was an exceptional evening."

"And you turned all your rage inward. You did not hit Mike. You *did* hurt yourself."

"Wait a minute, Dr. Mueller, you sound like you're siding with Abby."

"But, Mrs. Shields, here, during our time, you are the one who speaks of the importance of women being able to stand on their own. Abby is doing something you respect, something that you respect her for. Can you tell me why you don't want to learn?"

"The practice. Abby says everyone has to practice the hitting in a controlled way. I don't think I could do that."

"Do you know why?"

My arms by my sides, I lie on the couch not moving a muscle. I let my eyes wander up to the ceiling. I hear a plane overhead. There's no sound outside his office. In perfect tranquility, I confront for the first time my own murderous impulses. "I'm afraid I might kill someone."

"Where are the feelings?" asks Dr. Mueller.

"Locked up."

"Where?"

"Inside." I hear my voice growing childlike.

"Who would you kill?"

"Everybody loves a little razzle-dazzle." I can see my Big Daddy swing me up into the air. Every time he returned from a long abandonment, it would take him just minutes to lure me back to his side. Each time, anew, he could seduce me into forgiveness.

I hear Dr. Mueller clear his throat. The sound breaks my wandering train of thought.

"Let me put it another way." He rephrases the question. "Are you afraid someone will die from your anger?"

"You. Perhaps me. The next time you have to go away. I'm afraid I'll kill you—or die."

"There is time," he says calmly. "We have time to analyze all your feelings."

I slump on the couch in total exhaustion.

Chapter Forty-one

Registration has been brisk, spirits are high, and the Mother's Day weekend is sunny and bright as more than one hundred females attend the very first feminist conference to be held in the city of Boston since the suffragists last held theirs, in the Twenties.

In the gymnasium, Abby, Jayne, and their friend Dana move with the grace of young dancers, but their performance isn't a dance; it is a demonstration of the classic forms of tae kwon do, and they exhibit power and strength.

Thwack! Abby splits a pine board with one hand. Slam! Jayne splits a pine board with her forehead. In unison, the trio punch and block, their moves very stylized right up to the finale of balletlike flying side kicks.

They are met with a standing ovation from their audience, girls and women, all ages.

"Quiet, please." Abby tries calming the crowd. "I have an announcement." She brushes damp hair back from her face. "Starting next week, Jayne and I will be teaching an all-female class in self-defense. Those of you who want to join can meet with us in the rear of the gym. Jayne has the sign-up sheet."

The majority leave for the workshops, but, moved by their spirited performance, I stay behind to sign up for the class.

"You were marvelous, Abby." I give her a hug.

"I'm glad you'll be with us," she says with a smile.

* * *

Every workshop is tempting, but I choose the one titled "Women and Psychology." As the only one in my c-r group who is actually in psychoanalysis, I'm beginning to feel that I'm less of a feminist because Freud and all followers of his ideas come up for a perpetual onslaught by feminist theorists, and Abby herself has stopped seeing her analyst. "I can devote time to feminism or analysis. Doing both divides my energy," she explained to me when she quit. I try to do both, but with tremendous self-doubt. Perhaps there will be someone in the workshop with whom I can share my conflict.

"Present psychology will *never* liberate women," says our group leader, "so seeing a psychiatrist, especially a male, is the most damaging thing a woman can do to herself."

I scan the faces to see if I sense some dissent, but everyone seems to agree with what's just been said.

"My doctor makes me feel guilty that I can't find 'fulfillment' in my husband and children," volunteers one woman.

"Mine too," says another.

"Doesn't it make you feel as though something must be wrong with *you* to want more out of life?" asks the first woman of the second.

"Yes!" Her answer is emphatic.

I force myself to stay quiet and listen. It's not for me to defend sexist psychologists. They must answer for themselves the well-founded criticism of feminist theorists.

By the workshop's end, it's clear that all of the women have had bad experiences with doctors who encouraged them to conform to society's norm rather than seek their own definition.

"If we have each other," says one woman, "who needs the psychiatrists?"

"But women's liberation isn't therapy," I finally say.

"And therapy isn't necessarily liberating," she answers spunkily. "By sticking together in our consciousness-raising groups, at least we know we're not crazy."

"Consciousness-raising?" says the woman beside me, "If my consciousness is raised any higher, I'll disappear into thin air. Where do I sign up for consciousness-lowering?"

The workshop ends in good-natured laughter, but I am keenly

aware that dedicating myself to both feminism and Freudian psychoanalysis appears to be paradoxical.

"I hope Abby's teaching tonight," I overhear someone say in the dressing room.

"Me too," says another. "It's not that I don't like Jayne, but she runs the class like a drill sergeant and I feel like I've joined the army."

It's true. Jayne sets a pace and then expects us to keep to it. Abby seems to have more feeling for a pace we beginners can manage, and then she takes us through it.

The night is muggy and warm, and I cannot imagine that I'll survive the next two hours. Barefoot, we go out to the long, narrow classroom. No one is allowed to walk with shoes on the highly varnished wood floor. Upon entering our classroom, we bow to the Korean flag, a gesture some had protested, but we voted to honor the tradition of the Korean teacher whose *dojo* we use.

Abby comes to the front of the class, and we bow to her. In this formal manner, our class time begins. We line up in six rows of four, all in white uniforms and white belts—except for Dana, whose belt is gold, and Abby and Jayne, whose belts are green. Jayne and Dana take the first and second positions in the front row. That way, the rest of the class gets to watch not only our teacher but the very best students, whose positions mirror our own, whereas our teacher's are the opposite.

The warm-up, regardless of how humid the weather, is always done at a brisk pace. Leg raises, knee bends, stretches, and push-ups. For me, the push-ups are especially hard because we do *ten* on our knuckles!

We practice making fists. "You're going to have to cut your fingernails," says Abby to one student. "You'll hurt yourself otherwise." At least that's one problem I won't have!

"Square off your knuckles." Abby holds her fist next to mine. "Watch the angle of your thumb. You've got to protect it."

Abby directs us in the forms, and were it not for the kicks and the punches, it would almost appear to be ballet. There is no sparring for beginners, and for that I am grateful.

"Riding-horse stance," Abby says, and we all get into position and hold it while she comes around to check on our form. "Look at Dana. Do your feet line up the way hers do?" My turn comes and I do my best. "Look at Lou," she says. "Is your back as straight as hers?" The compliment thrills me, but I keep my manner as serious as Abby's.

Then we break for the bricks which are piled up in the back of the studio. Rope-bound, some are bloodied from previous users. Down on our hands and knees, a brick in front of each of us, we practice pounding our fists to the count of ten. The goal is the building of calluses, one I'm not sure I aspire to, so I punch lightly.

"I wish they weren't all so young," whispers a woman my age.

"I know what you mean," I gasp. "I feel faint."

"Me too."

"No talking in class," Abby says sternly.

When we are finally back in the dressing room, with me having made it through one more class, I look at the woman who spoke to me and she really does look faint.

"Wait here," I tell her, "I'll get you some water."

When I return to the dressing room, there's a commotion. "What's going on?" I ask Betsy, who's holding a magazine. "Look at this." She shows me an article in the current *New York* magazine.

Next to the article is a grotesquely caricatured Wonder Woman holding a man up in the air.

"This is how that sneaky reporter wrote up our conference," Betsy says angrily. "Listen to this description of Dana, Abby, and Jayne: 'a perfect chorus line except for their prison matron eyes, gritted teeth, clenched fists and war cries.' " The class groans, and Betsy reads on: " 'Witness the Liberated Woman: Her feet are swords. Her body is a weapon (it has to be; she is a revolutionary). She doesn't need to use her sex to get what she wants from men. She knows karate.' "

"But she wasn't supposed to write up what went on." I recall when we voted to let the reporter stay.

"That's what we asked," Abby says, with her usual acumen, "but if you recall, she never did promise."

"It's a hatchet job, that's all," says Betsy. "We should have known better than to let the press in."

"But she's a woman," I say.

"And we've just learned that all women are not to be trusted," says the woman to whom I brought the water.

We continue our classes undaunted, and one thing's for sure—Abby was right about tae kwon do changing my outlook on life. I feel a new sense of physical confidence beginning to surface. I am growing proud of my stamina. Developing it will be very hard work, but I want to do it.

Chapter Forty-two

"Boys are taught from childhood to be aggressive. When they grow up and become antisocial, they get sent to jail. Women," I announce authoritatively to Dr. Mueller, "are conditioned to be passive. When we're antisocial, we get sent to mental hospitals."

"But men go there too."

"Not nearly as often. Check the statistics. When men get sent to mental hospitals, they're either abnormally passive or criminally insane. Did you know that?"

"I can't say I ever gave it much thought."

"Well, I have, and I've learned that more than half of all mental patients in America are female, most of whom, one way or another, have rejected society's roles." I cross my arms on my chest and defiantly wait for him to refute me.

"Do you have someone in mind?"

Prepared as I'd been to argue in the abstract about society's treatment of women, Dr. Mueller's unanticipated question catches me unawares, and I have to think before I can answer.

"My mother, I guess." My tone is conciliatory. "The main complaint Tilly and Nana ever made about her was that she did not do her housework. When she came to my aunt's for home visits, my mother would spend the day cleaning as proof she was well. The index for my mother's sanity seemed to have been her neat appearance and her willingness to clean my aunt's house." I can feel myself seething with an anger I know has nothing to do with poor Dr. Mueller.

"Yes?" He urges me on.

"Think about it yourself, Dr. Mueller. After fourteen years of being locked up, my mother was finally set free because she was willing to work in a kitchen!"

"How does that make you feel?"

"It was a high price to pay," I answer bitterly, "for 'mental health.' "

He sighs and makes no comment to what I've just said, so we both share a time of silence.

"Have you ever heard of Naomi Weisstein?" I ask.

When he says he hasn't, I explain that she's a psychologist who presented a paper to the American Studies Association titled "Kinder, Kuche, Kirche as Scientific Law: Psychology Constructs the Female." Her paper is brilliant and brief and has been reprinted as a pamphlet which is circulating by the thousands in feminist circles all over the country. Her empirical data demonstrate that the ideas psychologists have about female "nature" coincide with society's prejudices. I read her conclusions to Dr. Mueller: " 'Until social expectations for men and women are equal, until we provide equal respect for both men and women, our answers to the question of what true liberation will mean will simply reflect our prejudices.' "

Dr. Mueller makes no response to my attempt to enlighten him. I interpret his silence as a defense of his profession.

"Women are called 'castrating bitches,' but, whenever men *are* castrated, it's other men who actually do it. Women are called 'ball busters' and 'man-eaters,' but it's men who rape little girls and women." I egg him on. "It's *men* who can't imagine being alive without a penis, so they foist their fantasies on us and say our 'ambition' is merely to get one."

I'm incited to fury by his failure to argue with me, but I'm not so angry that I do not notice that he does not deny my accusations. Talked out for the moment, I remain on the couch in tense, angry silence.

"Mrs. Shields," he asks calmly, after a while, "do you think I see you as a second-class citizen?"

"No . . ."

"Have I ever said or done anything to indicate that I want you to be one?"

"You've always been very fair." As quickly as the rage boiled up, it dies down. "I don't know why I get so angry with you," I say apologetically.

"I will not be destroyed by your anger." He pauses. "Nor will you."

"Are you really so sure?"

"As long as you keep bringing your feelings here to analysis, I *am* very sure."

"That's part of the problem."

"What is?"

"Bringing the anger here. Abby stopped her analysis because she feels her anger is justified. She is channeling it into fighting social injustice toward women. That way, she uses her anger politically."

"And how do *you* feel?"

"Me?" I hesitate. "I'm afraid of my rage. I feel too angry and I don't have a clear target. Anger simmers inside me day in and day out. I see injustice everywhere. I can't seem to have fun anymore, and the simplest things send me into a frenzy."

"Such as?"

"Having dinner served by a woman when I'm out at a party. The men sit around, the women help the hostess, and I usually shoot off my mouth and ruin the party." I try to think of other examples. "Oh, the children. Christopher comes home from school and tells me that the teacher asked how many boys wanted to grow up to be doctors. Chris raised his hand to say that girls could be doctors too, and the class laughed at him. And me—I can't even cook anymore!"

"What? He does sound surprised.

"In all this time I've been seeing Zygmunt, it just so happens we always eat out or bring in deli or Chinese. Saturday night he didn't have to work, so I decided to make dinner for Zygmunt, Abby, and my brother, Frank. Not only were the onions charred, but I ruined the sauce, one I've made so often I could do it blindfolded. The rice not only burned at the bottom but the burned flavor went all the way through, so none of it was salvageable. We made do with chicken and an extra-large salad. Abby and Frank said it was an off night. Zygmunt, of course, had no basis for comparison, and my brother knew there was a problem when he ate the mousse."

"What was so special about that?"

"Frank knows how I adore chocolate, and my mousse is fool-proof. Well, Saturday night it contained globules of egg white, and if that wasn't enough, I ended the evening with a big fight with my brother *and* Zygmunt."

"A fight over what?"

"The dishes. I asked them to wash them and they complained bitterly. They said they might have 'offered,' but when I 'commanded' them, I *forced* them to rebel. Abby and I joined together in a lecture about how many women through the ages were unsung cooks and dishwashers. My brother and Zygmunt sided with each other, and all I can say is it will be a long time before I cook anything but the simplest food for the kids. Zygmunt and I will continue to eat out."

"What do you make of not being able to cook anymore?"

"It's an obvious way to cast off an old role, but the trouble is I don't have a new one. Women's liberation causes me to challenge everything and leaves me with no place to hide. I have no more guidelines. I feel a new space. I want to walk into it. Not run away. Running away *really* would make me crazy."

"I'm not sure I see."

"The male view of females is pornographic. The choices are limited, and I refuse to play either whore or madonna, the mistress or the wife. I am Everywoman. I know that sounds crazy . . ."

"It doesn't."

"My mother cracked up over those choices. I see that now. She is damaged."

"And you?"

"Damaged too. I'm a victim. A new definition of me will have to include a new definition of all womankind."

"Are you telling me that you cannot change until society does?"

"Perhaps."

"Then you cannot be free"—Dr. Mueller enunciates every word carefully—"until all women are free, and for that you will have to wait until hell freezes over."

"You mean that I should be able to do my changing here?" I ask him, astonished.

"Why not?"

"You're a man."

"*One* man. Your pictures of male oppression are infinite."

"And for every dirty picture, there's a piece of self-loathing in me. The loathing some men have for women makes me loathe myself. Why can't you see that?"

"Because, here in analysis, I'm just a frame, a background on which you can project."

"Bullshit! You're a man like the rest of them. What makes you so sure you're not hung up with society's prejudices?"

"I've been analyzed."

"By a man?"

"Yes."

"Big deal."

"You're not being fair."

"Can you honestly tell me you spent a big part of your own analysis analyzing your unconscious sexism?"

"No . . ." He hesitates.

"And did your own analyst even give a damn?"

"It was never an issue."

"Aha!"

"What do you want from me?"

"I want you to concede that you and I are *both* shaped by forces far larger than we can ever fully comprehend or even begin to analyze here."

"And?"

"If we do, we can at least know what to challenge. How else will I know what to change? And in your practice there will be other women with similar problems. I'm sure of it. Do you see what I mean?"

"I'm trying." His voice falters.

"I'd like you to keep your mind open, suspend all your judgments, and yet hold some expectations for me that I can't yet hold for myself."

"You mean you're like Tinker Bell?"

"For Tinker Bell to become visible, someone had to believe she existed. I want you to be that one. I *do* want to trust you, and I will if I can be sure you are searching your own soul for traces of sexism."

"That's a tall order to fill."

"Not when you look at the damage some men have done to the women they allegedly love. Their wives, their mothers, their sisters, their daughters." I feel tears roll down my cheeks.

"Their patients," Dr. Mueller says softly.

I feel myself growing light-headed. "I will offer you no more resistance. I don't have the strength. I can't trust all women— only some. I have to either give up and die or learn to trust one human being totally." I begin to feel dizzy. "I'm not sure I'm going to be able to stand up at the end of the hour," I tell Dr. Mueller.

"There will be no hurry."

"I'm asking you questions beyond my own reach, perhaps beyond anybody's. I believe they're worth asking. The only relief I expect is to know whether or not I am crazy." More tears fill my eyes.

"You're not crazy, Mrs. Shields." Dr. Mueller speaks the words with kindness and sends forward his box of tissues.

"The way people see me has always affected how I see myself. All I want to do now is to be able to see myself as I am. I want to be able to jump off from this place my own mother has brought me to. I want to live out some part of her unfulfilled dreams. I have DeeDee, Abby, my brother, my 'sisters.' And, of course, I have you. You don't have to work *everything* out, you know. If you say you have, I'll believe you, but if you tell me some things are too tough to do here, that's okay too. Just as long as I know where we stand."

I turn around on the couch and get up for what I know must be the end of the hour. "You said that I may have to wait until hell freezes over."

He nods.

"What if you're right?"

Chapter Forty-three

"It's Zygmunt's idea, not mine," I tell Dr. Mueller defensively.

"But can you afford it?"

"Just barely. I've been on a strict budget since Mike and I split, and my bills are all current, but it's my tax return that's the sudden windfall."

"How much is it?"

"Three hundred and fifty dollars. It's more than I usually get back, because of my change-over to divorced status."

"Do you have any idea what the fare is?"

"The travel agency across the street from the store trades discounts with us, and they've found me a rock-bottom fare from Boston to Paris on a scheduled flight for two hundred and fifty dollars."

"That won't leave much to spend."

"I have two weeks' paid vacation coming to me from the store. Zygmunt says I won't need more than that. If I decide to do it, he'll take his family's Volkswagen and drive from Frankfurt to Paris to meet me. He'll bring his tent. He's done lots of camping. He says it's cheap and it's fun. Besides, he's been saving all winter, so he'll have money too."

"Well, it seems as though you've worked everything out." Dr. Mueller speaks hesitantly. "Can you tell me why you are so apprehensive?"

"Zygmunt hasn't been home for three years. He's planning a

trip to the Black Forest to be with his mother and father when they have their vacation."

I sense Dr. Mueller waiting for me to go on.

"The best time for him to meet me in Paris," I say, my whole body tensing, "is the week before you go away." That said, I stop talking.

After some time passes, Dr. Mueller speaks. "And you assume that my late departure makes the whole thing impossible."

How is it that he's gone straight to the heart of the matter?

"Doesn't it?" I ask—sure that it does.

"Not necessarily."

"Wouldn't it be odd for the patient to take off before the doctor?"

"Unusual"—I hear him tapping his pipe—"but not out of the question."

"You're kidding."

"I'm not."

"What's involved?" I seem to have developed a lump in my throat.

"We must first analyze the whole situation. If you can do that, you are free to do what you want."

Zygmunt's trip has been planned for a long time. He'll be in Europe for almost three months. I'd never have gathered as much information as I've gathered this far if Zygmunt had not put so much pressure on me. Since I have the time and the money, the trip seems easy and natural—to him.

I was certain that Dr. Mueller would be concerned with what it would mean for me to go away before he did. I never expected him to mistake a mere possibility for a feasible plan. He wasn't supposed to.

Zygmunt wants me to join him. Dr. Mueller's not stopping me.

I'm left with nothing to do but consider this trip as a real possibility. And it seems I must confront my reluctance to travel.

Paris and Florence—I've always wanted to see them.

Other people are able to travel.

Why, then, am I so afraid to leave home?

* * *

The trip to Europe is something I must break to my mother gently, so—arm in arm in the Common—I try to explain to her. "Flying is pretty safe nowadays, Mum, and just think, I'll be able to send you postcards from Paris and Venice, Bologna and Florence. Won't that be exciting?"

Her grim expression gives me not only her answer but a new subject to bring up in my sessions with Dr. Mueller.

"How much of my life is planned around staying close to my mother?" I ask Dr. Mueller when next we meet.

"Hmm," he says in a tone which translates to "How about that?"

"The commitment must have been made in my unconscious."

"The unconscious is where many of us make our deepest commitments," he observes, unsurprised.

"I always wanted my mother and brother to know where I'd be in case they needed me. Perhaps"—my voice drops to a whisper—"even my father."

I hear Dr. Mueller let out a sigh.

Discussing what it means for me to have Dr. Mueller go away becomes easy compared to discussing what it means for me to leave the country.

"Boston and Cambridge are the only two places I really know."

"So then," he says, "you've decided to remain here for your whole life?"

"It's not that." I dismiss his comment. "It's the children. My mother. They need me."

"They can't manage three weeks without you?"

"I'd reached a point of thinking I might be able to leave for two weeks, but when I checked with the agency, I learned that the special fare stipulates three—absolutely.

"I'll be away for Lizzie's fifth birthday. It's the thirteenth, and I have to stay until August fifteenth."

"Can't you bring her something special from Europe? Won't Mike give her a party? I thought you trusted him with the children."

"Of course I do."

"Then it's Jeannie?"

"No. She's offered to do all she can to make it nice for the kids."

"So?"

"So what?" I ask snidely.

"There's not much else left."

"What are you getting at?" His attitude irritates me. I don't quite know why.

"Your real reason for not being able to leave."

"And what's that?" His comment piques my own curiosity.

"You seem to be trying to tell me that you are indispensable."

"Jesus, Dr. Mueller. What are you trying to do anyway? Push me into this trip?"

"I'm trying to 'push' you to analyze the reasons you say you can't go."

"Oh," I grumble, and then confess, "The children are actually excited that their Mummy will see the 'real' Eiffel Tower. But my mother *is* worried, that's for sure."

"Are you aware that there *is* mail from Europe?" he asks sarcastically.

"Okay, okay. I'm afraid! I'm the one!"

"It is frightening to take such a long trip all alone."

"And I'm going to have to lay over in London before going on to Paris to meet up with Zygmunt. I wish I could fly straight through."

"Perhaps making connections is part of why your fare is so low?"

"I think so."

"Well, why don't you try to analyze your own resistance?"

He is definitely pressing, so I try to rally. "If I can make myself take this trip, I'll feel it's a triumph. I'll feel strong being able to be the one who leaves you rather than being the one left behind. The choice is one I want to make, but I've had so little practice."

"You had a difficult childhood."

"And most of the time I stayed where I was while the people I counted on left me behind."

"Including me."

"Including you," I say softly, relieved to be able to say it out loud, not just feel it way down deep inside. "Money. What will we do about money for the week that you're here and I'm gone?"

"Last week you made an excellent point when you said that patients have to work out their vacations around their analysts' time. Your plans are complicated and I know that you tried to coordinate them with mine, so I don't see why you should have to pay for that week. The whole period will be our joint vacation time, and you can resume my fee upon our return."

"God, I feel good. So many things are worked out. It all seems very fair, and I'm about to get to do something I've dreamed of all my life. I don't even feel selfish and rotten."

"Like that 'bad little girl' who always deserves to be punished."

"Not at all."

"That's a big step forward, isn't it?"

"For me, yes it is."

"Caio," DeeDee wires me from the Vineyard, "here's fifty dollars. Spend it all in one place. Bring Firenze my love."

"But, Mary Louise, what if you never come back?"

"What are you worried about?" I ask, concerned for her fear.

"Something *terrible* could happen."

"I'll be all right." I hug my mother. "And I'll bring you back something special. I promise."

"Oh, Sonny," I say when they call my flight to London, "I'm scared."

"So am I," he says tearfully, "it's a big step, but take it—for both of us." Like me, my brother, too, always stays close to home. He kisses me brusquely and pushes me off in the direction of the boarding passengers.

Chapter Forty-four

"I'm so pleased you like it." Zygmunt reaches into the bucket of ice for what will be my first glass of French wine on French soil. "Welcome to Paris, darling Lou," he says as we toast with crystal he carefully carried from home.

What I had imagined would be a pup tent turns out to be a tent large enough to stand up in. A "bedroom," screened off with mosquito netting, is equipped with a double air mattress. The "living room/kitchen" has a table, two chairs, and some cooking gear. An orange awning, staked about five feet away from the tent, extends the living space and offers protection from rain and shade from the sun.

"Germans are very big on camping," Zygmunt says proudly, "so we make very comfortable tents."

"I've never seen anything like it," I say in genuine admiration.

"Location is very important when camping, so I arrived early in Paris, as the campgrounds were emptying. I drove to several, but this one was best."

Zygmunt has pitched the tent in a secluded spot under a tree next to the Seine. No one else is nearby.

"What can I say?"

"That you missed me. Did you?" Before I can answer, he says, "It's been a month, and I must confess"—I see he is blushing—"that on my long drive from Germany, never have I been so excited. 'Lou is coming,' I sang to myself, 'soon she will be here.'

My heart is so full of joy," he says tenderly. He holds out his arms for me to come into them, and we abandon our wine for an even simpler pleasure.

Through the screened window in our sleeping space, an afternoon breeze from the river cools the whole tent. I fall asleep happy.

Paris is all I expected and more. Montmartre, on Saturday night, brings tears to my eyes. We mill in the streets with the people, and we stop in sidewalk cafés. I am reminded of Boston's North End and New York's Greenwich Village, and I come to see that what I love best in America is European in origin.

Day trips to Chartres and Versailles exhaust me emotionally, and I am left with the feeling that I've slipped into paradise.

"Do we have to go?" Even I hear the whine in my voice.

"There's so much more." Zygmunt pulls up the stakes. "And you are the one who so desperately wants to see Italy. How can we get there if we never leave Paris?"

As we travel through France, I perceive a new Zygmunt. He reads maps well and easily and is an excellent driver. Nothing fazes him, and when the French mistake him for American, their error pleases him. He negotiates our needs in either French, German, or English, whichever is called for. What I'd mistaken for an innately shy personality back home turns out to have been Zygmunt's reaction to being an immigrant in a strange land. I make this observation now because I, with my poor high-school French, have undergone something of a personality transformation myself. No longer outgoing, I shyly let Zygmunt order with waiters. I let him ask for directions and prices. I follow his lead, and the role reversal is edifying.

On our approach to Marseilles, we ferry through the yellow marsh grass of the Camargue, and I feel like a wanderer inside a canvas done by Van Gogh. I'd always thought he dreamed up those colors; it had never occurred to me that what he painted was real.

Our last day in France is spent on the Riviera in an uncrowded campsite high in the hills overlooking Cap Ferrat.

"That's where Garbo lives," says a fellow tourist, pointing out a villa on a peninsula not far from our beach.

"We could almost swim to it." I marvel at being so close to a legend. "Do you suppose she'd serve us tea?"

Zygmunt fastens my goggles, and instead of swimming to Garbo's, he teaches me snorkeling in the gorgeous blue water of the Mediterranean. An experienced scuba diver, he's also a patient teacher, and once I get the hang of it I enjoy myself very much.

"From here, you will act as our guide," Zygmunt announces in San Remo as we cross the border into Italy. Zygmunt was in Italy only once, as a boy; he hasn't been back since, and his Italian is minimal, but we are both aware that Italians are more forgiving of foreigners.

"Before seeing what Michelangelo carved out of stone, I'd like to see where he quarried."

"A fine idea," Zygmunt says, but the burden of the long drive falls on him. We arrive in Carrara too late to check into a campsite and too weary to do anything but roll out our sleeping bags and sleep on the beach until sunrise.

Once we recover from that miscalculation, our trip through the treasures of Italy is well paced and goes smoothly. In Florence, thanks to DeeDee's generous gift, I'm able to treat Zygmunt to a fine dinner and a bed in a hotel. In the morning, we both send her a card: "Firenze says 'Ciao' and we both say 'Grazie.' "

"Madam," says the clerk in the Alitalia office in Venice, "we have no flights to Paris."

"But we called from Bologna and we were told that there were several."

"Ah, yes, but they have all been reserved."

"But we can't be this close to Venice and not see it," I'd begged Zygmunt just a few days ago. "This is no time to take risks," Zygmunt warned me, "when there are so many vacationers." "Oh, Zygmunt," I'd pleaded, "you've never seen Venice either. Please say we can do it. I have lots of money left over. I'm happy to spend it on the air fare to Paris."

Now, in the Alitalia office, I cannot fully comprehend that the question is not one of money.

"There must be some way," I plead. The clerk seems friendly and competent, and she speaks perfect English.

"Maybe tomorrow. Let me see your ticket to Boston."

I hand it to her in its folder. She scans it, does not look happy, and then leaves our part of the counter to make a few phone calls. She speaks in rapid Italian.

She returns with my ticket in hand and shows both Zygmunt and me the print across my connecting flights: ABSOLUTELY NO CHANGES. "I cannot help you," she says, "it's out of my hands. There is no way Alitalia can have you in Paris by eight-thirty tomorrow morning."

I read the ticket myself. The print is quite clear. August 15: ABSOLUTELY NO CHANGES.

"Could she fly direct to London?" Zygmunt's face lights up with this new idea.

"Perhaps." The clerk brightens too. More phone calls in Italian, during which Zygmunt whispers, "Whatever it costs, I'll loan you the money."

When she returns to us at the counter, we can tell by her expression that no flights are available. "I *am* sorry."

"What will it mean if I'm not on my plane tomorrow?"

"It is not good. You will forfeit your ticket and have to buy a one-way fare back to Boston." Shaking her head, she says, "Very expensive. Almost the price of your whole excursion. You had a very low price."

It's true. Back in Cambridge no one could believe how good a price it was.

"It is understandable that they cannot allow changes," she says sympathetically.

How did I let myself get into this situation? Every time Zygmunt urged me to be realistic about the trip's end, I talked him down. I sounded as though I knew what I was talking about. I never showed him my ticket.

Why did I do it?

The magic. I wanted it never to end.

"What would you do in this situation?" I hear Zygmunt ask the clerk from my dreamlike trance.

"I'd rent a car—" she begins.

"I have one," Zygmunt interrupts.

"Good. Where is it?"

"Mestre."

"Excellent."

I've lost track. I feel my heart pounding rapidly. It's in their hands now. After all, I'm the one who refused to even look at the map to see the long distance between Venice and Paris.

"Take the Vaporetto. It will get you there fast." She looks at her watch. "If you leave now, you can make it to Milan in time for the *Orient Express* to Gare de Lyon. The Signora"—the clerk smiles sweetly at me—"can taxi to Orly and catch her plane to London."

"Bravo!" exclaims Zygmunt, reaching over the counter to give her a hug. "You have solved the problem! Thank you so much. Come, Lou, there is no time to lose."

"Thank you." I smile gratefully but I know any minute I'm going to burst into tears.

"Good luck," she says. "I think you will make it."

"But, Lou, why are you crying?" Zygmunt asks when we're outside in the piazza. "You'll make it. I know I can get you to Milan."

"I don't want you to leave me. Please drive me to Paris."

"I can't do it in time, and," he says gently, "when there's a train, it doesn't make sense."

"Doesn't make sense?" I shriek. "Doesn't make sense?" I cover my face with my hands so people won't see the tears. "I *can't* do it, Zygmunt," I cry, "and that's what you don't understand."

"Why, Lou." Zygmunt's face, for the first time, registers shock. "I had no idea you were so frightened of travel."

"I've been all right up to now because we've been together. How will I manage the train? Change lire to francs? Find the taxi? Get to the airport? I'm scared, Zygmunt," I sob. "I *know* I can't make it home all alone."

"For now," he says in his calmest voice, "let us go to the

Vaporetto. I will see you safely to Paris." He takes my arm. "I will not abandon you."

Abandonment.

Can that be why I'm in a cold sweat?

I'm in over my head, but it doesn't really make sense. It was always our plan that Zygmunt would go back to Germany to return the car to his parents, and although we never pinpointed my exact place of departure, I always knew I would have to continue alone.

The separation. I feel it only now. I had not been able to foresee how I would feel. That must be why I'm reacting like a child being abandoned.

The ride to Milan is a hair-raiser. As much as I don't want Zygmunt to put me on the train, even I have to face that he could not keep up the pace the whole way to Paris.

Zygmunt, usually so precise about everything, parks the car in the middle of traffic outside the train station. He grabs my suitcase in one hand and pulls me along with the other. In broken Italian, he orders my ticket. I hand him my wallet to pick out the lire. A whistle blows. The seller gestures frantically toward the gate. Zygmunt gets to the train first, hands my bag to the conductor, and says, "May I board her?" "Vite, vite," says the conductor.

Zygmunt hurries me into the first empty couchette we come to. "Tip the night porter. That way, you can sleep through the last border and he'll call you before Paris."

The train starts to move.

"You'll make it, my darling, you will." He kisses me quickly and then nimbly jumps from the train.

I wave from my window even after I don't see him.

The train picks up speed, and for the first time I let myself look around. The little private compartment I'd seen only in movies; it's really quite nice. And, after all, the *Orient Express* has to be one of the world's most glamorous trains. This is an adventure. I'm safe. I'm all right.

My sense of release from the terror began when Zygmunt used

the word "abandon." It was perceptive of him to observe that my tears were those of a child scared of being abandoned rather than the tears of a grown-up frustrated by a change in travel arrangements. During my hysteria, reason played little part in my feelings. I felt pushed out. On my own. Not enough preparation. Before I was ready. Those feelings go back to childhood. I take out my journal and begin thinking things through. The process is tranquilizing. This ordeal has taught me one thing for sure: comings and goings are traumatic for me, regardless of who comes or goes.

Outside my window, the blanketing fog lends the distinctive rooftops of the Domodossola a surrealistic beauty. My passport is checked at the Swiss border, where I miraculously manage a conversation in French.

As Zygmunt has instructed me, I tip the night porter generously when he comes in to make up my bed. He makes up the one although there are three others.

He smiles broadly. "Madame, the compartment will be yours for the night. I shall see that you are called a half hour before Paris," he says, closing the door and drawing the curtain. "Sleep well, Madame."

Soon the clickety-clack of train wheels on track lulls me to sleep.

Chapter Forty-five

"Do you have room for me?" Lizzie asks.

"In my bed?"

"In your heart," she snuffles. Her head is stuffed up from the flu. She's home from school sick on Valentine's Day and she's miserable.

I wrap her in her favorite blanket—"my fuzzy," she calls it. I pick her up in my arms.

"Wait." She snatches her stuffed lion and sketch pad. "I want these too." She reaches down to grab up her Magic Markers.

I stagger into my bedroom and we flop down on my bed.

"Dearest girl." I cradle her in my arms. "Forever and for always, there's a place for you in my heart."

She perks up and smiles for the first time all morning. "Am I too big to snuggle?"

"Nobody ever is."

We lie together, and she nestles close to my bosom.

"My bottles." She touches my breasts.

"Not anymore."

"I'm too big for nursing?"

"I'm afraid that you are. Besides, the milk goes away when the baby grows up."

"Too big to nurse but not too big to snuggle?"

"That's right." We cuddle together, her head on my breast.

It's been so long since we've had such a quiet morning alone, just the two of us.

"Oh, Lizzie." I stroke her feverish brow. "I know I'm away a lot what with work and my meetings, but that doesn't mean I don't have room for you." In my obsession with all womankind, am I forgetting the littlest? The one I love best? "Women's liberation is so the world will be better when it's your time to grow up."

"Mum. About women's liberation."

"Yes?"

"Can *you* do it for me? I'll see how you do it, *then* I'll decide if I want to or not."

"Fair enough." I laugh. "I'm trying my best, but for you I'll try harder." I give her some medicine.

What I want is for neither Elizabeth nor Christopher to have to recapitulate my life's mistakes. I'd like to bring them along so they start one rung higher than I did. But so many of my days feel like backsliding. How can I, as a mother, give my kids a fresh start?

I kiss my sleeping daughter's forehead and tiptoe out of the room.

"It's bitter cold," my mother says in the hall. "Feels like snow," she says on her way up the stairs. "Hmm," she says at the top, "what's that wonderful smell?"

"Guess." I help her off with her coat.

"Not apple pie?"

"That's just what it is."

After lunch, while Lizzie still sleeps, my mother and I sit in the living room drinking coffee and eating pie.

Next to the window, my mother is suffused with winter light. How can it be that after so many years sealed up alive in untended back wards she still remains such an exquisite beauty? I gaze at her in awe.

Her hair, lightly tinted with Roux, looks the way it has ever since I can remember. Nurse May sells my mother products from Avon: enough lipstick to make her smile rosy and tints of mauve and sky-blue for her eyelids. In her steady hand, cosmetics merely enhance my mother's natural loveliness.

"I'm an old lady now, Mary Louise. I won't last forever."

"Don't say that, Mum. You're still so beautiful." And because it is true, I add, "No one can believe you're sixty-six."

"Sixty-seven pretty soon."

"That's right. All the more reason for you to be proud of yourself."

No, neither her face nor her figure reflects her long years of suffering.

Her eyes.

They say it all.

"Look at Nana." I try cheering my mother up. "She lived to be eighty-six."

"She was stronger than I was."

My mother sounds serious.

"I don't have much time left, Mary Louise."

Except for her bout with pneumonia, my mother's hardly been physically sick in her life. And she does look well.

Nana, although she always complained, was rarely ever what you'd really call sick.

This is a bad time of year, winter's end, and so many of my friends have the flu, just as Lizzie does.

I calculate odds. It must be the weather.

"Don't you think we'll all feel better when spring comes around?" I say optimistically.

"You're probably right, dear." She sighs. "We'll all feel better when the weather changes." She puts out her cigarette. "Let's have some more of that pie, then I better be getting on back to the nursing home before it piles up." I follow her eyes to the snow out the window.

"I'll walk you down to the bus."

"No, dear. You stay here with your sweet baby daughter." She tiptoes into my bedroom to kiss the still-sleeping Lizzie.

From downstairs, I hear footsteps. It's Chris, home from school.

"Hi, Grandmummy. Leaving already?"

"I don't want to get stranded."

Chris takes off his Mighty Mac. "Boy, I hope there's going to be enough so I can go snow shoveling."

"Chris, I'm going to walk Grandmummy. You stay here with Lizzie, okay? There's some pie out in the kitchen. Why don't you go have some?"

"Yum," he says, hugging my mother good-bye.

My mother and I walk the short block to the bus. The snow swirls around us, but the day is nowhere near as chilly as it had been when it started out.

"Look after the children," my mother says, boarding the bus.

"Take care of yourself." The commonplace farewell suddenly takes on specific meaning. "I mean, I hope you feel better." I blow her a kiss as the bus door closes between us.

The bus pulls away.

I watch it even after it's out of sight.

Back home, I call Mike and tell him Lizzie is too sick to travel and Christopher wants to go shoveling. Mike says he'll stop by to read Lizzie a story.

"Saratoga Nursing Home," the night nurse answers.

"Mary Frazier, please."

"She's downstairs. Give me a few minutes to get her."

She made it back safely. I sigh with relief.

"Hello."

"Mum, it's me. I just wanted to make sure you got back all right."

"No trouble at all. There were more trains than usual."

"That's good. I'm glad. How do you feel?"

"Just tired, dear. I'm on my way to bed now. I don't think I'll even watch any TV."

Fatigue. Winter weather. It's getting all of us down. That's what it is. I feel it myself.

"You take care of Lizzie," says my mother, "I want to see her all better next week."

"You take care, too."

"Goodnight dear. Thank you for calling."

"Goodnight, Mum. I love you."

Chapter Forty-six

"It's for you," Billy says, calling me to the phone at the store. "It's a Mrs. Peretsky."

What can she want? I wonder. I saw my mother just a few days ago.

He hands me the phone.

"Mrs. Shields, your mother is dead," she says abruptly. "You better get over here and let me know what to do with the body."

Click.

She never gave me a chance to say a word.

I run down to the basement.

"Oh, Mike," I wail, "it's my mother. She's dead!"

Mike drops what he's doing. He leads me to the back room. "How did it happen?"

"I don't know. Mrs. Peretsky just called. She sounded angry . . . as though I'm at fault. I need a few minutes to think." I sit down on a stool. I feel myself trembling. "She knew it."

"Knew what?"

"That she was dying." I clasp my hand to my mouth.

"Are you okay, Lou?" Billy peeks in on us.

Mike speaks for me. "She just got word that her mother died. Is it all right upstairs? She can't come back up."

"I'll manage. Don't worry."

And Billy is gone.

* * *

"I don't know what came over me," Mrs. Peretsky explains when I pull myself together enough to call her back. "Patients die on me all the time. It goes with the job. It's a big part of the responsibility—death. I called you the minute it happened. I think I was in shock. It was different with Mary."

"And you were angry with me."

"What makes you say that?"

"Your tone. My guilt. I think we both thought she should not have been alone at the end."

Mrs. Peretsky pauses, says nothing, and then, over the phone, I hear her sigh. "Mary had just finished lunch cleanup," she begins. "She went down to her room for her break, like she usually does. May had some cosmetics for Mary, so she went down to deliver them. Mary was there on the floor, a cigarette burning beside her. It happened that fast."

I cover the receiver to muffle the sounds of my crying.

"She was probably dead before she hit the floor. Sometimes it happens that way," says Mrs. Peretsky. "It's merciful, really, when you think about all that the poor woman suffered."

I've never been to a crematorium before.

"Mr. Huggins?" I ask the man who greets me at the door.

He looks vaguely the way I'd remembered from childhood except his hair has gone gray.

"Mrs. Shields?"

"Yes."

I guess he must not be expecting anyone else.

"I've come for my mother's ashes." The ordinary words convey neither the bizarre nature of my request nor the strange way I feel.

"Come in." He throws the oak door open and steps aside.

"No, thanks. I'd rather stay out here—if you don't mind."

"Certainly."

He bows and disappears.

FOREST HILLS CREMATORIUM, reads the bronze plaque by the door.

In East Boston, right now, at the small chapel my mother attended, they are having a memorial service for the patients and staff.

Today would have been her sixty-seventh birthday, I think as I wait. At least the day is beautiful, I try to console myself.

Mr. Huggins returns carrying a brown cardboard box, not very large, more square than rectangular, taller than wide, and tied up with a string. The tag looks like the kind the shoemaker gives. MARY FRAZIER, it reads.

I am stunned.

Can this be all there is?

At Plum Island, I lead my brother and Zygmunt to the spot where, so often, Abby and I put in the canoe. The place is deserted, the day cold but not bitter.

I divide the bouquets three ways.

Tea roses. Her favorite.

I untie the box and, from the water's edge, tip it toward the outgoing tide. The ashes are chalky and easily visible in the clear water as some sink to the bottom.

Ashes.

I thought they would be gray, but they're unexpectedly white.

Release her from pain, I think to myself as I scatter the last of her ashes.

Frank, Zygmunt, and I take turns tossing roses, one by one, to the outgoing tide. Without having planned it, we all wordlessly stand by the water until the last rose is carried way out of sight.

"But why didn't you put Grandmummy into the ground?" asks a bewildered Christopher.

I considered taking the children along to Plum Island, but Frank and I decided against it. We'd never known anyone who buried their dead in this manner. I'd read about it in books, but that's about all. I wasn't sure I'd have the strength to survive it myself.

Mike spent the day with the children, and they spoke of Grandmummy, recalled all the good times they'd had with her. It was the children's memorial.

"It was what Grandmummy wanted," I explain to the confused Christopher. "I like to think that her spirit is free."

He smiles. "I like to think that, too."

"I admired your mother's power of concentration," Mrs. Peretsky says as we sit in my mother's room and go through her belongings.

"No one ever put it that way, at least no one I remember. My mother's 'power,' whatever it was, is to be envied and feared." I gently pick up a Florentine frame of my mother's, one of her favorites, which she'd had many years.

Mrs. Peretsky lovingly touches a pure white linen handkerchief whose edges my mother had crocheted in lavender lace.

"Would you like to have that as a remembrance?"

"Very much." She presses it to her breast. "It's so like Mary. Lovely and delicate. It even smells of her perfume."

There, in the drawer, are the beads I'd so carefully chosen for my mother in Venice. Small glass beads of mauve, hand-painted with tiny pink roses. I hold them up to the light. Their color is changeable. A little like sunset.

"You knew, didn't you," asks Mrs. Peretsky, "that your mother fainted the night you left for Europe?"

"I didn't."

"It was more of a swoon than a faint. It happened when a plane went overhead about the time of your flight. She was so frightened. We gave her smelling salts and put her to bed. We watched her that night. She cheered up when she got your first postcard, but she wasn't really herself until you came home."

"It was hard for me to leave her, too," I murmur. "It was a first."

"Mary was so proud of these." Mrs. Peretsky picks up the beads. " 'My daughter brought them to me from Venice,' she told everyone proudly."

A tear rolls down my cheek.

"She loved those beads—and she loved you and your brother."

"I know . . ." I clear my throat. "And we're both so grateful to you. You gave my mother the only freedom she knew in her lifetime—at least that I know of. We're in your debt for the rest of our lives."

"Don't be foolish. What I mean is, you don't have to feel that way." She looks around the room. "Mary and I sort of opened this place together. She worked hard and well. The only time she ever was sick was that bout with pneumonia. She paid her way, Mary did. She owed no one here anything." Mrs. Peretsky chokes up herself. "I'll leave you now so you can finish alone. Thank you for the handkerchief. I'll cherish it always."

Into a few shopping bags and boxes, I put the things that I want, her papers and letters, the things that I'll cherish. The Venetian glass beads.

Frank had been afraid he'd break down, so he hadn't come with me, but he's meeting me soon, picking me up in his car.

"The rest I think you should offer around," I tell Mrs. Peretsky upstairs. "There are some very nice dresses and some brand-new cosmetics. My mother loathed waste. It would please her to know someone got use from her things."

Nurse May walks Frank and me to the front door. "If your mother had any one fault, it was her generosity. Did you know that the night before Mary died, she treated the whole staff to ice cream?"

"That doesn't surprise me." I smile at Nurse May.

"Her heart was too big, if you ask me, and *that's* what it was done her in." Nurse May presses my brother and me to her bosom. "God bless you both."

Part Four

One would like to think that when the flames freed her spirit, they transmuted all that was mortal of her into her natural elements of fire and air.
—SARA MAYFIELD
about Zelda Fitzgerald in *Exiles from Paradise*

Chapter Forty-seven

It's not that I stop grieving for my mother, but I do come to terms with the loss. It was a blessing that death came to her quickly, I tell myself. It is some consolation to me that she was spared the nightmare of a long-drawn-out hospital death. She died quickly, like Nana. I hope I'm as lucky.

Zygmunt faithfully endured my grief for my mother. Although I mostly see him on the nights the kids are with Mike, Zygmunt recently went out of his way, on a day off, to take Christopher boating with some friends. He is patient with Lizzie and plays little games with her which make her laugh. Both children accept him as Mummy's "good friend."

Zygmunt now shows signs of fatigue and depression, and I'm fairly sure I'm the cause. After my consciousness-raising group Sunday nights, I usually meet Zygmunt at his place or mine, and I harangue him with a ruthlessness I've never known myself to express. I can't understand it and I don't seem to want to control it.

"I can't take any more, Lou," Zygmunt says one hot Sunday night in July. I've just finished telling him that *no* man and woman can have an open, honest relationship. "I'm unable to distinguish what you must do to cleanse yourself and what you do

to me." He gets a beer from the refrigerator and comes to sit
next to me at the table in the kitchen of Mead Street.

Zygmunt has just come from the shop, but the night's muggy
humidity seems not to have affected him. He looks clean and cool
in white cotton trousers and a short-sleeved white shirt, the
whiteness emphasizing his fair hair and complexion. Typesetting,
Zygmunt tells me, is dirty work, but off the job you can't tell it
to look at him. He wears white more often than not, and how he
manages to stay spotless in white is beyond me.

I'm in my blue wraparound dress. I feel tired and cranky and
worn down from the heat of the day.

"You ask me the hardest of human questions." Zygmunt pours
his beer into a glass. "Questions I have neither the intelligence
nor information to answer. If I were ever to ask such things of a
person, I would hope I could have a gentler hand."

I light a cigarette.

I say things to test him, I try to drive him away, but now that
it appears he might actually leave, I feel sick to my stomach.

When we argue, I make Zygmunt accountable for man's injustice to woman. I turn him into a stand-in for all mankind since
the beginning of time. Sometimes I do it unconsciously, but even
when I'm aware that I'm doing it, I don't try to stop myself; I do
it compulsively.

"Many men look at women and see only 'the hole' and good
feelings. I've never looked at a woman that way."

"It's true," I murmur.

"I've tried for you, Lou. I've honestly tried. I've never been
with one woman so long. I've seen how you hurt, and I've loved
you the best that I can."

I cover my face with my hands. I dread what he'll say next.

"Things are getting worse between us," he says quietly, "and
I can try no harder."

"Oh, Zygmunt, don't say that!"

"One moment you ask for my love. The next moment you
scream at me. When you apologize, my brain hears your words. I
believe what you tell me. But my heart tells me otherwise. And
. . . my heart can't make this vital turn."

I go over to him, kneel down on the floor, and put my head in
his lap. He strokes my hair tenderly. "I've told you things from

my past," he continues, "things I'm not proud of . . . ways I hurt other women that I now regret. Then, when we argue and you throw these things in my face, I ask myself why did I bother to tell you?"

"I can't help myself . . ."

"And I can't take any more. I see no sign that you'll change."

There is a certainty that I've never heard before in Zygmunt's tone of voice.

"I don't mean to hurt you. I get crazy sometimes." I look up at him with tears in my eyes. The end feels perilously close.

"I can never forget that night you threw me out. You told me to go away and never come back."

I move back to my chair and try to subdue the anxiety I feel coming on. "I felt helpless that night."

"And I saw a woman whose eyes burned with fire."

"I don't see myself that way . . ."

"But I do—and you frighten me. I can't forget it."

I heave a deep sigh. My own sense of fair play begins to take over. "You shouldn't forget it," I say in a whisper.

Zygmunt looks puzzled.

"You shouldn't forget it, and I don't think you *should* trust me." I suddenly remember that Zygmunt, too, has had his fair share of problems in life. He grew up in Germany during the war. His father was gone for four years, came home a stranger. Zygmunt's mother kept him and his sister alive by fleeing to distant relatives in Poland.

"Zygmunt,"—I now reach for his hand—"when that anger comes over me, that blinding rage, it comes from deep inside me . . . has little, if anything, to do with you. You must decide what *you* have to do to save your own self. I can't help you do that."

Zygmunt makes no reply.

"You say you don't think I will change, but what neither one of us really can see is that I am *already* in some kind of transition. All these years of analysis soon to come to an end. My women's group. The women's movement. All these things add up to inner turmoil and change. You've got to believe me that what goes on between us is as hard on me as it is on you. Do you believe it?"

He nods.

"We've tried to exist on some new kind of plane that's not

just tired old male/female roles. We've tried, you and I, and maybe we fight all the time, but we've always been honest."

"Maybe lies would be easier." For the first time all night, Zygmunt smiles.

"I don't mean to threaten you. I'm seeking out my best interests, and it only just now has occurred to me—they may not be yours."

Our eyes meet, he nods again, and I can tell that this new revelation makes sense to him.

"I am in transit, Zygmunt, but from where to where, I can't tell you because I don't know myself."

We embrace and stop talking.

"How are you feeling today?" asks Dr. Mueller.

It's our last session before his month of vacation.

"A little shaky," I confess.

"It's the first time I won't be around since your mother died. Are you sure you can handle it?"

I sigh and stare up at the ceiling. "It would be a lie if I said I wasn't scared. I am. I wish Zygmunt and I weren't having such a rough time." I raise my voice because, outside his open window, a power mower cuts grass. "Don't close it," I say, "the breeze feels too good. I'll just talk louder, okay?"

"Fine with me," he replies. "Now what were you saying about Zygmunt and you?"

"When I fight with him, I feel self-righteous, but when we're through I feel ashamed of myself. Zygmunt claims I blame him for every injustice done to women."

"Uhmm?"

"He's right. I admit it. I think that what's at the bottom of all of it is I don't really love him and I think he loves me . . . or thinks he does. I'm deeply fond of him and very grateful that he stood by me when my mother died." I pause.

"And?"

"Gratitude isn't love, and perhaps I even use his strong feelings as leverage against him. I use him as a scapegoat . . . almost to punish him for being fond of me. Isn't that odd?"

"Perhaps it's you who has trouble liking yourself?" Dr. Mueller pauses, and I take a new tack.

"I've thought of something that may even be more important than that." I hesitate, then continue. "You agree that for some time now, you and I have devoted our sessions to discussions about how we shall terminate the analysis?"

"Yes," he replies, "I'd say that's true."

"Well, while you and I discuss termination here in your office, back home I seem to be trying to drive Zygmunt away."

"Do you know why?"

"Not yet—but I do know it has something to do with wanting to be independent of men."

"Am I missing something?" he asks. "I don't follow your logic."

"I never had a boyfriend until I was in college. I got three consecutive D's on some essays in freshman English, and after that I started going steady with Wally."

"Now you really have lost me."

"At what point?"

"The connection."

"Between the D's and the boyfriend?"

He doesn't answer.

"Men—the prospect of some man to marry—the idea suddenly had some appeal. Until the D's, I'd always imagined myself single —free to travel and write."

"Can you explain a little more so I can see how things fit?"

"You have to know how I was then."

"How were you?"

"Insecure. Uneducated. Lower-class, compared to my classmates. I was the only one I ever saw on the campus with cavities in all her front teeth—and, if that wasn't enough, I had a Boston accent."

"What's wrong with that? Didn't some of the others?"

"Mine was the accent of the poor—like the kids I grew up with—not the broad 'A' of the Cabots and Lodges."

"You're losing me again," he says, and I hear him move in his chair.

"Okay, back to the D's. After the third one, I worked up my

nerve to have a private tutorial with the teaching assistant who'd graded my papers. Outside his office, I felt faint and anxious—worse than waiting outside the dentist's office. I was getting ready to leave when he opened the door. Alone with him in his office, I tried not exposing my teeth, made myself try to speak 'properly,' but, all in all, I think that I bordered on hysteria. All I really wanted was to find out how to improve my grade . . . learn what I was doing wrong."

"And?"

"He never did respond to my questions, but I must tell you that although this man was a lowly teaching assistant, his father was a world-famous professor, and—even to my then-unpracticed eye—I could tell that he thought his father's position made *him* superior. He spoke of his father and took cheap shots at the other assistants . . . said how grateful we should be to have him." My tone turns bitter. "Now I can see that he was an arrogant snob."

"Then?"

"He intimidated me."

"How?"

"I recall one time in class daring to speak up about Thorstein Veblen's theory of conspicuous consumption. Miss Hargreve had given me my first cashmere sweater, so I said to the class, 'A sweater is a sweater, but a *cashmere* sweater is what one should buy if one wants to conspicuously consume.' "

"Not a bad example." Dr. Mueller laughs.

"Now I know that"—I laugh myself—"but what an embarrassment at the time."

"Why?"

"Most of the class was wearing cashmere—and so was he! Anyway, that scene preceded our tutorial, so I just kept asking him what I could do to bring my grade up." I pause, and then the memory washes over me full force: " 'How did they ever let *you* in here?' To tell you the truth, after all these years, that's all that I can actually remember him saying. 'How did they ever let *you* in here?' "

"He said that?" Dr. Mueller now sounds astonished.

"He said that." I pause to reflect. "Yes, that's what he said. Not a word about my papers."

"How did that make you feel?"

"Second-rate. Substandard. Inferior. And then—for the first time in my whole life—right then and there I considered the possibility that I might not be able to write."

"And?" Dr. Mueller wants more.

"Then came the boyfriends—nonstop until Mike."

"Ah." Dr. Mueller sighs sadly. "*Now* I see how it all fits. You went to Radcliffe in the hope of becoming independent—the same reason you came into psychoanalysis—and now that we're nearing the end, you're pushing Zygmunt out because you're afraid that you won't achieve what you set out to do. You *still* want to write!"

"That's it in a nutshell."

"Have you told Zygmunt all this?"

"Not in so many words, but the other night, after I pushed him too far, we decided to take a little trip to the ocean. Somewhere on the Cape. I haven't been near the water since my mother died. It might do us both good, and . . ." Outside, with a blast, the mower runs into some foreign object and the machine clangs to a stop. I speak normally now. ". . . And, to tell you the truth, a big part of me is looking forward to a vacation from *this*." I point to the couch. "These sessions are sometimes excruciating for me. You do know that, don't you?"

"I do. Three and a half years of analysis has weakened your defenses. We're closer to your vulnerabilities, so you feel it more."

"That's for sure."

"Well, our time is up for today."

"So soon?" I sit up on the couch but don't stand immediately. I face Dr. Mueller. "I really do think I'll be all right."

Dr. Mueller removes a small piece of notepaper from his clipboard. "Dr. Anson will be here the whole month of August. Should you feel the need for someone to talk to, please feel free to call him. I've spoken to him of you."

"That's thoughtful." I take the piece of paper. "I don't think it will be necessary, but I'll keep it—just in case."

"And remember that when we resume, we'll meet in my new private office in Belmont Center."

"I know where it is." I walk to the door, Dr. Mueller behind me.

I give in to impulse and kiss him on the cheek. "Have a good vacation. You deserve it."

"You too." He appears not to be flustered, and we take leave of each other with a firm handshake.

Chapter Forty-eight

On the Tuesday after Labor Day, Zygmunt drives me to Dr. Mueller's new office. It's a short half block up the street from the bus stop in Belmont Center. The three-story modern structure is a medical building. I see from the board in the lobby that Dr. Mueller's new office is on the third floor. I take the elevator.

Upstairs, it's deserted. No secretary or receptionist. At the end of a narrow corridor is a door with his name on it. A few magazines that Dr. Mueller subscribes to are scattered on a small table, a few chairs next to that. At the other end of this narrow room there is a bathroom. The glass window of a door to a fire escape lights up the area. From my chair I can glimpse the autumn-red treetops.

Zygmunt dropped me off a few minutes early. I can hear no voices coming from Dr. Mueller's office, no telephone ringing. I must be his first appointment.

Somewhere a clock starts to strike nine. I hear footsteps. Dr. Mueller walks from the hall into the waiting room.

"Good morning." I smile.

"Good morning." He arches his brows, and his eyes take in the cast on my leg and the crutches next to my chair.

He unlocks the outer door, throws it back wide, and gestures to me to come into his office.

I get to my feet, stabilize on my crutches, and hobble past him into the office. As he closes the doors, I take it all in. This new setting is sparse; it has the dry wall and acoustical tile of modern construction—not the old plaster and wood paneling of his office at McLean. The office is smaller but brighter, and it's furnished the same: the old couch, his nice chairs, and the same painting of the sailboat. Only his desk is brand-new.

The wall-to-wall carpeting absorbs the sound of my crutches, and I'm glad to reach the couch and be able to lie down.

"I guess you're wondering what happened," I say right away.

"Yes, I am," he replies. "Tell me about it."

I explain the trip to the Cape with Zygmunt. We went on the first weekend of Dr. Mueller's vacation. On our first day at the beach, I went in for a swim while Zygmunt sunned himself up on the blanket.

"I was standing in three or four inches of water. A wave knocked me over. Neither Zygmunt, the bystanders, nor I, myself, could believe that such a short fall on soft sand could break a bone—but it did. This"—I point down to the cast—"is the first broken bone of my life."

"Exactly what broke?" he asks.

"My ankle. A hairline fracture, but I'll be in this cast for another two weeks."

"I see," he comments without much affect.

"There's more to it," I continue. "I'd just had a dream about my mother. It was a sexual dream and it upset me."

"Do you want to tell me about it?"

"Not today, if you don't mind. I'd just like to get used to having you back. I'll tell you tomorrow, if that's all right with you."

"Whatever you feel more comfortable with."

"One thing I *can* tell you."

"What's that?"

"Having one leg in a cast has been quite an experience. I'm not saying the accident was unconsciously deliberate, but it has put certain unconscious feelings right out in the open."

"Such as?"

"With you gone, I felt vulnerable. I wanted people to handle me with great care. Actually, it's my head that's unsettled, but the cast on my leg alerts friends and strangers alike that something is wrong. Luckily I didn't have to miss any work. They let me stay upstairs, handle the customers and answer the phone. Everyone else does the running up and down stairs. They've all been very kind."

"What about you?"

"What do you mean?"

"Have you," he asks, "been kind to yourself?"

"This leg"—I point to the one in the cast—"I call it my bad leg."

"And?"

"The bad leg reminds me of the bad little girl. . . ."

"The one who believes she drove her own mother crazy?"

"That's how I still feel. I failed my mother, and for that I believe I *should* be punished."

"So." He pauses. "You still live with that guilt about your mother dying alone."

"And that I did not take her in." I sigh. "She gave me some warning. She could have lived with us for that short period of time. I feel so terrible. . . ."

"And you cannot get on with the business of your own life until you work these feelings out."

"I know." I sigh. "Boy, do I know. Oh, by the way, were you surprised when I kissed you good-bye?"

"Were you?"

"Yes. It surprised me that I felt free enough. I feel you've been like a father to me and . . ."

". . . I won't seduce you." He finishes my thought correctly.

"I feel safe with you, and"—I look down at the cast—"and not so safe when you're not around. Is this part of my unconscious resistance to termination?"

"Until I hear about the dream you had about your mother, I don't think I can tell. What we both know for sure is that there's more under the surface than you can bring up verbally. Perhaps a break in a bone will help lead us to it."

"I'm so glad you're back. Really I am."

❀

Chapter Forty-nine

❀

The next day is Wednesday, and yesterday I'd been so grateful to see him, I'd forgotten to ask Dr. Mueller whether we'd keep Wednesdays at eight now that he's in his new setting. When he opens his door, from inside, at the first stroke of nine, I've already been sitting outside his office for more than an hour. This being the very first time I'd ever preannounced a session's agenda, I wanted to take no chance I'd be late.

"I'll get right to the dream," I say nervously. Once again, I hear the familiar sound of the page going into the clipboard as he prepares to take notes.

"In my dream, I watched a movie about a mother and her young daughter. The little girl followed her mother everywhere, and at first the dream movie seemed to be nice. Then it got creepy. 'Your body's unclean,' said the mother. 'Mummy, I love you,' the little girl said. The mother caressed her daughter and fondled her clitoris. The little girl smiled. The mother hugged her. 'You experienced pleasure and that was *bad*,' said the mother. She beat the young child—and the girl understood."

"That's it for the dream?"

"Except that you should bear in mind that I dreamed it in a motel bed next to Zygmunt. He'd registered us as Mr. and Mrs. It was my first time close to the ocean since I'd scattered my mother's ashes."

"Is there anything else?"

"The night before we left for the Cape, Zygmunt and I went to a foreign film which included a scene of lesbian lovemaking. It was the first explicit lesbian sex I'd ever witnessed."

"And?"

"I felt guilty."

"Why?"

"I'm sure that being so easily orgasmic with men somehow makes me less of a feminist. As close as I feel to all women, I also believe I'm incorrigibly heterosexual. I prefer my friendships with women *because* they're nonsexual. No sex makes everything less confusing. Then I have a dream which mixes everything up."

"And what you've told me is all you remember about the dream?"

"From the moment I woke up in the bed next to Zygmunt, I tried to put the dream out of my mind."

"Then, a few hours later, you had the accident in which you broke your leg?"

"That's right. Zygmunt and I were on the verge of 'walking away' from each other and I have an accident which means I literally cannot walk. And then there's the mother part. Can a dream have more than one meaning?"

"Of course."

I sense a certain edginess I've never heard before in Dr. Mueller's attitude and tone of voice. "Is something the matter?" I ask.

"Our time—it's almost up."

"That can't be," I protest, "we just started."

"It's my mistake. It's almost nine-twenty, and I have a meeting up at McLean at nine-thirty."

"Are you trying to tell me that today was an eight-o'clock morning?"

"Exactly."

"But you were right inside your office and I was outside your door."

"It was my mistake—and I apologize."

"Well, Dr. Mueller," I say, getting up on my feet, "we're certainly going to have to talk about *this!*"

"Yes, we are." He nods, conceding my point.

"I've come to certain conclusions," I start Thursday's hour.

"Such as?"

"In three and a half years of analysis, yesterday's session was the only one where I preannounced subject matter: a lesbian dream."

He makes no comment.

"I have to conclude that some part of you is threatened by lesbianism."

He doesn't deny it.

I feel slightly ambivalent, but mostly triumphant at having caught my own analyst in an unconscious slip. "I must also conclude," I continue, "that you, too, have a 'few dark corners' your own psychoanalysis failed to illuminate."

"What makes you so sure?"

"Your own perfect record. You must have had me down on your calendar for eight and I was right outside your door, yet you never checked either. The 'mistake' was unconscious."

Still no denial.

"Why don't you say something?" I ask.

"I do not dispute you."

"You're kidding!" My tone is flippant.

"No," he replies seriously, "I'm not."

"Well, where do we go from here?"

"Do you have any suggestions?"

"*Me?*"

"Why not?"

"I consider you a good man—one of the best. Do you believe that?"

"I do."

"Feminists believe that the bonding of women—lesbianism in particular—threatens *all* men, even the best."

"And my 'slip' gives some evidence . . ."

"That you're not exempt. Even though, as it turns out, my

dream is probably more about other things than lesbianism itself
—but you couldn't have known that yesterday."

"That's correct."

"As far as I'm concerned, your slip, as we call it, validates what
I've been saying to you all along."

"Which is?"

"Women's liberation and the issues it raises upsets even the
unconscious premises society's built on. And that's why everyone
gets so upset about it."

"I agree with all that you've said, but one thing disturbs me."

"What is it?" I'm really curious.

"That you will want to interrupt your own analysis in order to
analyze me."

"But you did slip up."

"I don't deny it."

"Should we ignore it?"

"Not exactly."

"Then what?"

"You've done enough reading on the subject," he slowly begins, "to understand that no analysis is ever finished—not even an
analyst's. During the actual analysis one masters only the process."

"That's what I hope I'm doing," I interrupt him.

"Once the process is mastered, analysis becomes an ongoing
thing for the rest of one's life, long after the formal analysis
stops."

"I do understand that, and I hope I turn out to be able to do it
after we terminate, but I'm still not sure I get what you're driving at."

"We should not use your time—the time that remains—to
analyze *me*."

"But the slip?"

"I will work on it on my own time—that is, if you trust
me."

"I do."

"You are correct when you point out that this analysis, which
has involved so much feminist theory, has pushed me into places
where my own analysis didn't go. But it would be self-destruc-

tive on your part to want to analyze me when you still have so much of your own work left to do—and when I am able and willing to work out my own problems."

"Dr. Mueller?"

"Yes."

"I respect you for your honesty. I'm sure many analysts would not be so forthright, would play that old bullshit game of 'what do *you* think it means?' You've never done that to me, and it just now occurs to me how much I appreciate that part of how you have always dealt with me."

"Then we can proceed?"

"With what?"

"You. *Your* unconscious."

"And you'll work on yours—on your own time?"

"I promise. Do you doubt me?" he asks.

"You give me no reason to."

"Back to the dream . . ."

On my own time, I, too, indulge in recollection.

As an infant, my mother nursed me. I have no conscious memory of this, but I'm sure the sensations were pleasurable and—obliquely—referred to in my dream.

As a young child, I grew up between two parental extremes: a mother who didn't like to be touched and a father whose touching was hypnotically sexual.

As a grown-up, I'm a toucher, a hugger, a hand-holding person. Even a back-slapper, on rare occasions. As for sex, my focus is men, and if I demand intense sex from men, I demand a "correct" ideology when it comes to feminism.

The mother in my dream is more like a feminist consciousness. That I enjoy sex with men makes me feel like a traitor to my own philosophy.

The return to the ocean was a return to my mother. For many, men and women alike, the sea is a "she," but—for me now—the sea as my mother takes on a slightly more literal meaning.

If I'd had more guts, I'd have let Zygmunt make the break that hot July night. Instead of a breakup, I insisted on a trip to the ocean, where I—right away—break my leg. How can I walk away from a man when I can't even walk?

I just *had* to drag it all out. I couldn't let go, even though I knew it was time—and certainly not with Dr. Mueller about to go away too! So I acted out my deepest fears on an unconscious level. I owe Zygmunt an apology. Sometime I'll give it to him.

Zygmunt cares for me deeply, and I was the one who precipitated most of our arguments. He even joined a men's consciousness-raising group, but nothing he did ever satisfied me. No, I can't say that: the sex was always delightful. The thought that I might have preferred the sex to the man makes me feel ashamed of myself.

I continue to work with Dr. Mueller—on me, not on him.

"Before any little girl can grow up and give herself completely to a man," I tell him, "she has to have had *some* man she cares for value her for herself, not see her as a sexual being. If her father, or some fatherly figure, won't value her beyond sex, then she will forever mistake sex for approval and be doomed to seek it from all men at random."

"Are you speaking of any one little girl in particular?" Dr. Mueller asks in a tone that's gently sarcastic.

"Me." I sigh. "We both know it. My father's attempts at seduction when I was so young gave me the sense that sex was my only value. I fought him and fought the idea, but not until you *and* the women's movement did the pieces fit together. I was eighteen and I believed I'd failed as a writer at Radcliffe when I first turned to a boyfriend and sex. I had no self-esteem left, and it didn't matter to me that I passed the rest of my subjects. I'd begun to get self-esteem from sex, and not work, and since then I've learned that countless women have done the same thing—and for the same reason."

"And now?"

"The day I felt free to kiss you was a great moment for me. I felt you to be the father I never had, the father who values me for myself." I turn around on the couch and flash him a smile. "You want for me to become a first-class citizen."

He nods and smiles back.

"I love you for that," I say, turning around again. "Fathers are men with great power. As their daughters approach adolescence, fathers can continue to hug them and love them *or* they can seduce and abuse them and fuck their minds up forever. Some men solve the problem of developing breasts and emerging womanhood by turning their backs on their daughters, which makes the girls feel guilty for growing up. Other men simply start fucking girls their own daughters' ages."

"And?"

Dr. Mueller senses, correctly, that I'm holding something else back.

"Psychoanalysts. Father figures. We both know," I continue, "that some of them exploit their female analysands the same way some men exploit their young daughters. That seems even a greater crime to me."

"How so?"

"When a woman signs up to be analyzed, she's signing up for a process which cannot progress unless she lays bare *all* her vulnerabilities. If the analyst actually sleeps with her, she gets it both ways."

"I don't understand."

"She pays *and* she pays—and she's left with even more guilt than she may have started out with."

"Speaking of guilt, before we can leave your dream behind, what about the guilt you felt with regard to your mother?"

"As a child growing up, I sometimes forgot that she was taken away against her own will. She never abandoned me; I'm not sure I forgive myself yet for ever feeling she did. My first return to the sea should have been all alone—to communicate with her."

"Don't you think it was natural to go there with Zygmunt?"

"Perhaps. Perhaps not. Anyway, since the trip and the dream I've come to see that sex with men who care for me gets me other things that I need. I hadn't wanted to face that before. Mike helped make a home for my grandmother, my brother, the new baby, and me. Zygmunt has been kind. You might even say that I've exploited him, in a manner of speaking. Because of you—

your fairness and honesty—I'm able to analyze men and sex a little more clearly."

"And how does that help you see the dream's meaning when it comes to your mother and sex?"

"With Zygmunt, I found sex *and* mothering. I didn't want to give it up, not at all, even though I knew I didn't love him. So I tried to walk away—and broke my leg."

"That's how you see it?"

"At this moment, I do. It's from men that I want mothering."

Chapter Fifty

Through what remains of my convalescence, Zygmunt eagerly trades his role of lover for nurse—and I let him. On the nights he stays over, we use my cast as the reason we cannot make love; we both know the cast is not the reason.

The break was The Break; it's clear to both of us now, and every so often we lock in embrace to commiserate for what cannot be.

With neither of us emotionally able to endure the relationship's abrupt rupture, my convalescence gives us both the time we need to agree to our differences. We struggle to maintain mutual compassion.

"Dearest Lou"—Zygmunt leaves me a letter on the kitchen table on the morning that the cast is to come off—

> I am sorry our relationship is over and I shall always hold you in the highest esteem. I wanted to understand you. I tried and I couldn't.
>
> That night you banged your head on the wall, I didn't understand what I had said to provoke you. I *still* do not understand. Perhaps, because I am a man, I never will. When you screamed at me, I was frightened. I was very much afraid that you were losing your mind.

Losing my mind? I look up from the letter. And here I am afraid that Zygmunt—or some other man—will drive me crazy. I know there's a joke in here somewhere, I muse on the irony, but right now I can't laugh. I return to the letter:

> The bombs from the war still go off in my head. I am frightened of trust. Communicating with people will always be hard for me.
>
> With you, I built bridges, yet you seem convinced you are not the woman I should marry. "She should be younger," you tell me, "and want to bear you the child you desire." Perhaps you are right but I am sorry I was not the "right" man for you.
>
> Our arrangement gave you security, it gave me security, too. It's a security I know I will want again.
>
> We had a wonderful two years. Probably the best of my life. Important. Impressive.
>
> You were always too much for me. Too far out of my reach. I just couldn't "catch" you.
>
> And so, dearest Lou, what I see clearly now is that you prefer your "perfect" philosophy to this "imperfect" man.
>
> My love always,
> Zygmunt

"We tried, Zygmunt, really we tried," I tell him outside the hospital later that afternoon.

"It could have been different," he says.

"If we had been different."

I take my first steps in nearly two months without the weight of the plaster.

"I'm sorry it's over, Lou," says my brother. "I liked Zygmunt a lot."

"I did too."

"When why did you do it?"

"Oh, Frank, Zygmunt feels he's ready to marry, and he wants a child. I'm beyond all that now."

"You were too hard on him."

"Maybe I was."

"Are you sure you're not still angry at Mike? Or Daddy, for that matter?"

"What's that you once said about Daddy?"

"I called him a heartbreaker."

"And look at the two of us. Aren't we a pair? But you never risked marriage and children. I did. You saw for yourself what happened with Mike. I could never go through that again. That scene has to be a 'once' for my lifetime. Once was enough!"

Frank puts his arm around me. "How about dinner? My treat. Let's celebrate the fact that you're back on your feet."

"You're on."

"Where to?"

"Your treat, your choice."

And my brother takes my arm as he helps me down the stairs to his car.

"What will you do now?" asks Dr. Mueller.

"Take a rest."

He says nothing.

"Nowhere in society are the sexes equal, so how can a man and woman be equal in bed?"

Still no response.

"I've probably just stated the case for homosexuality, but Gloria says I'm too queer to be gay."

"Does that mean you're giving up on men?"

"Not giving up *on* them—giving them up for the time being. I don't have the energy to give to someone new, and I've had it with casual sex, so I just took myself off the pill."

"Oh?"

"My doctor advised it. I was showing stroke symptoms."

"There are other methods."

"Tell me about it. I nearly bled to death on the coil. Christopher was conceived while I was using a diaphragm. Come to think of it, I'll tell you a man who *would* interest me."

"Who would that be?" He sounds interested.

"A man with a vasectomy. Oh, Dr. Mueller, don't worry about me. I have so much consciousness that I think I'm breathing rarefied air, and I also think I've just made myself sexually unemployable."

He laughs.

I laugh too.

"I'll tell you one thing, though."

"What's that?"

"I'd rather have no man at all than one who can't meet all my needs. Until then, I'll be just fine with all my friends and my family—and . . ."

"Yes?"

"It's great to be back on my feet."

Chapter Fifty-one

"How's your writing coming along?" Dr. Mueller asks me one February day during a lull. For a change, we have no major life trauma to discuss.

"The work is tedious," I reply.

"You've been at it all fall and winter. Do you have anything yet?"

"A title."

"What is it?" He sounds eager to hear.

"*Sexist Semantics.*"

"Good title."

"The problem is that I don't think I can write the book to go with it."

"How come?"

"I have lots of research on language, and dozens of lists, and none of it shapes itself up into an outline."

"Why not get one of your writer friends to help you?"

"At this point I don't know enough about writing to know what kind of help to ask for. Besides, I think I'm working out an obsession."

"Excuse me. You just lost me."

"I'm tired of going to demonstrations. My arms"—I hold them up over my head—"ache from all the pamphlets I carry to feminist meetings. Physically, I'm a wreck, I'm worn out, but my brain, it keeps speeding along. That's why I go to the library so much nowadays. The tranquility permits me to think. I like the reduced stimuli. It takes great discipline to put what I feel on paper. I'm trying to focus my thoughts *and* my anger."

"Why do you call that an obsession?"

"The proof it's obsessional, and not professional, is my lack of organization."

"Isn't writing like anything else?"

"Now *you* just lost *me*."

"Shouldn't you allow yourself time to learn how to do it?"

"Even *trying* to write a book is so different from keeping a journal. It's like the difference between a person who knows how to swim and the swimmer who is a champion."

"But isn't training and time what transforms the swimmer to champion? Big changes don't come overnight."

"Well now." I burst into laughter. "Of all the people in the world, aren't you just the *perfect* one to be telling me that? And how long have we been working away at these 'little' changes?" I ask self-mockingly.

"Four years next month."

"Somehow it really doesn't feel like it's been that long, and I know in my bones that one of these days I'll be ready to walk away. Not today." I turn around on the couch so I can see his expression. "Okay?"

"Okay." He smiles. "Not today."

Chapter Fifty-two

Dr. Thomas Szasz, a New York psychoanalyst, became a hero of mine years ago, when I first read his classic work *The Myth of Mental Illness*. Szasz, the widely published author of books and articles about law, ethics, and psychiatry, is giving a lecture at Boston University, and I'm thrilled at the prospect of being able to hear him in person. I've also signed up for a seminar that he will be giving on the Saturday after his Friday-night lecture.

He is an exuberant speaker, whose dark eyes twinkle from beneath graying temples. He both outrages and dazzles his audience.

"You were right," DeeDee says, "I wasn't bored for a minute, but he's not a man who leaves people much middle ground, is he?"

"He's way ahead of the rest of us."

"I'm not so sure about that," comments the ever-cautious DeeDee.

"I'm a fan. I admit it. I'll call you tomorrow to fill you in on the seminar," I say as she drops me off at home.

The next morning, I'm back at the university, this time in a classroom. The seminar starts at nine sharp. Half women, half men. I count us all up. Sixteen. I'm pleased that the seminar group is so small.

It's worth every penny of the thirty-five-dollar registration fee to be in the same room with Thomas Szasz, a man whose theories I have so taken to heart.

When four policemen cast my mother from our home, they left me behind. I was not quite twelve years old, and I thought, "I'm an outcast too." To this day, I'm shocked when people assume I'm worthy and capable. "But wait," I try to say, "let me prove it." In that sense, I'm never off duty.

Social injustice perpetrated upon the so-called mentally ill is primary in Dr. Szasz's social theory.

"So," Dr. Szasz begins, "may I assume you all know who I am since you are each thirty-five dollars poorer for being here?"

We all laugh and nod yes.

"Well then, before we begin, why don't we go around our circle and each of you can tell me a little about who you are and why you are here."

When my turn comes, my throat has gone dry. "I'm a feminist concerned with psychiatric discrimination against women, and" —I clear my throat—"my mother spent nearly a third of her life involuntarily committed to a state hospital here in Boston."

The others all have professional reasons.

"Last night you referred to yourself as 'hired help.' " The graduate student in psychology starts us off, asking Dr. Szasz, "Do you *really* see the patient as 'boss'?"

"I sell services; my clients pay me: I *am* the hired help."

"It can't be that simple," she replies.

"Why not?" he asks with a glint in his eye. "You tell me."

"Imagine a patient who comes to you as a drug addict."

"Does this imaginary patient come to me because he wants to stop taking drugs?" asks Dr. Szasz.

"No," she replies, "but wouldn't you try to make him give them up anyway?"

"If he didn't want to, how could I make him, and why would I want to?"

"What about all the junk kids buy on the street?" she persists. "It's not even heroin. If they ever get the real stuff, some kids overdose. Don't you feel any responsibility?"

"If drug overdoses are your concern, you should get after the Food and Drug Administration. If the FDA did its job, one ounce of heroin would equal one ounce of heroin—and we'd have fewer drug deaths. If it's the young man's use of his body that concerns you, his body is his own, and so is the choice of substance he puts into it."

"Clean needles. Pure stuff. Over the counter." The group's lone psychiatrist now takes charge in an arrogant tone. "It's that simple, is it, Dr. Szasz?"

"Almost."

"And what about kids?" the psychiatrist asks snidely.

"Cigarettes. Alcohol. They're adult-only vices. We set purchase age-limits." Dr. Szasz, refusing to be baited, maintains his matter-of-fact tone.

"Alcohol isn't like heroin," the psychiatrist says.

"That's true," Szasz agrees. "We have *evidence* that alcohol can destroy human brain cells."

The psychiatrist misses this point entirely.

"Just let anybody stuff anything into their bodies," mocks the psychiatrist.

"Do you know the largest known group of users?" Szasz asks the psychiatrist, who previously boasted of his medical qualifications. "Doctors," Szasz answers, before the psychiatrist can. "So you"—he directs his attention to his antagonist—"should think about purity and availability as factors in drug use."

"Isn't this drug issue a false one?" I finally find the nerve to speak up. I look to Dr. Szasz. "Aren't you really saying that when an analysand comes to you for treatment, you want her or him to end up fulfilling his or her own dreams—not yours?"

"Precisely." Szasz smiles. "Dr. Freud himself once said that the less like the analyst the analysand is when the analysis ends, the more likely it is that the analysis can be called a success."

"And how do *you* conduct an analysis?" asks the psychiatrist.

I speak up even before Szasz does. The psychiatrist irritates me. In the group, next to Szasz he's the highest professional, and he seems confident that he can use his status to monopolize the group's time. "If you're *really* interested in Dr. Szasz's technique, he's written it all down in a marvelous book, *The Ethics of Psychoanalysis*. You can read it in a couple of hours. It's all there.

Believe me—I've read it. Why should Dr. Szasz rehash what he's already written down in a book?"

Is that really me speaking?

"She's right." Dr. Szasz smiles. "Thanks to my editor and secretary, it's better said in that book than I could do for you in the time that remains to us." He looks around at the group. "All those who'd prefer to skip technique, raise your hands."

The show of hands is unanimous. The psychiatrist is the last one to vote, and as he raises his hand, he glowers at me.

"Dr. Szasz," asks our hospital attendant, "last night you said you would never treat anyone involuntarily hospitalized."

"That's correct."

"But what if you could cure them?"

"When therapy is forced, there can be no cure."

"Then what *would* you do for someone locked up?" asks our young lawyer.

"Hire someone like you."

Dr. Szasz scans our faces and, accurately, reads our expressions as puzzlement. "Do you know," he asks, "which group in society is least likely to be committed involuntarily?"

"Neurotics," announces the psychiatrist.

"Rich people," says the attendant.

"Stop guessing." Dr. Szasz holds up his hands. "I won't waste our time. The group least likely to be committed are those persons who have a lawyer present when the commitment attempt is made."

His answer stops the group cold.

I can't help but think of my mother. Four cops and a paddy wagon, plus a cruiser. How would it have been different if she'd had a lawyer?

The hospital attendant is the first one to speak. "Are you saying that being locked up has *nothing* to do with being schizophrenic?"

"A man could be dressed up as Napoleon, with papers to prove that he is, but if he's got a lawyer when they come to get him, he probably won't get taken away."

"Dr. Szasz." It's the psychiatrist again. "Am I correct to quote you as saying 'I don't dispense treatment'?"

"You are." Szasz nods.

"Then, if I may be so bold," he asks, "whom *do* you treat?"

"Those who seek me out freely, those with whom I can come to some contractual understanding of mutual terms, and, of course, those who can afford to pay my fee."

"Aha!" exclaims the psychiatrist.

"You work free?" parries Szasz.

"Ahem." The psychiatrist clears his throat. "Er, no."

"Neither do I."

The medical student speaks up for the first time. "If you refuse to call mental illness a disease, Dr. Szasz," he asks, "what *do* you call a disease?"

"Myocardial occlusion. Cancer of the breast. Shall I continue?"

"No." The student shakes his head. "I understand what you're saying. What about the homicidally inclined?" the med student asks as an afterthought. He seems to be trying to tune in to Dr. Szasz's point of view.

"The courts handle them, and by the way, a lawyer rarely lets a judge hand down an indeterminate sentence. A criminal gets specified time *and* parole. Once someone is locked up in a mental hospital, he or she may not even come up for review in ten years."

"That's what happened to my mother," I interject. "It wasn't until this new wave of social workers flooded state hospitals to review back-ward patients that anything was done for my mother. A social worker found my mother to be more normal than not; she got her a job in the hospital's cafeteria, and that job led to one on the outside. My mother was sixty when she was discharged."

"That kind of story is one I hear all too often," Dr. Szasz comments.

The woman in our group who works as a hospital attendant now looks distressed. "So who *should* be hospitalized?" She slumps back in her seat looking confused.

"Those who wish to be," Szasz answers simply.

"If asylums were *real* places of sanctuary"—I reach across and touch the attendant's hand gently—"we'd all fight to get in, wouldn't we?"

Everyone laughs.

"It's not the concept of an asylum that's bad," I continue, "places of shelter and refuge are good. It's what 'asylums for the mentally ill' have become that's so evil; that's what we must protest. If anyone here today doubts me, may I suggest"—I look into each and every face—"that you sign yourself in at random to any state hospital for a few days. The experience should clear up your doubts."

"I agree," says Dr. Szasz, "we all should sign in for a while. Then the answer to the question: is this a good place to be? . . . it comes more clearly." He pauses and changes his tone. "Life is a struggle," he says compassionately, "and we aren't all champions. The poor, the female, and the people of color, they fill our prisons and mental hospitals. Statistics prove it, and, like it or not, the fact is that mental institutions have become warehouses for the unwanted and homeless. I consider it criminal that human beings are sent there."

As visions of Boston State Hospital flash to mind, I feel myself close to tears. And I'd been so in control. Hang in, I tell myself. Don't start to cry now.

But it's such a relief to have my childhood perceptions confirmed after so many years. No one ever could convince me that what went on in that hospital was good for my mother.

In spite of myself, my eyes brim with tears. I look down at my notebook, start scribbling, and hope no one will notice.

"Why, it's twelve-thirty." Dr. Szasz looks down at his watch. "We're a half hour over our time. I'd like to stay, but if I do, I'll miss my plane back to Syracuse."

After the good-byes and the shuffling, I'm the last to assemble my belongings.

"Mrs. Shields?"

"Yes, Dr. Szasz."

"Is your mother still alive?"

"She died a little more than a year ago."

"Did you ever learn why they locked her up in the first place?"

I shake my head no. "It was sometime around 1930. She was in for a short time, then they let her out. After that, she gave birth, first to me, then my sister, and I always had the idea that having babies drove her over the edge. And if it wasn't having the ba-bies, it was my sister's death. It seems to me she never recovered from that."

"The law allows you access to her records, you know."

"What are you suggesting?"

"That you look them up. They might yield"—he hesitates—"some peace of mind."

"How are you getting to the airport?" I change the subject.

"By taxi," he answers.

"Let me give you a hand." I go over to him. "I'll walk you down and we can hail the cab together."

"Good." We gather his things. "This gives me a chance," he says as we walk down the corridor, "to thank you for your contribution to the seminar. I guarantee you they're not usually so lively. And thanks for the book plug."

We both giggle.

"It did shut him up, didn't it?" I laugh.

"Nicely done, too. You liked that book, did you?"

"Very much. My analyst follows your guidelines. I don't know whether or not your book influenced him, but that's how he does it."

"Glad to hear it." Dr. Szasz moves his overloaded briefcase from one hand to the other. "These feminist pamphlets you gave me. I'll read them," he promises. "And I'll let you know what I think."

"I'll look forward to hearing from you."

"By the way," he says as we position ourselves on a heavily trafficked corner of Commonwealth Avenue, "both you and your mother were up against a formidable system. I think you should know that it took institutional psychiatrists three hundred years to get society to go along with them. First came the nomencla-ture of madness, then came the victims."

"Speaking of nomenclature . . ." I see an empty taxi coming our way, so I quickly work up my nerve. "I'm at work on an outline for a book titled *Sexist Semantics*. I don't have it yet, but I do have an essay."

"Would you like me to read it?" he volunteers—before I can ask.

"Very much. And would you critique it?"

"I do it for students all the time. It's part of my teaching job. Send it along when it's ready, but just allow me some time. I have quite a backlog."

"Oh, Dr. Szasz." I shake his hand and help him into his cab. "What a pleasure it's been."

"For me too. I assure you."

We both wave farewell.

I know what I've done is take a big step. To show my work to a real writer—and one I respect—is progress. Whatever his comments, I know I've chosen the best.

I'd better start revising that essay.

I run for the trolley and head for the library.

Chapter Fifty-three

"Dear Dr. Szasz," I write in July, two months after our meeting, "the essay's not ready yet but here are some more pamphlets. Shall I keep sending them? MLS."

"Dear Mrs. Shields," Dr. Szasz answers immediately, "keep them coming! If the psychiatric journals printed more stuff like this, they would be much improved. Best regards. TSS."

"Dear Dr. Szasz," I write in September, "I'm still working on it but the essay is not ready yet. MLS."

"Dear Mrs. Shields," he replies promptly, "you choose a rough path when you choose to question assumptions so basic that people mistake them for absolutes. Good luck and warm regards from this 'old warrior.' TSS."

Hilles, the library at Radcliffe, is open six nights a week; every night that the kids are with Mike, I work there until closing at midnight.

Organization. I'm convinced that's my problem. The piece seems poorly organized, but I can do no better unless I have help.

I don't know how to type. I was always afraid that if I learned how to type, poof!—I'd turn into somebody's secretary. However, my handwriting is rotten. I can barely read it myself, so I hire a friend to type it up for three dollars an hour. She makes it look gorgeous and is pleased with her pay. "It makes sense to me," she comments, handing it back to me.

On a crisp day in October, I mail the essay to Szasz from the Harvard Square post office.

In less than a week comes his terse answer: "I received your essay today. Will get to it as soon as I can. TSS."

"We're going out to dinner," I announce to the children, "even though it's a school night. Dr. Szasz got that essay I mailed to him, so I feel like celebrating."

"Goody," says Lizzie, "let's go for pizza."

"Pizza," says Christopher, "at the College Grille, where they have that swell jukebox."

We walk down Mass Avenue, toward Harvard Square and the College Grille.

"Will they send you money for the essay that you wrote?" Lizzie asks when we're in our cozy booth, the kind with the jukebox on the wall next to us.

"Not at this stage, dear. Dr. Szasz, he's the man whom I sent it to, he's going to tell me where I'm on the right track and where I go off."

"Mum, you sound like a train." Christopher laughs.

"Train. Train of thought. Not bad." I chuck Christopher under the chin. "You, my dear boy, you're right *on* the track, that's for sure."

"Where do you get money when you're grown up?" Lizzie asks.

"From work," I answer.

"Is that how I'll get it? When I'm grown up, I mean?"

"Yes, but you're just six years old, so you have some time to go before you start to worry how you'll earn your living. Dad and I will take care of you and Chris until then. That's our job as parents. We share with you kids until you're ready to go out on your own."

"You mean if you have four dollars, I have two?" Lizzie persists on her theme.

"That's dividing," says ten-year-old Christopher. "Mum said she'd *share*."

"Chris is right," I say to Lizzie. "It's not exactly two for you, two for me, two for Chris. It's more like Dad and I share with the two of you, try to provide what you need. Then, when you're ready, you can do it for yourselves."

"That's good," Lizzie says. "I'm not ready to grow up anyway. I still love to swing, and Melina and I love to play in the backyard. Do you think Melina and I will be friends for always?"

"Might be." I hug Lizzie. "The both of you have been friends for almost your whole lives."

"I hope we stay grown-up friends, like you and DeeDee."

"Well then, maybe you will."

"How will I know when I'm grown up?" she asks.

I start to speak and then stop myself. I wanted to say that she didn't have to grow up one day sooner than she was ready to. Then I remembered: No parent can make that guarantee. "The important thing," I say to her instead, "is for us to move fast through the bad days and let the good days go on forever."

At the Central Square Theater, we drag this good day out by seeing *King of Hearts* for the third time.

The movie takes place in France during World War I. The inmates of a mental hospital are left behind when the town is evacuated. With the villagers gone, the inmates don the clothes of the villagers, and with them the roles. One becomes a priest, another a barber, and one the town madam. An English soldier, arriving on the scene, takes them for real, doesn't know they are "crazies."

"I just love that movie." Christopher skips up the aisle of the theater.

"Me too," Lizzie and I say in unison, as she and I pirouette the way the young tightrope walker did. Christopher imitates the knight who comes out of the church clock to strike midnight.

We all go home happy.

In early December, the manila envelope I'm expecting arrives in my mailbox. A glance at the essay shows the margins to be covered with comments. He must have read every word!

"If you're shocked by my title," I'd written to Dr. Szasz in my cover letter, "I intend you to be. I chose it with care: 'Castrating Men.'

"Men fear castration, the loss of their testicles," my letter continued, "and, to the best of my knowledge, the verb's most popular usage is as in 'castrating bitch.'

"Now," I'd gone on, "I don't pretend to be an expert in psychology, but I *am* a careful reader, and *nowhere* in my research do I find theories concerned with a girl's fear that she will be 'defeminated.' If the concept does exist, it's hardly in the popular culture. I suggest that if we were to ask 'the man in the street' what a 'castrating bitch' is, he'd know right off the bat. As to 'castrating man,' my guess is that he'd be perplexed. My theory, then, is that 'castrating men' 'prune' and 'deprive' the little girl of her 'vigor' so as to ensure that an entire human being will be sufficiently 'castrated' so that she can be jammed into that narrow thing—the FEMALE ROLE."

Attached to my essay is a cover letter from Dr. Szasz. I set the essay aside and read:

In my judgment, this material has the makings of a good paper (or possibly two, see below) but is, in its present form, not well enough organized. As I see it, you touch specifically on two themes; one: the semantics of feminine oppression; two: woman as role or a mask rather than person. I think it would be better to separate these and write a shorter, crisper paper on each.

The semantic issue is quite fresh (and it's not easy to say something fresh on this subject at this point) and I think you have the makings of a first-rate piece here. I think you should not have trouble finding a publisher for the essay on 'The Semantics of Femininity' (though certainly less 'shocking,' it might also serve as a title).

I hope you find my remarks helpful. Best wishes for the holidays. Cordially, Thomas Szasz.

Did he say "first-rate"? I go back and read his letter over again. Yes, he said "first-rate."

My first attempt at serious writing since those D's on my essays in freshman English almost twenty years ago.

Encouragement. In black-and-white.

With his letter and his careful critique, Dr. Szasz has renewed my hope that I might yet learn how to write—not just learn to write, *be* a writer. It was always my only ambition.

In the time that remains with Dr. Mueller, I can work at bridging the gap between my thoughts and my emotions—always a problem in college. There, my personal experience felt like an abyss; I kept my mind on the books and what they taught me for fear of falling into the past. But I need an emotional bridge, so to speak, between that past and my present. Perhaps writing will do that for me—even after the formal phase of my analysis ends.

I guess I'll have to bring *this* subject up in my analysis!

Chapter Fifty-four

New Year's Day, 1972. It's hard to believe that in March I'll have spent five years in analysis. I want to terminate in spring or in summer, so Dr. Mueller and I discuss my plans endlessly. Soon we'll decrease my sessions from five to three, and if my plans succeed—as I intend them to—this will be my last New Year's with Dr. Mueller.

Just before Christmas, along with some friends, I'd gone to the New York Radical Feminists' Conference on Prostitution. The weekend event, held in a high school in Chelsea, was well attended, and the issues were hotly debated.

The first issue was rather easily solved: How do we identify ourselves?

"I consider myself a feminist, but I'm also a prostitute," said a tall, slim young woman with good features and a strong jaw. "I'd like to be referred to as a 'working sister.' "

The other women "in the life" agreed with her, and those of us not "in the life" decided to identify ourselves as "straight feminists."

Nomenclature was our first—and last—easily resolved issue.

"But why *should* prostitution be legalized?" asked one puzzled straight woman.

"We want it decriminalized," answered a working sister. "That's something you straights could help us to do. That's why we got up so early this morning to come here to talk with you. By the way," she went on, "when you want those of us in the life to show up at a conference, next time don't call it for Saturday morning at nine!"

From the floor, a straight woman who said, "I'm married," got to her feet and challenged the working sister.

"What's your question?"

"I don't have a question," the married straight woman said, "I just don't see how a prostitute can be a feminist."

"I was a secretary once. I was straight," the working sister replied. "Men control jobs and men control the economy. As long as that's true, all women sell it, one way or another. I earn more this way."

"That's not true," protested the woman from the floor.

"I sell my ass piece by piece for a price." She looked out at all of us from the auditorium's stage. "Married women give it away. You may get allowances, a roof over your head, but you have no guarantees—and lots of dirty socks."

"That's not what I mean," the married woman rebutted. "Our husbands respect us. "*You* can't say that!" She remained standing.

"Who do you think our customers *are?*" The working sister stared the woman down. "Our johns are *your* bosses, yes, the ones who lay you, too. They're your brothers and lovers and husbands. Who else did you think our customers *could* be?"

I found myself upset and in conflict, but when one of the working sisters broke down and cried because she felt scorned, I went to her side, as did two working sisters and two other straights.

"I want to get out of here," said the crying working sister, so we left as a group and adjourned to a restaurant nearby.

"It kills me that the reporter from the *Village Voice* will write this damn thing up," said the crying sister, "and get it all wrong."

"Then let's write up how we see it . . . what we think the issues are," I suggested.

"What a good idea," said a straight woman named Marsha.

In a notebook, brand-new, bought for the meeting, I'd taken copious notes. When the others saw what I'd already written, they appointed me, on the spot, the editor for whatever statement we would produce.

"The *Village Voice* has that other section, 'Press of Freedom,' I think it's called," Marsha said. "Let's write it for that."

Over coffee and sandwiches, I continued my note-taking—not that we all agreed, but we were able to itemize the issues we felt had been eclipsed by the emotional intensity the conference had evoked.

Back in Cambridge, after several long-distance calls, I clarified our separate viewpoints and wrote it all up. Mailed special delivery, just before Christmas, the piece was published immediately.

"You must be feeling pretty proud of yourself," Dr. Mueller begins our first session of the new year.

"You mean because the *Village Voice* published our piece and wants another next week?"

"That's what I mean. You're not any less proud because the piece was collectively written?"

"Not at all. To tell you the truth, it pleases me even more. It was far harder, I think, to edit—and get approval from—so many women with so many perspectives. To tell you the plain honest truth, I'm thrilled."

"I read those *Village Voice* articles that you gave me, and I have one question."

"What's that, Dr. Mueller?"

"I'd like to read you one phrase and have you tell me the author."

"Go ahead," I say, but I am puzzled.

"'A woman,'" Dr. Mueller reads, "'cannot simply fit herself into a feminist mold. She has been educated in this sexist society, just as the men have. She must, therefore, re-educate herself *every day*. Personal feelings and prejudices *must* be revealed in order for them to be eliminated. They are no different—nor less important—than any group's prejudices.'"

"Is that it?" I ask.

"That's it," he replies. "Did *you* write that paragraph?"

"Is my style so apparent?" I ask.

"It is to me," he answers.

* * *

Both articles are published in the *Village Voice*—the first in December, the second in January. The *Voice* chooses the titles: "Guilty of Everything They Accuse Men Of" for the first; "Myths About Prostitution in a Sexist Society" for the second. Our six names appear as co-bylines, the three working sisters with first-name-only pseudonyms; the three straights, including me, have our full names in print.

"This article may not be my book—"

"But," Dr. Mueller interrupts me, "isn't a writer's first time in print a big event?"

"Yes," I agree, "but this episode has led to something even more significant."

"What could that be?" he asks.

"If I'm going to become a serious writer, I can't keep on paying a typist."

"I can understand that."

"So I've just bought myself a Smith-Corona portable. A ten-day touch-typing course on tape came with it."

"I see."

"Everything that I write out in longhand, the good *and* the bad, is easier to edit and change when I type it myself. I think it will be a big help to my writing."

"By the way, did the *Village Voice* pay you?"

"I think it's enough we got published," I tell him. "We were in a reader-speakout column. Besides, it's a little too soon for me to think about being paid for my writing. I think that it's enough to have made it into print on my very first try. Of course, the subject matter was there."

The *Village Voice* subsequently runs several pieces about the conference, and as controversy rages, I enjoy for the first time a new sense of exhilaration: I've made my opinion known—publicly—on an issue that I care deeply about.

Chapter Fifty-five

"Could I ask why you're pushing yourself so hard with your writing, Mrs. Shields?"

"I don't want the analysis just to end," I reply. "When it's over, I'd like to be different."

"And you are sure about setting June for a deadline?"

"Absolutely."

"Do you have a particular reason?"

"Remember that summer when I left before you did, the summer I went to Europe with Zygmunt?"

"I do."

"With June as our deadline, I'll be all finished before you leave for vacation."

"I see. . . ."

"And, just in case you were wondering, that leaves me a month out of analysis—with you still in town—before you leave for your own vacation."

"The acrobat's net?"

"Sort of." I smile.

"The 'when' *is* up to you. Just remember that."

"Will I be able to write to you?" I ask him.

"I don't think that's wise," he answers cautiously. "When an analysis ends, it should end—and the analysand should begin to incorporate the process into her own life."

"I just thought of something ironic."

"What's that?" he asks.

"Prostitution." I don't really want to be mean to him, but that *is* the thought that just flashed to my mind.

"I don't get the connection."

"It's tricky. Bear with me. When I was looking up all those words, I spent some time on 'prostitution.' The concept is fascinating, comes from the Latin—'to stand in for.' Are you with me so far?"

"So far."

"The working sisters rent by the hour, they don't get involved, and they walk away when it's over. The sex is impersonal. The whore's body is there, but she is a stand-in for God knows what fantasy the john is having. In that sense, she is not there at all."

"You're losing me."

"This analysis, to the extent that it has worked—and I think it has—works because our souls have actually touched. Day in and day out, we've learned to perceive each other in ways we can only begin to understand. I'm in tune with your head, with your being, but I don't even know you." I grapple with myself to make the point clearly. "You are a man in a field that's male-dominated, which serves mostly women—and for a fat fee. Am I right?"

"Generally speaking."

"Whoring, the rental of bodies—not souls—is done mostly by women for men, and for a better price than the wages society offers its best-qualified, highly trained, and college-educated women. Now do you see what I'm getting at?"

He pauses and takes a deep breath. "I rent by the hour? Is that what you're saying?"

"It may sound crude, but in a subtle way it is true. The irony, of course, being that analysts are looked up to and whores are looked down on. If I had to rent one or the other, I'd choose the body; my soul is a little too personal."

Dr. Mueller makes no response.

"I'm not trying to be mean, honest I'm not. It's just the way the whole thing suddenly strikes me. Now you're here—now you're gone. No phone calls. No letters. It's just like I'm a 'jane.' You 'service' many; to me you were *one*."

"Mrs. Shields, the analyst as whore," says Dr. Mueller, "while it's an interesting thought, is hardly the situation you and I face. Any analyst worth his salt knows that any analysis is a two-way street. The process has to work both ways to be good." He hesitates. I wonder why. "You," he says slowly, "and your feminism drew me into confrontations with myself I don't think I'd have otherwise had, and I'm certain that my future female patients will benefit from what you and I have gone through together."

"Do you mean that? Seriously?"

"I do." He laughs. "And while we're on the subject, let me tell you there were days you put me through the hoop."

"You're kidding."

"Oh, no I'm not. I can tell you that now because we're so close to the end."

"Do you know what's so great about you?"

He doesn't answer. I bet he's embarrassed.

"You never let on about that. To me, you were always your good old reliable self."

"That's an analyst's role."

"You're good at your job."

"I take that"—he pauses—"as a very fine compliment."

"It's intended as one."

"Do you have any suggestions about what we can do to make the termination process easier on you?"

"I would like us to have a denouement."

"Excuse me?"

"Like in the theater, after the play, when the actors come center stage."

"You mean that you want us to part as human beings, not as the roles we've been playing?"

"That's what I mean, and if we had our last week face-to-face, I think I would like that. After all, psychoanalysis *is* a little like theater. The face-to-face will acknowledge that the roles we've been playing are separate from life. Can we do it?"

"I don't see why not."

Chapter Fifty-six

From the outset and throughout the analysis, Dr. Mueller appealed to my healthiest side. During the crisis with Mike, when I pleaded for tranquilizers, Dr. Mueller said, "If you want them, go to a doctor. I don't prescribe drugs." Yet, when I fled to the Vineyard, where, by coincidence, Dr. Mueller was vacationing, he made two house calls to DeeDee's to make sure that I was okay. And when even DeeDee considered having me hospitalized the night I cracked up after Ben and Ramona's wedding, Dr. Mueller's question to me over the telephone was not "Do you want to go?" but "What do *you* want to do?"

In that one question, Dr. Mueller revealed both the subtlety of his own perceptual apparatus and the confidence that, at all times, I should be the one to decide my own fate.

If I am to fulfill my life's ambition, I must try to write. Dr. Mueller and the work we've done together has brought me to the starting point, as I now see it.

On our last morning, Dr. Mueller is five minutes late, a "slip" I notice but do not refer to. Our parting is difficult, and the difficulty works both ways. I see that now, too, but I feel no compulsion to mention what we both know.

How I love his face. Those compassionate eyes. The lines which show that somewhere he, too, has known sorrow. How strange it is that I know so little of his "real" life. That part of analysis, I must confess, I cannot get used to.

"You should be proud," I start us both off.

He looks at me quizzically. With his elbows on the arms of the chair, he rests his chin upon folded hands.

"I've grown to trust my own perceptions so much that I don't have to shoot my mouth off all the time to prove what a wise-ass I am. Wouldn't you call that progress?"

"I would." He chuckles.

"Until this analysis"—I grow serious now—"I felt that I'd spent my life walking between doors that weren't really open."

"What comes to mind?"

"The corridors between the locked doors of the violent wards at the state hospital. As a teenager, I had to walk through them to get to my mother. Sometimes an attendant would let me in one door and then she'd lock herself out on the other side. I walked what seemed miles down the corridor, past people who'd ask, 'Have you come to see me?' 'Are you my daughter?' 'Do you have any cigarettes?' Some of them made nasty remarks, but those I seem to have forgotten. It's the pathetic ones that stick out in my mind. But what I remember the most is how long it would take for some other attendant to hear my knock at the other end of the corridor. 'Oh, God,' I used to think as I stood at that door, 'I'll *never* get out. What if I don't look like a kid? Like I'm *not* crazy?'"

"It must have been terrifying." Dr. Mueller lets out a sigh.

"I wasn't sure the attendants would know that I was a patient's daughter and not a patient myself. I always wore my best clothes, such as they were. I tried to recognize the attendants and learn their names, but over the years so few ever lasted."

"How *did* you manage?"

"Instinct for survival, I guess. Early on, I'd noticed that most— not all—patients looked down at the floor or off into space."

"That was very perceptive."

"I think it's what saved me. I used to stand tall, make lots of eye contact, and smile or look stern—whichever was called for. I do the same thing today when I'm in troublesome situations with strangers."

The morning is quiet, no sounds at all from outside his office, the way there used to be at McLean.

"We've weathered a good deal together, haven't we, Dr. Mueller?"

He nods. "And we share something I've never discussed with you before. You probably never gave much thought to the fact that I was a young resident once. I, too, walked those corridors. I was a grown man, a doctor, and I held all the keys, but, I'll confess to you now, I was terrified. When I saw in your application to the Institute that you'd spent your adolescence going back and forth to such places, I knew you had to be a person with fortitude."

"That reminds me," I interrupt him.

"Of what?"

"Our situation. Most people choose their analysts, but not so in our case. You had dozens of applicants, and one time slot to fill. Why did you choose me?"

"For one thing, the two senior analysts who interviewed you were impressed."

"What do they look for anyway? I always wanted to ask you." I scratch my head. "I never was sure."

"Strength."

"It can't be that simple."

"In large part it is," Dr. Mueller replies. "Not all those who seek to change themselves have the strength to endure an analysis. The senior analysts and I were struck by how many of life's difficulties you'd already survived—and admirably."

"But what made you choose *me?*"

"It was clear to me that you were in some sort of crisis. You spoke about having dropped out of graduate school, but there seemed to be more to it."

"How did you know?"

"You never once said you had a desire to teach; you said 'it was a good thing to do,' 'a way to pay back society for all the good teachers who'd helped me.'"

"That's what I said?"

"That's what you said." He smiles. "And only in passing did you mention that you'd hoped to grow up to be a writer."

"You noticed that?"

"You must give me some credit for my long years of training," he says facetiously. "Anyway," he continues, "it struck me that teaching, for you, was a compromise—a way to do something socially useful and a way to avoid the creative side of yourself, the part that both you and your mother believed drove her mad. In my eyes, you'd failed at your compromise, and *that* was the real conflict bringing you into analysis."

"Was I so transparent?"

"You were to me."

"This is quite a revelation," I tell him. "It means that you knew more about me than I knew about myself—at that point in time."

"You seemed afraid of what would happen next. You were afraid to move on to a new phase in your life. I was certain you could be helped by psychoanalysis."

"And?"

"I chose to try."

"Gosh, I was lucky!"

"Me too," he replies without missing a beat, "your analysis taught me a lot too."

"You know that Dr. Szasz has been very helpful with the writing?"

"Yes."

"I think of him as my mentor. He does things you can't."

"Nor could he, were he your analyst."

"I've got the best of both worlds. That's how I see it. Anyway, Dr. Szasz claims that psychoanalysis isn't a medical treatment; it's not like getting cured of a disease—it's more like learning a game or a language. Do you agree with him?"

"On that point, I do, but," Dr. Mueller continues, "I sense in you some disappointment. What's on your mind?"

"The end," I confess, "it's anticlimactic."

"In any particular way?"

"The writing, I suppose. My good luck with the *Village Voice* was followed up with rejection of my book outline."

"But you told me that the editor called you from New York and suggested several ways to make the book outline salable."

"She did."

"Refresh my memory . . . I've sort of forgotten exactly what her recommendations were."

"She liked the material very much but she told me that *Sexist Semantics* lacked a narrative voice. She said that if I could find a more personal voice, she'd be happy to look it over again."

"Then I don't understand." Dr. Mueller shakes his head. "Why don't you just follow her suggestions?"

"I can't."

"How come?"

"I lack the skills."

"Are you sure?"

"Positive. I've been trying too hard, and the one thing I know for sure is that I have lots more to learn about how to write." I sigh. "Do you want to know something else?"

"Sure."

"I don't even know what a personal voice is!"

"So what will you do?" Dr. Mueller's face registers concern.

"Keep at it. I like the challenge. There's lots of attention to detail, movement through time . . ." I pause. "Like psychoanalysis."

"Writing does seem to suit you. Do you think you'll stick with it?" he asks.

"The process absorbs me."

"*Like psychoanalysis!*" We say it in unison, and then we both laugh.

"Our time"—he looks down at his watch—"is almost up, but we can run a little over the hour."

"Those closed doors I mentioned?"

"Yes," he replies.

"There was one open door I never walked through."

"Which one was that?"

"Radcliffe. Do you remember me telling you that I never attended my own graduation?"

"I recall that distinctly," he says. "I never understood why you didn't go. It was quite an achievement to have been able to graduate."

"Do you really want to know why I didn't attend?"

"Yes." His expression is all curiosity.

"I wasn't ready to 'commence.' Today, fifteen years later, I am."

He takes a deep breath.

"You do know that June is a month of commencements?"

"The parallel did *not* pass me by."

"Would you say I finally figured out how to do it?"

"What?" He looks puzzled.

"Psychoanalysis."

"What else did you think you were doing?"

"Sometimes I wondered."

"Let me assure you, it *was* psychoanalysis."

"That's good."

"Why is it so important to you?"

"Because if I can teach myself to do psychoanalysis, then maybe I can teach myself how to write." I pause. "It gives me some faith in myself."

We both rise as though on cue.

"I will miss you, though." I blink back a few tears.

We both shake hands firmly.

"I *will* miss you." I give him a hug. "*Very much.*"

"Why don't you," he says gently, "give yourself some time to recover, some time to let the 'dust' of analysis settle?"

❀

Chapter Fifty-seven

❀

On the Vineyard with DeeDee, she and I hold our glasses high.

"To Zelda!" We toast with champagne and then flop down on the couches, opposite each other.

I've come for a visit to celebrate the end of analysis. During the bus and the ferry ride, I finished reading Nancy Milford's biography, *Zelda*, and happened to notice the date of Zelda's birth: July 24, 1900. July 24? Why, that's today, I'd thought. Had she lived, Zelda would have been seventy-two.

"I don't want a party to celebrate the end of analysis. Let's have it for Zelda," I said to DeeDee when I arrived. "It somehow feels right."

"She would have had a good time, Zelda would," says DeeDee, putting up her feet. "She would have loved it, especially, I think, because she was so sure that it was only Scott the world would remember."

"These flowers"—I touch the bouquets DeeDee and I had selected—"zinnias, baby's breath, and the small tea roses. Zelda would have loved them . . . just as my mother would have."

"They were the same generation, your mother and Zelda," DeeDee observes. "They both grew up in the Twenties with romantic notions of life."

"You're right about that. The funny thing is that the pictures that my mother drew could have been illustrations for Zelda's own life. I just wonder if she had any fun."

"Who?"

"My mother."

"Oh, Lou." DeeDee puts her arm around me. "I wish you could stop your mourning for her."

"My sadness will pass—at least, I think it will. Reading *Zelda* has just brought it all back. Somewhere Milford has written that Zelda once said, 'I don't write, I don't paint. It takes most of my resources just to keep out of the hospital.' Who does that remind you of?"

"Your mother," DeeDee says softly. "You described the day she burned her artwork so vividly to me that I almost believe I was there."

" 'Hold on to your little job. Take care of your children. Don't ask for more.' That's the last advice my mother gave me before she died."

"Not such bad advice," DeeDee says.

I find myself admiring, all over again, the photographs which line the wall of her living room. DeeDee took them in Europe. "Did your psychoanalysis help you to be able to work?"

"It helped me to be able to live with myself. After that"—DeeDee looks at me closely—"the work comes more easily. Something's on your mind. Now why don't you just spit it out?"

"I'm quitting my job."

"You're not!" DeeDee exclaims. She's not wild about sudden change, of any kind.

"It's been thirteen years, DeeDee."

"It hasn't."

"Oh, but it has. I came to the store two months pregnant with Christopher. He's now twelve, and Lizzie will be eight in just a few weeks."

"I hadn't realized it had been so long," DeeDee murmurs.

"Time creeps up on us all."

"If you give up your job, what will you do?"

"Write."

DeeDee flinches as though I've just slapped her in the face. "And," she asks snidely, "how will you support yourself?"

"Dr. Mueller was costing one hundred dollars a month."

"What does that have to do with anything?"

"That's less I now have to come up with to get by," I say, "and I've talked to the store's owners in New York. They'll give me severance pay."

"How much?" DeeDee perks up.

"Twelve hundred dollars."

"Peanuts. You'll go through it in no time."

"Listen to me, will you?"

DeeDee sits back on the couch, but she does not look happy.

"I can support the kids with the money Mike gives me. The new tenant's rent just covers the mortgage. I'll put the twelve hundred into the bank and draw no more than one hundred a month for necessities. In other words, the severance pay will buy me a year to work full-time at writing. Until I quit my job next month or the month after, I'll save all I can. I'll do my writing at Hilles. I've thought it all through."

"Oh, God," DeeDee laments, "you always were an all-or-nothing girl. How I wish Dr. Mueller could have cured you of *that*."

"He's just an analyst, not a magician."

DeeDee pours from a new bottle of champagne. "Now I need a drink. I don't like the sound of this plan," she says as she pours, "not one little bit. No." She sets down the bottle. "It's nonsense, that's what it is. Not one writer I know earns their living by writing. They all hold down other jobs to support what they call their 'habit.' You're crazy, that's what you are! You have no training, no experience, and—may I point out—your 'big success' in the *Village Voice* paid exactly *zero*. Why, in the name of everything dear, do you have to give up the only security you really have—your job *and* your health?"

Before I can say anything in my own defense, DeeDee is off again.

"You live on the edge . . . on the brink—and you know you do. What would you do if you got sick and had no income? Oh, Lou," DeeDee pleads, "can't you learn from your mother? Her job is what saved her! Goddammit, you know that!"

"I don't think I can hold down a job and write."

"And I don't think you can write!"

"What a cruel thing to say, DeeDee. How can you say it?"

"I'm not running in any popularity contests this week." Her

tone is caustic. "This whole idea stinks. You'll ruin your life and you *will* go crazy, just like your mother—*and* Zelda, for that matter."

"DeeDee." I clasp my hand to my breast. "You, of all people, how can you say that to me?"

"Who else has the guts to confront you? This idea is a fantasy, and I don't approve of it. The world you live in is too harsh and too real."

"I can't believe you're being this rotten."

"Rotten? I'm not being rotten. Don't forget, I'm a professional. I was writing advertising copy when you were in high school. I was head of the department by the time I was twenty-three. I know what professional writing looks like . . . what it takes to meet deadlines, and believe me, you don't have it." She comes to sit next to me. "Please, Lou, keep your job. Write in the morning, write at night, work part-time. Do anything. Just don't give up your job."

"I think I need some time to reflect . . ."

"Oh, Lou, please don't cry. You know how I hate crying. I love you. We all love you. No one cares that you work in a furniture store. No one cares what you do."

"But I do. I want more. I care where I work—and what I work at. I've dreamed of being a writer the whole of my life. If I don't at least try, what's the meaning of life? When my mother died, some part of me went with her. She and I were both dreamers. I'm still alive. I can still dream . . . for the both of us."

DeeDee shakes her head sadly. "You've made up your mind. I know all the signs. Will you make me a promise?"

"What is it?"

"If you can't make a living by the end of the year, promise me you'll get some kind of a job."

"I promise."

"Oh, Christ, let's finish this champagne and wish you good luck in your new venture." She holds high her glass. "God knows you'll need it."

"Oh, DeeDee, I love you."

Part Five

I know scarcely a beautiful woman of Zelda's generation who has come up to 1938 unscathed.

—F. Scott Fitzgerald

Chapter Fifty-eight

In my dreams, I still hear my private Greek chorus. Aunt Tilly and Nana come back to haunt me. "You are just like your mother," their words echo in my brain, "so you better watch out. Look what happened to Mary."

Then another voice speaks, Mrs. Peretsky's: "What I admired most about your mother," she told me, "was her power of concentration."

Now that I'm doing work that's creative, I need to know: what was it? The power of concentration—or madness?

What if Mrs. Peretsky was right?

A power of concentration, put to use in my lifetime, would be a gift. A legacy. From my mother to me.

It's time.

Dr. Szasz was probably right when he suggested I look through my mother's records to find out why they locked her up in the first place.

A dear friend of mine from Radcliffe, Bonnie Harrigan, works for the state mental health department. Thanks to her, my mother's records are pulled from an old warehouse in Grafton only days after my first request. (As a private citizen, I could have requisitioned them, but Bonnie's efficiency speeded up the whole process.)

It's eight in the morning when she calls to say, "They're right here on my desk—your mother's records—but I must tell you one thing."

"What's that?" I ask sleepily.

"There's less here than I expected after so many years of confinement."

"I see."

"I just didn't want you to be disappointed."

"Oh, Bonnie, words fail. How can I thank you?"

"No trouble at all. When will you be here?"

"An hour okay?"

"Fine. There's just one more thing. Until we have a lawyer's release, you can't remove them from the grounds, but I'll see to it that you have a private office to read them in—for the whole day if you like."

Here I am back on the bus again heading toward Waverly Square, this time to go on to Met State—not to McLean to see Dr. Mueller.

I am lost in old memories.

I have never been able to forget the day they took my mother away. After so many years, the scene is as vivid as if it happened yesterday instead of when I was eleven or twelve.

A police car was at the end of the alley in front of my house. The paddy wagon too. But it was daytime.

What could the matter be?

In a sweat, I came to a stop at the stoop.

No hello from the neighbors. Not one word of greeting.

My mother! It must be my mother! I thought.

"Don't go up," someone shouted, "don't let her go up!"

Too late. Already in the front door, I was on my way up the front stairs.

On the second-floor landing, I bumped into a policeman. "Hey, kid, where you goin'?"

"Upstairs." I slipped past him. "That's my mother up there."

Up one more flight. Light streamed into the dark hall from our open kitchen door.

Hunched in the corner, back by the window, my mother stared at four policemen, who looked ready to pounce.

For the moment, she's safe, I thought.

"Look," she said to them, a card cupped in her hand. "I'm an air raid warden. You can't take me! I'm doing my job," and she flashed at them the card which proved she was an air raid warden.

Arm outstretched, hand slightly cupped, she leaned toward the men. She showed each of them her identification.

"My identity card," she used to call it.

She leaned into the men—all of them bigger than she—as though she were a lion tamer. They *did* appear mesmerized.

Was she trying to use her power to neutralize theirs?

She gestured to the church out the back window.

"Ask those priests. Shillitoe spies." She pointed her arm, machine-gun-like, out the window. "Shillitoe spies." She made a sound like the ack-ack of a gun.

Seeing their chance, one man nodded to another. Those two lunged before I could do anything. They pulled my mother from the chair she had leaped up on, by the open window.

"Let go, you dirty bastards!" she cried. She groaned in their grasp. "Let go of me!"

I can't let them take her away. I threw myself on her feet, adding my weight to hers. The men swarmed and subdued her. I held on very tightly to my mother's legs.

Bang! I'm across the room—on the floor, stunned. She must have kicked me off, not knowing it was me, not the men.

Panting and grunting, the men grabbed at my mother, their bodies moving to keep hers from writhing out of their grasp.

Pulling together, they dragged her and themselves down the three flights of stairs.

Stumbling to my feet, I ran after them.

By the time I got outside, the door to the paddy wagon was already closed. From inside, my mother banged out.

"Don't let them take her away," I pleaded to the neighbors. "She must have been nervous. Something must have upset her."

The paddy wagon motor revved up.

I ran to the driver. "Don't take her away," I screamed, over and over, "don't take her away!"

"Get her out of the way," shouted a policeman to the neighbors.

From behind, I felt myself pulled away from the driver's door of the paddy wagon.

"Where are you taking her?" I finally shouted.

"Boston State." The driver pushed me into the arms of Mrs. Brandon, a neighbor my mother particularly disliked.

"Come on. Come on," said one of the cops, "get that kid out of here."

People I couldn't seem to recognize held me until the paddy wagon pulled out of the alley.

To this day, I can hear my mother's screams and my own cries of despair.

Suddenly I remembered my brother! Where was Sonny?

Leaping the stairs two at a time, I followed his bawling to the open door of the kitchen.

I scooped him up into my arms and held him close to my breast. I swayed back and forth, nuzzling his baby-soft hair close to my nose. "I'll take care of you always," I said to my two-and-a-half-year-old baby brother. "I promise you that."

I righted the chair where my mother had been, only moments ago—my brother still in my arms.

I stared out the window. There was just one place to go. Aunt Tilly's. She and Nana will take us in—they have to, I thought.

At Waverly Square, the January wind is fiercely cold. I tighten my scarf as I wait for the shuttle bus to Met State. Fortunately, I don't have a long wait, and within fifteen minutes I'm seated in Bonnie's light, airy office.

"This place isn't as bleak as I'd remembered," I tell her.

"There have been lots of changes since your mother's day."

She points to the record in front of her. "Here it is, but, before you start reading, can I tell you one thing?"

"Of course." I look into my friend's kindly face. Her blue eyes and sad expression exude sympathy.

"What happened to your mother," Bonnie says gently, "couldn't happen today."

"Couldn't or wouldn't?"

"It couldn't. There are laws, lots of changes. Commitment procedure has drastically changed. For example, what happened to her could *never* happen to you."

"So." I smile at Bonnie. "You know what's at the bottom of this search?"

"How many years has it been now that we've been friends? And how dumb do you think I am?"

"Not very."

We both laugh.

"Let me give you just one *for instance*," she says, "before I hand you these." She points to the records. "When you came here to visit your mother"—we both look out the window to the bleak buildings—"there were about two thousand patients here. How many do you think there are now?"

"I can't begin to imagine."

"Four hundred eighteen—exactly—and those patients still with us are the old and the homeless, the ones who've been here so long, there's no adjustment they *could* make. They're actually happy here—or at least they feel taken care of—and they are."

"Dear Jesus" is all I can say.

"I have a meeting to run to." Bonnie hands me the records. "This conference room won't be in use the whole day. Stay as long as you want and just"—she opens the file drawer of her desk—"put the records back here when you're finished, okay?"

"I will." I nod. "You've made this whole thing much easier."

"Well, what are friends for?" She gives me a hug and she's gone.

Chapter Fifty-nine

All alone in the conference room, the frayed folder in front of me, I wonder: where to begin?

How did it happen that very first time?

That's what I want to know. I start to read.

"*January 10, 1929:* This attack," wrote a neurologist, "began a few days ago, according to patient's friends. We have here a young woman who has become irritable and unreasonable over a period of time and, finally, when the one she is most interested in leaves town, she becomes acutely disturbed. The cause seems to be a broken love affair."

"What? I can't believe what I'm reading." Oh, my God, I just said that out loud. I'd better watch out . . . especially here.

I continue to read.

From the information in the record, I gather my mother was a nineteen-year-old virgin when she met George, a reporter whose ambition was to write books.

I flip back and forth to get a fuller picture, and George emerges as a man who "freely admits to being addicted to alcohol" and in "the year and a half prior to patient's admission introduced her to alcohol too."

Someone enters a description of George as a southern gentleman, handsome and several years older than the patient. My mother's best friend, Agnes, reported: "George introduced Mary to the ways of 'free love' and they lived as though married without benefit of clergy. Mary told me she and George wouldn't marry until they 'each did something with their lives.'"

Another record reads that George reported, "When we both drank to get drunk, friction between us increased."

George's career, I gather from the records, was very important to him. He very much wanted a job on a New York City newspaper. On January 5, 1929, an offer came through from a New York wire service.

My mother, according to the record, wanted to go to New York and continue living with George as they had been. George said no to that, but proposed to her. My mother refused, saying to one of the doctors, "I thought he was doing it because he thought he *should*."

The record shows that my mother was in Museum School when she met George and that their relationship lasted for seven years. "There was an accidental pregnancy," says one doctor, "but it was followed by an abortion."

That's interesting to me. Since my mother was seven months pregnant with me when she married my father, I always wondered if the marriage was "my fault," but if my mother knew where to get one abortion, presumably she could have done it again. Could she have wanted me after all?

"When patient speaks of George," one page of the record reads, "tears come to her eyes. 'He's the only man I ever loved, the only man I've been intimate with. I always thought he loved me, but now I'm not sure.'"

On January 5, 1929, without saying good-bye, George left for New York. "It is about this time," reads the admission record, "that family and friends noticed the onset of patient's present symptoms.

"She [the patient] doesn't know why this occurred, but admits they've been devoted to one another. 'We didn't want to get married until we'd done something with our lives.'"

When asked why he left as he did, she answers, "I really don't know. We just disagreed."

"Right now," says the admitting record, "this event is of great importance to patient:

" 'I'm not clean,' she says, 'George ruined me.
" 'I might as well die now.' "

So, there it is. It wasn't art that drove my poor mother crazy, but a man. (I can't help but think back to my own reaction to Mike and the breakup of our marriage. I, too, nearly went around the bend.)

If my mother was nineteen when she was "introduced" to "free sex," the year was 1922. I think of poor Zelda, the "quintessential flapper," as she was called; if she had trouble, why shouldn't my mother, a poor immigrant's daughter? My mother's social circle in Boston was surely less sophisticated than the Fitzgeralds' world.

"Patient does not know the name of this hospital," reads an entry on Boston Psychopathic letterhead, "but she thinks it's an 'insane asylum.' "

RECOMMENDATION
This girl should be hospitalized for a time and it is to be hoped that in the near future she will accept help from someone else in solving her problem.

Then, to my astonishment, come the following words:

Patient has mismanaged her ambition and has a mismanaged sex life.

2/12/30: PROVISIONAL DIAGNOSIS: Dementia Praecox.

From there, the record bogs down in day-to-day trivia, but a letter toward the end catches my eye.

Dearest George honey:
    Have been feeling rather rotten since you left last Sunday.

Have had a nervous crying spell. I'm terribly discouraged and feel like the end of the world. Do you suppose I will ever really get out of here? At times this hospital feels hopeless. This is a terrible way to feel on Good Friday but nevertheless it is true.

Have just had that awful pain near my heart for the last five days and it just knocks me out. I was very happy to see you last Sunday. Everything would have been marvelous except that old house of mine. It always upsets me even though it's the best that I have. You must hate coming over there after all the nice things you are accustomed to in New York.

Have you got a new woman George? I hope so. I hope that she is someone useful and nice and not an old stick in the mud like I am. Do you have any feelings at all toward me George outside of pity? At times I feel like the end of the world. You don't love me any more and I just don't know how you feel toward me. Have you had any woman after me George? You've had one before and I nearly die when I think of that. Sometime I wish you would talk to me about things like that. You always knew so much better than I did.

I don't trust people enough I guess. Without you it seems like the end of the world. I used to see you so often and the routine was regular sort of. Now it seems all very useless. I have spells when I don't mind anything except being by myself. If I'm not going to be with you I don't want to be anywhere.

Did you run away from me George so you would never see me again? Why did you go away at night with Bill so no one would know? Or were you drunk? Some day it will be as clear as mud. I still don't understand about all that awful New Year and Christmas spell. I know it keeps me here worrying and moping. If everything is all over why don't you say so in so many words so I can get cured and have it over with.

Will you please come up to see me again George? You

know there is nothing I would rather have now than a visit from you. Please come to see me soon.

Love.
S.

I close this folder with tears in my eyes.

❈

Chapter Sixty

❈

The Boston State Hospital folder, a much later set of records—a timeworn elastic band snaps in my hands. I look through the pages quickly for the entry I want to see in black-and-white. Ah—May 3, 1947. My mother was forty-four, my brother had just turned three, and I was eleven and a half.

Four police officers from Station Thirteen brought an agitated forty-four year old white woman to the hospital for admission. She'd been up on the roof—before she returned to her apartment—she reported bombers overhead in the sky. Neighbors feared she might jump so they called the police.

The sister, a rather placid person, speaks of the patient in an offhand manner but describes the husband as never being reliable. "He promises the world but never fulfills his promises."

Well, that's no news to me, is it?
The next entry is, however:

Following the birth of the patient's first child, Mary Louise, patient and husband separated for six or seven months but then reconciled. A second daughter was born but died a year or so later of a strep throat. Following the child's death, patient became upset and developed peculiar ideas. The child's death brought on an acute episode—but a rapid recovery was made.

As background, the Boston State Hospital record of my mother's hospitalization at Boston Psychopathic summarizes:

She had fallen in love with a newspaperman, and—in 1932— patient received news that George had married a Southern woman of his own social class. Six months later, he died of a sudden heart attack.

During that hospitalization, the one where I, as a kid, made so many visits, Miss Foster, the occupational therapist, was one of the only staff members who worked there regularly and had an interest in my mother. In a very nice letter, Miss Foster suggests to the staff that my mother's state is not one of "acute withdrawal" but, rather, "the state of concentration that an artist at work requires."

God bless you, Miss Foster, I think.

In a particularly poignant entry dated 1948 (when I was thirteen and Sonny was four) a doctor is recorded as having asked the patient, "What is your ambition in life?"

"To go home," my mother answered, "and bring up my children."

I may have at times felt abandoned by my mother, but these records document, once and for all, that she never abandoned us—she was taken away.

"It couldn't happen today," I hear Bonnie saying.

How sad that it could have happened at all.

There's more to read but I stop, satisfied that I've found my mother's "breaking point"; that same breaking point could have been mine. God knows I freaked out over Mike. She didn't survive the crisis with George, but, like the "sea run," my mother also found her way back to the outside world, slowly, and had

at least a few years of happiness, free from money worries and
free to enjoy the love she and I managed to salvage.

A sheet of paper catches my eye, a follow-up summary on
Boston Psychopathic Hospital letterhead. The single sheet is re-
markable—it has graph summarizations from the years between
1932 and 1938.

In 1932, it is noted that "patient lives with sister and parents.
She does not return to her art work. George marries, dies six
months later and patient is 'glad no one can have him.' "

In 1934, "patient becomes interested in another man. Marries
him. 'He thinks he's a big shot,' patient says, 'esteems anyone
with money and likes to talk of Einstein as if he understood it all.' "

In 1935, a few months after the marriage, it's noted that "patient
has baby girl." (There I am!)

In April 1937, "patient is pregnant again [that's Baby Sissa],
likes children—wants more. Patient says that if something were
to break up her marriage, her heart would *not* be broken. 'I will
never feel for anyone what I felt for George,' patient says."

A social worker records that "neither patient nor her husband
are practical in money matters. They have no regular income."

The final entry in May 1938 is a social worker's report on her
home visit:

> The home situation has continued economically unsound
> for patient but, although shabby and living in a sordid tene-
> ment, patient appears to be placid and undisturbed. She now
> has *two* daughters of whom she is very fond and of whom
> she takes excellent care although she is frequently without
> money, fuel, light or food and has been evicted from one
> tenement after another. Her husband works for the Puritan
> Ice Cream Company, earning $50 bi-weekly but giving pa-
> tient only a dollar of it—and paying no bills which he can
> avoid paying. He drinks. Patient no longer drinks. Recently
> she did some drawings for a former teacher who sought her
> out, receiving a liberal payment for them. She occasionally
> speaks of returning to her profession when her children are
> older. Patient does not look well physically. She will not see
> a doctor.

I put my head on the table and sob a long while, grateful for Bonnie's gift of privacy.

I finally pull myself together and try to console myself that at least she'd had *something* with George—and it did last seven years. My mother once told me that she kept a black lace negligee tucked away in the back of her drawer—"just in case."

I bind up the folders, brush back my hair, and peek into Bonnie's office. She's gone, so I put the folders in the drawer she had shown me and leave her a thank-you note.

Men. A weak point in my mother's life. A weak point in mine. "It couldn't happen today." I repeat Bonnie's words just to make sure that I get the message.

All these years in analysis, all these years in the women's movement—I'm different now, I reassure myself.

Chapter Sixty-one

I return home from Met State with the courage and curiosity to go through those papers I'd taken that day from my mother's room at the Saratoga Nursing Home, the day after her "burial at sea."

I find the shopping bag full of papers in the back of the closet where I had put it the day I brought it into the house.

It saddens me, but does not surprise me, to find blank books, all sizes, all kinds: bound and unbound, lined and unlined, with not a sketch or drawing in any of them. A red alligator pencil case is filled with colored pencils, each razor-sharpened to a fine point. I can never remember my mother without a pencil case. During hard times, the cases were cheap leatherette; during good times, they were fine leather, and my mother always used a single-edged razor blade to sharpen her pencils.

But then I come upon a folder whose contents do surprise me. I handle them gingerly: newspaper clippings and a few of my mother's full-page artworks of the now-defunct *Boston Post*.

The hair on the back of my neck stands on end and I'm covered with gooseflesh as I unfold the first one.

The front page of a Sunday edition of the *Boston Post* has mostly ads and a single news story. I turn the page over to see a bold headline set in type even larger than that on the front page:

WHAT PART DOES ROMANCE PLAY IN A GIRL ATHLETE'S LIFE?
Helen Wills Scorns Psychologist's Claim that Athletics Damage a Girl Champion's Chance of Matrimony

The date? July 17, 1925.

The nearly full-page story has four photographs to go with it, and two of my mother's illustrations!

To prove that athletics don't damage a girl's romantic potential, Wills cited the case of Eleanora Sears, who, "back in 1906, was engaged to Jack Saltonstall and a few years later was rumored to be going to marry Harold S. Vanderbilt. Sears made a name for herself in tennis, horsemanship and swimming. She was the first of her sex to try aeroplaning, polo and squash. Whatever the causes of her remaining unmarried," the eminent psychologist concluded, "they certainly cannot be laid to her interest in sports. Nor can it be said that her activity in sports made her 'unattractive' to the male."

Originally, the Sunday edition of the *Boston Post* used illustrations for its cover—and my mother did these too. I unfold another clipping with trembling hands.

EASTER BATTLE BETWEEN BLONDES AND BRUNETTES, reads the bold banner of the Sunday *Post* pictorial section for April 14, 1927. "Drawings by Mary Smilga."

The page is filled with beautiful flappers, those glamorous women my mother so loved. The colors, even faded with age, are still lush and gorgeous.

When the *Post* switched the Sunday pictorial format, it went to a magazine form, newsprint in texture, and its size a little larger than that of *Life* magazine, and, again, a cover of illustrations—not photographs.

The one I so tenderly lift from the folder is actually a visual pun. A cover headlined PLANE JANE OF TODAY AND PLAIN JANE OF YESTERDAY shows my mother's small signature in the lower right corner.

A young woman sits back on the fuselage of an ascending biplane whose prop is in motion. She wears brown jodhpurs, high black boots, and a white collar. Her black hair is short and windblown. Clearly, she is "Plane Jane."

Falling through air down below, looking up toward the aviatrix, is an old-fashioned girl, her petticoats and skirt blown up around her, revealing dainty black pumps and, on one knee, a red garter. Her long curls are in disarray, her beribboned bonnet is sailing aloft, and her parasol is falling down toward the ground. "Plain Jane" is apparently on her way to becoming passé.

The date on this is November 4, 1928.

Wait a minute. That's less than three months before they took my mother to Boston Psychopathic. Come to think of it, somewhere in the record I'd seen reference to the fact that even while she was hospitalized, the paper kept sending my mother assignments, which, one doctor noted, she worked on "diligently 'until they were right.'"

The last of the clippings is from the *Boston Daily Record*, a now-defunct Hearst tabloid. A page-three story about "the dramatic Costello trial" is half filled with four of my mother's courtroom illustrations. The story, continued, shows three photographs—including one of my mother! She is in profile, at work at her drawing board. "Mary Smilga," the caption reads, "whose intimate sketches of central figures will be a daily feature."

Amazing.

My mother, at work at her board—just as I always remember her—but *here*, in a newspaper!

Oh, what I'd give to have my mother's trunk . . . but at least I have these. Visible proof of what a farsighted and talented woman my mother was.

❀

Chapter Sixty-two

❀

I've been sitting for hours now in a single-desk cubicle on the third floor of the library at Radcliffe—not that I have much on paper to show for my time. I feel moody, but not depressed. I have no concrete ideas, but it's almost as though I trust that they will come. The wall of glass just beyond my desk provides a vista of Cambridge rooftops and sky.

I really owe Dr. Szasz a letter, I think. Reading my mother's records *did* give me "peace of mind"—and much more.

I have an idea, a possible route to that personal voice the editor asked for. For the time being, even after all the work that's gone into it, I'm going to set *Sexist Semantics* aside. The subject matter itself is so impersonal, it makes finding a voice of any kind much too hard, at least at this stage of my writing skills.

When my mother sat at her drawing board, she told me she heard voices. Now that my grown-up eyes have seen the exquisite art she produced, I must consider that some of her voices were one voice—her Muse.

The clouds outside have been billowy all afternoon, but, looking skyward again, I notice—for the first time all day—the extraordinary blue of the sky.

White clouds and blue sky somehow remind me of Mummy and her whimsical fairy-filled fantasy skies. How could I ever have forgotten the Blue Fairy?

* * *

"Look, Mummy, look," I said as I pirouetted to my mother, who was bent over her drawing board. She'd been sketching ballerinas for days.

I was just home from school, maybe ten or eleven years old—not much older than that.

"Look at this." I showed my mother the newspaper, folded to a page in the middle.

"A doll-carriage parade," she said when I pointed out the announcement, "how nice."

"Can I enter?" I asked.

"As what?"

"Help me decide," I pleaded.

"Let's go through my trunk," she said, "perhaps we'll get some ideas."

"Ooh, look at this one." I handed my mother a drawing of a fairy-filled sky.

"I think I know just what we'll do," she said, suddenly closing the trunk.

"What?" I jumped up and down, for I knew her idea had to be good.

"You'll see." Then she began humming, "When you wish upon a star . . ."

"Makes no difference who you are." I sang the words.

"Everything your heart desires will come to you." Together we finished singing the song we both knew by heart from Walt Disney's Pinocchio.

Pinocchio was a wooden puppet who longed to become a real boy, so the Blue Fairy, the cartoon movie's heroine, turned him into one—complete with a conscience in the form of Jiminy Cricket.

"The Blue Fairy," my mother announced. "You will be the Blue Fairy."

That week, while I went to school, Mummy used up yards and yards of blue crepe paper she'd bought from the five-and-ten. She covered my doll carriage in blue right down to the spokes of each wheel.

She tinted an old bed sheet blue with Rit dye, and when she cut it up, it became part bedding for the doll in the carriage and part of a costume for me.

I came home from school one day to find her bending coat-hangers. Once she'd covered them with blue crepe and wrapped them with tinted blue gauze, the wings of a fairy materialized.

She wound blue crepe around my old baton and, topped with a silver-foil star, the baton turned into a wand, the Blue Fairy's wand, the one that "did magic."

Saturday morning finally came, and my mother unwound the rags from my hair. Tight curls fell to my shoulders—a transformation to the perfect fairy look!

Over the dress of blue sheeting she draped more blue theatrical gauze before attaching my wings. She tied the gauze at the waist with silver cord.

My heart sank when we arrived at the playground. Of all the contestants, I was the tallest. I felt gawky and out of place. No chance of me winning, I thought, and, indeed, first prize went to the little canary who wheeled the tiniest wire carriage I had ever seen. She was all fluff and feathers.

"Mummy." I ran up the stairs after school the next week, the newspaper in my hand. "Look at this," I cried.

"What is it?" Her own voice sounded excited.

"Me. My picture." I held up the newspaper. "There I am."

She took the paper out of my hand and stared at the picture, titled "Trio of Winners From Local Doll Carriage Parade." She read aloud from the caption: " 'Mary Lou Frazier, second prize winner as the Blue Fairy.' "

"Isn't it wonderful?"

My mother looked pleased.

"All day at school, I was a star. Even a few grumpy teachers said, 'Oh, Mary Lou, it was a wonderful costume.' " I hugged my mother with all my might. "Oh, Mummy, I was in the paper, and it was all because of the costume you made me."

*"Mary Louise." My mother touched my face tenderly. "It was
you who won the prize—not the costume."*

Yes, the Blue Fairy—that's a good place to begin.

Back home all alone (the children are with Mike), I take my
scribbled notes out of my satchel. Up on the wall, over my desk,
I pin the newly discovered tabloid photo of my mother at work at
her board when she was so young and so productive. I take my
place at the typewriter.